A Primer on German Enlightenment

A Primer on German Enlightenment

With a Translation of Karl Leonhard Reinhold's
The Fundamental Concepts and Principles of Ethics

Sabine Roehr

University of Missouri Press
Columbia and London

Copyright © 1995 by
The Curators of the University of Missouri
University of Missouri Press, Columbia, Missouri 65201
Printed and bound in the United States of America
All rights reserved
5   4   3   2   1   99   98   97   96   95

Library of Congress Cataloging-in-Publication Data

Roehr, Sabine, 1957–
    A primer on German Enlightenment : with a translation of Karl Leonhard
Reinhold's The fundamental concepts and principles of ethics / Sabine Roehr.
      p.   cm.
    Includes bibliographical references (p.   ) and index.
    ISBN 0-8262-0997-1 (alk. paper)
    1. Enlightenment.   2. Ethics, Modern—18th century.   I. Reinhold, Karl
Leonhard, 1758–1823. Verhandlunger über die Grundbegriffe und Grundsätze
der Moralität aus dem Gesichtspunkte des gemeinen und gesunder Verstandes,
zum Behuf der Beurtheilung der sittlichen, rechtlichen, politischen und religiösen
Angelegenheiten. English.   II. Title.
B2621.R64   1995
193—dc20   94-44811
                                                                           CIP

∞ This paper meets the requirements of the American National Standard for
Permanence of Paper for Printed Library Materials, Z39.48, 1984.

Jacket Design: *Kristie Lee*
Text Design: *Rhonda Miller*
Typesetter: *BOOKCOMP*
Printer and binder: *Thomson-Shore, Inc.*
Typefaces: *Minion and Clairvaux*

*To Hans Wolff in the Old World
and Alexander von Schönborn in the New World*

Contents

Preface

This book provides the English translation of a work that has not been translated before and that has even been forgotten in the country of its origin. Its author, Karl Leonhard Reinhold, was a famous philosopher, renowned for his interpretations of Kant; about his *Letters on the Kantian Philosophy*, Kant himself noted they "were unsurpassed in their graceful thoroughness."[1] He was active all his life as a firm promoter of enlightenment, not only as a thinker, but also as a teacher, as a citizen, and as a letter writer who corresponded with many important philosophers. Finally, his writings on theoretical philosophy were decisive for the development of philosophy after Kant. Fichte at one point described him as "the most ingenious thinker of our age."[2]

The work translated here—in German, *Verhandlungen über die Grundbegriffe und Grundsätze der Moralität aus dem Gesichtspunkte des gemeinen und gesunden Verstandes, zum Behuf der Beurtheilung der sittlichen, rechtlichen, politischen und religiösen Angelegenheiten*—was published in 1798, a time when the movement of German enlightenment was on the brink of dissolution. It is not a philosophical work in the strict sense, but one that in truly enlightened fashion tries to spell out the basic ideas of enlightenment thought in a manner accessible to a wide audience. Thus it is more interesting as a social and moral testimony than as a theoretical work. Philosophers will find not much new in it.

My historical-analytical introduction follows the same approach. It sheds no new light on the German enlightenment but follows current views. Like Reinhold's book, it is meant to be introductory,

1. Immanuel Kant to Reinhold, December 18, 1787, in Karl Leonhard Reinhold, *Korrespondenz 1773–1788*, 298. From here on cited as *Korrespondenzausgabe*.
2. Fichte to Reinhold, March 1, 1794, in Ernst Reinhold, *Karl Leonhard Reinhold's Leben und litterarisches Wirken*, 168.

suited for a wider audience interested in the German enlightenment movement as a historical phenomenon and maybe also in personal enlightenment with regard to particular moral, social, or religious concepts.

Contrary to common practice, the introduction does not restrict itself to the immediate time of Reinhold. It goes far back to the beginnings of the enlightenment, attempting to give an overview of the entire movement. It does so not only for the benefit of those who are novices in this field. I also am convinced that the ideas of the late German enlightenment can be fully appreciated only when seen against their historical background. In one way or another, the translated work deals with all the important ideas of the late enlightenment, in an affirmative or a critical manner. It illustrates that the Kantian concept of enlightenment, which Reinhold shared, was in no way the only one or even the most influential.

Since the rendering of the historical background is lengthy, the usual in-depth study of the contents of the translated work is omitted. As I mentioned, from a philosophical point of view, it does not provide much that is new. There are two exceptions, though, to this strategy. A more intensive treatment is given to two issues that— among others—deserve special attention: first, Reinhold's political views, which have been dealt with in a less than adequate manner. One commentator sees him as a reactionary; another, as a radical, an instigator of the French Revolution. Second, Reinhold's concept of free will is examined in more depth. It seems to offer an alternative to Kant's dilemma of moral freedom, a problem in the limelight during recent discussions of Kantian philosophy.

Of course, these are not the only aspects of Reinhold's work that deserve special attention. His epistemology certainly requires more study than it has attracted so far. However, these are best studied in his other works, which, it is hoped, will be translated in the future. Insofar as his theoretical views are important for his practical views, I include a brief overview.

Reinhold's *Fundamental Concepts* is well suited as a primer on enlightenment, not only because it deals with many important ideas of that movement, but also because it does so in a special way.

Many works by enlightened thinkers addressed a wider audience with the aim of educating the public. The popular philosophers, for instance, popularized philosophical ideas for lay readers, thus once more providing proof for those modern critics who deem the movement superficial and shallow. Reinhold took a different approach to communication. He developed a version of "popular philosophy" that did not oversimplify difficult concepts. Instead, he attempts to argue solely on the basis of common sense, which is supposedly shared by all rational human beings. Whether or not this attempt was successful, it remains of interest to those who try to philosophize on the basis of some common feature, be it common sense, everyday language (Reinhold tried that too), or something else.

Naturally, I have consulted the German literature on the subject of German enlightenment. Wherever available, I quote from an English translation; otherwise, I translated the quotations myself. Since I translated all quotes from Reinhold's work, I left out indications to that effect. Reinhold uses highlights to an extent that makes his texts unreadable. My translation, therefore, leaves them out, though I have kept those of other authors.

Finally, I would like to thank those people without whose support this work could not have been completed. It was my adviser Alexander von Schönborn who first brought the importance of the philosopher Karl Leonhard Reinhold to my attention. His immense knowledge on the subject, which he generously shared with me whenever I needed help, was invaluable. Much specialized literature from Germany was needed. I am grateful to Hans E. Bödeker, who helped me in the selection of the relevant books and articles, and to my parents, who sent book after book. And I would like to particularly thank my old friend Hans Wolff in Hannover, who made many trips to the library. To him and to Alexander von Schönborn I dedicate this book. Also many thanks go to Elly Knox for editing the translation. And to Beverly Jarrett at the University of Missouri Press, who did not lose faith in this project. Last but not least I wish to express my gratitude to my husband Abudi Zein, who edited the whole work and then typed the final draft.

A Primer on German Enlightenment

I. Historical-Analytical Introduction

Chapter 1

Salvaging the True Enlightenment

The Historical Phenomenon

The movement of enlightenment started in the seventeenth century and developed and spread throughout the Western Hemisphere in the eighteenth. It was a movement hard to describe in general terms, since it took widely different forms in different nations. It was by no means a purely philosophical movement—an impression that may arise from works focusing on the intellectual history of that time. As an eminent scholar of the eighteenth century in Germany puts it: "To see it, as is widely done, as an intellectual, philosophical and literary movement, is to cover only a part of it. Economic, social and political changes are part of its conditions as well as its effects." Rather than consisting in a certain theory, enlightenment could be more adequately described as a "style of thought and behaviour," a "philosophy of life,"[1] or as a set of "shared premises"[2] that had practical consequences for all spheres of life—from moral behavior to agriculture.

However, a closer definition of these shared premises proves difficult, owing to national differences. Another difficulty is that during the period in question, the concept 'enlightenment' had no uniform meaning, but was claimed by diametrically opposed philosophical and political thinkers. Nevertheless, the attempt to describe some basic common features has to be made if the various national movements are to deserve their common name, enlightenment. In the most general way, then, the movement of enlightenment rose on

1. Rudolf Vierhaus, "The Historical Interpretation of the Enlightenment: Problems and Viewpoints," 24, 26.
2. Norman Hampson, "The Enlightenment in France," 41.

the basis of a new confidence in the power of human reason, which was a result of advances in the natural sciences. These advances, in turn, were based on new epistemological perspectives, making the human subject—possessing understanding, reason, and sensibility— a decisive factor in the process of cognition. The new methods of thought, of scientific theory and practice, which had been developed in the seventeenth century, were now applied to society, politics, religion, morality, and economics. Adherents of enlightenment believed that it was possible to create a rationally ordered society, one in which people would find happiness. A utilitarian and hedonistic view of ethics dominated enlightened moral thinking, and natural law and social contract theories were influential in political theories. In Germany, these were utilized to formulate the ideal of enlightened absolutism. People were optimistic about the future of humankind; they thought that through proper education every human being could become enlightened. They were convinced that human beings, through the power of their understanding, could distinguish truth from falsehood and thus purify reason of its distortions. They believed that humankind could do away with superstitions, prejudices, and dogmas maintained by secular and ecclesiastical authorities. Religion, thus purified, would be based on a rational morality. Religious toleration was thought essential in an enlightened society. And people believed in the actual power of reason represented in the power of *Öffentlichkeit*, the public discourse of the educated members of society.

National Contexts

The reason for the differences in the national and regional manifestations of the enlightenment movement can be found in the respective social, political, and historical situations in each country. England was politically rather advanced. The Glorious Revolution of 1688 had already introduced enlightened ideas into the constitution. Personal freedom, representative government, religious toleration, and the right of property were guaranteed.[3] Therefore, it

3. I rely here on the excellent article by Roy Porter, "The Enlightenment in England."

was generally not necessary for English proponents of enlightenment to put forward radical claims.

The French admired England for these achievements and considered it a model of enlightenment. France itself was ruled by an absolutist monarchy, which—after the death of Louis XIV in 1715—became "more open to change and to new ideas from across the channel."[4] In the long run, however, the French political system proved to be incapable of dealing with social, political, and economic change, a fact that was decisive for the outbreak of revolution near the end of the century. Although it was not the case in England or Scotland, the power of church orthodoxy was a problem in France, where the second estate was rich, powerful, and allied with the first estate. Here Voltaire's demand "Ecrasez l'infâme!" was understandable.

Germany's situation was altogether different. Its political and religious partition made social, political, or economic progress more complicated and questions of different faiths more urgent. On the other hand, at times the country thought of itself, and was seen by others, as the most enlightened European country, especially when enlightened rulers such as Friedrich II and Joseph II came to power.

Accordingly, the carriers of the enlightenment movement also differed from country to country. Enlightenment can be described as the movement of the rising bourgeoisie only to a certain degree, if the bourgeoisie is seen primarily as an economic class. In England, educated people gathered, irrespective of their social standing, in clubs, coffeehouses, taverns, Masonic lodges, friendly societies. They discussed the new ideas, which were put forward in the journals of enlightenment—Addison and Steele's *The Spectator, The Tatler,* and *The Guardian*—or in the works of such theoretical thinkers as Locke, Hume, Shaftesbury, Smith, Ferguson, Hutcheson, and many others. Hume and Burke, for example, held public office and thus had practical experience and also some influence in politics. In Scotland, the universities also were seats of enlightened thinking.

The French enlightened philosophes and their supporters were in a different position. The places where ideas were exchanged—

4. Hampson, "Enlightenment in France," 43.

aristocratic salons, academies—were "socially exclusive," mostly restricted to members of the nobility and the clergy.[5] Businesspeople
had no access, and neither did the new bourgeoisie. As much as the
members of these exclusive circles were removed from the economic
scene, they were as distant from court politics. Their ideas had
no political influence whatsoever, a fact that made them prone to
generalization and abstraction in their thinking.

As in other countries, the enlightenment movement was carried
by the educated strata of German society. The difference in Germany
was that the proponents of the movement were closer to the state, as
they often worked as public servants, officers, university professors,
schoolteachers, judges, or clergymen. Others were private tutors,
writers, or publishers. These people stemmed from the nobility, the
middle class, or even lower social strata. With the new economic
bourgeoisie—which was very weak in Germany—they had in common their financial dependence on an earned income. The old estates
did not offer them "a fixed place in . . . society."[6] Therefore, they had
to create such a place for themselves.

As the German states developed toward absolutism they depended
more and more on a centralized administrative bureaucracy, no
longer on the old noble estate. As a consequence, the princes promoted schools and universities from which they could recruit state
officials who would be better qualified and more loyal than the independently wealthy aristocracy. During the first half of the eighteenth
century these schools and universities became the major seats of enlightened thinking. From there, enlightened ideas entered the sphere
of political decisions. The necessity of loyalty to the state for those
who worked in its service created a specific kind of enlightenment—
one that believed in the benevolent ruler, in the king as philosopher,
in reform from above.

Freemasons' lodges were another place where adherents of enlightenment could meet and discuss—and partly live—their ideas. Unlike

5. See ibid., 44.
6. Rudolf Vierhaus, "Deutschland im 18. Jahrhundert: Soziales Gefüge, politische
Verfassung, geistige Bewegung," 180.

the universities, which represented a purely academic environment, the lodges were open to people from different social backgrounds. They offered a refuge from a society that was still strictly organized on the basis of social rank. So great was the importance of Freemasonry to German enlightenment that one of its most famous representatives, Gotthold Ephraim Lessing, wrote a whole series of dialogues on the subject, praising it as "the essence of man and of bourgeois society."[7]

Important Stages of German Enlightenment

There are three main phases to be distinguished in the development of German enlightenment: first, its beginnings and its rationalistic culmination; second, a romantic reaction against the dominance of reason; and third, the movement's self-reflection on "true" and "false" enlightenment. These different phases nevertheless have in common a focus that was characteristic of German enlightenment—religious problems. This focus can only be understood in the context of German history. The sixteenth and seventeenth centuries had been dominated by religious controversies, revolutions, and a most violent denominational war. In the sixteenth century, the Reformation and the consequent Peasants' Wars took place. The latter, despite their sociopolitical and economic origins, were strongly influenced by religious ideas. A century later, the Thirty Years' War devastated Germany, and its development fell behind that of other European countries in every respect.

During the second half of the century, a second great religious reform occurred—Pietism. It channeled all anti-orthodox ideas and movements that had developed since the establishment of Protestantism through the Reformation. By now, Protestantism had also become orthodox, but it could not cope with the social turmoil after the Thirty Years' War. The Peace of Westphalia (1649), which confirmed and extended the older principle of *cuius regio eius religio* (whose

7. Gotthold Ephraim Lessing, "Ernst und Falk: Gespräche für Freimäurer," 453.

rule it is, his religion it is), had not solved the problem of different denominations. Practiced by all denominations, and sometimes more rigidly by Protestants than by Catholics, religious intolerance represented a serious social and economical problem. Social discrimination against religious minorities inhibited social peace, economic and population growth, economic innovation (often brought by foreign immigrants), and foreign trade. Pietism, as a subjective kind of religious practice that was centered on the individual's inward relation to God, presented an escape from the situation in which a king determined his subjects' creeds.

Pietism was extremely successful in Germany. Eventually it developed into a dogma itself—against which, in turn, German enlightenment revolted in the eighteenth century.[8] At the same time, it paved the way for German enlightenment by driving scholasticism from the universities, by providing a more tolerant atmosphere for thought in general, and by raising society's conscience. The Pietistic movement retained its importance in the eighteenth century, when it influenced major thinkers of the romantic reaction to the rationalism of enlightenment, as well as critical thinkers of late enlightenment.

The Rationalistic Phase

Against the background of political and denominational partition, thinkers such as Gottfried Wilhelm Leibniz, Christian Thomasius, and Christian Wolff began to search for unity. Leibniz developed a rationalist metaphysics on the basis of which the existence of God could be justified. If the quarrel between different philosophical schools regarding the one sufficient metaphysical proof of the existence of God could be resolved, then the possibility would arise to build a unified, "true religion, which is always the most reasonable."[9] The reasoning of such a proof had to be as completely secure as the reasoning in mathematics. Leibniz's idea of a systematic demonstrative

8. L. W. Beck, *Early German Philosophy: Kant and His Predecessors*, 158.
9. Leibniz to John Frederick, Duke of Brunswick-Hanover, fall 1679, in Gottfried Wilhelm Leibniz, *Philosophical Papers and Letters*, 402.

symbolic logic, fashioned after the model of mathematical reasoning, proposed to make such a deduction possible. Once the proof of God's existence was grounded in human reasoning and had thus been rendered independent of divine revelation, it could function as the basis for a unified religion that could become common to all mankind.

By giving a rational philosophical proof for God's existence, Leibniz's *Theodicy* tore orthodox theology apart, though not the Christian religion itself.[10] His doctrine of preestablished harmony, which stipulates a parallelism between mind and matter, enabled him to assert the strictly physical explanation of natural phenomena while at the same time maintaining metaphysical (teleological) explanations consistent with religion.

In a certain regard, the world becomes independent of God. Eternal truths are still dependent upon him, but only upon his understanding. Consequently, he cannot change them at will. In creating the world, God is committed by the principle of sufficient reason to choose the best of all possible worlds. And once the world is created, he is bound by the internal teleology (entelechy) of his own creation.

The fact that the world possesses a nature of its own explains its imperfections, but its perfections originate in God. Man's knowledge of these perfections has a moral value in that it gives human beings insight into God's perfection. "In thus grounding true virtue in knowledge, Leibniz posed for the entire Aufklärung, the 'clearing up of the understanding' as the primary ethical task."[11] Here lie some of the roots of the German version of enlightenment in its emphasis on religion and morality, as well as on the clarity and distinctness of thought.

Thomasius, unlike Leibniz, was not concerned with founding a metaphysical system; he was more interested in practical knowledge. Philosophy, for him, had to be oriented toward worldly concerns,

10. Wilhelm Schmidt-Biggemann, "Emancipation by Infiltration: Institutions and Personalities of the German 'Early Enlightenment,'" 46–47.
11. Henry E. Allison, *Lessing and the Enlightenment: His Philosophy of Religion and Its Relation to Eighteenth-Century Thought*, 29.

away from the esoteric preoccupations of scholastic theologians. His approach to knowledge and truth was eclectic, although in a sense different from the known eclecticism of some seventeenth-century natural philosophers whose anti-Cartesian approach was based on experiment and selection of truths according to probability.[12] Thomasius's kind of eclecticism meant the reflective selection of ideas with the help of "sound understanding," or common sense, a concept that would be important throughout the enlightenment, right up to Reinhold. Free, independent thought could transcend the boundaries of philosophical, theological, or political systems and select historically given knowledge according to its truth and its usefulness for practical reforms. The purpose of these reforms was to promote human happiness.

Thomasius himself helped advance the reform of university education. Probably he is best known as the first professor at a German university to give his lectures in German and not in Latin, as was traditionally done. He also contributed to the reform of legal punishment, especially in the removal of torture and the abolition of witchcraft trials.

Thomasius's promotion of the German language not only questioned the educational monopoly of academic scholars and the power of orthodox scholasticism, it also revalidated German culture for the middle class, opposing the aristocratic overvaluation of French language and culture. With the publication of a learned journal, the *Teutsche Monate* (later called *Monatsgespraeche*), in 1688, Thomasius took another step toward the enlightenment of the middle class. This monthly periodical was one of the first in Germany and can be seen as a forerunner to the moral weeklies of the eighteenth century, which played such an important part in German enlightenment.

By promoting independent thinking, Thomasius took a stance against prejudice, superstition, and authority, which was characteristic of enlightened thought. The emphasis on the freedom of thought—in contrast to its clarity and distinctness—was another

---

12. Michael Albrecht, "Thomasius—kein Eklektiker?" 79–81.

major feature of German enlightenment. In 1690, Thomasius was expelled from Leipzig for his critical views. However, by about 1710, his philosophy was already taught at most German universities.

During the first half of the eighteenth century, Christian Wolff became the most influential philosopher and promoter of enlightenment in Germany; by the 1730s, his ideas were taught at all German universities and at many institutions abroad. Wolff, the systematic thinker par excellence, brought to Germany the "spirit of thoroughness."[13] On the basis of some of Leibniz's metaphysical assumptions and a mathematical method, he created a system of knowledge built on empirical facts and rational proof. As "worldly wisdom," philosophy consisted of the knowledge of all things in this world; but as the "science of the possible," it transcended factual knowledge toward the conditions of the possibility of things, thus creating knowledge of reasons, or rational knowledge. Ultimately, this led to knowledge about the ultimate reason of the world, or God. Wolff emancipated the discipline of philosophy from serving as an introductory course in the curricula of theology and jurisprudence, elevating it to being the superior science. All other disciplines, including theology, were subject to its rational method. Wolff's rationalism in regard to religion promoted in Germany the emergence of a rational theology, which had thus far been influential only in England and France.

Norbert Hinske sees one reason for Wolff's immense influence in the new confidence he placed in reason as a result of denominational conflict (as we saw earlier, for Leibniz and Thomasius). Another reason was his expulsion from the University of Halle in 1723 (an experience that he shared with Thomasius), which turned him into a martyr of the enlightenment movement.[14] Others have claimed that Wolff's greatest importance consists in his having "first introduced the German public to philosophical thinking."[15] Thus he created the leading role of philosophy in German intellectual life—particularly

13. Immanuel Kant, *Critique of Pure Reason*, B XXXVI.
14. Norbert Hinske, "Wolffs Stellung in der deutschen Aufklärung," 314–15.
15. Allison, *Lessing and the Enlightenment*, 34.

outside the universities—and helped reawaken that life. An indication of this is the foundation of Wolffian societies all over Germany, private societies through which his philosophy gained great influence on practical as well as political life. Beck mentions the Gesellschaft der Wahrheitsfreunde (Society of the Friends of Truth), founded in 1736, which took as its motto *Sapere aude!* (Dare to think!), which Kant later called the motto of the enlightenment.

By the middle of the century, the German enlightenment as a whole had broadened its basis and become something of a popular movement beyond academic life at the universities. All kinds of societies and associations sprang up, where educated people from different strata of society met for the exchange of ideas or for the practical purposes of charity or educational work. Their objective was the common welfare of society, the creation of a new, civic morality that, in its promotion of a moderate style of life, a social attitude, and sympathy for all fellow-creatures, was diametrically opposed to the aristocratic way of life.[16]

Moral weeklies, following the model of English journals such as *The Tatler* and *The Spectator,* were an expression of and directed toward an educated upper middle class, which sought its own place and recognition in society and tried to challenge the aristocracy's privilege of education. Common sense, moral strictness, and sober rationalism replaced aristocratic form, taste, and classicist wit. One objective of the weeklies was to close the gap between scholars and nonscholars by providing instructive, readable, and entertaining treatises. Although not in confrontation with religion, they stressed the independence of reason from traditional authorities.

The audience for the weeklies consisted of the educated middle class, including women. Reinhold was the co-publisher and chief editor of the *Allgemeine Damenbibliothek* (1785–1789), which aimed at instructing "ladies" (*Damen*) in fields from ethnography to moral philosophy. Common people, such as craftsmen and peasants, were not addressed. The weeklies encouraged their readers to participate

16. See Wolfgang Martens, "Bürgerlichkeit in der frühen Aufklärung."

by writing letters or their own essays, thus creating a public discourse, indeed, a civic public *(bürgerliche Öffentlichkeit)*. Private correspondence between friends also became an important forum for the discussion of enlightened ideas.

When in 1740 Friedrich II, the epitome of the enlightened ruler, became king of Prussia, a period of relatively free thought and writing began, with Berlin as the center of intellectual life. The Academy of Arts and Sciences—originally founded by Leibniz—was promoted again. Many French enlightenment thinkers—among them Voltaire, La Mettrie, and d'Alembert—became members. As Beck points out, the introduction of French and English thought to Germany was "equivalent to setting up rivals to the dominant Leibnizian and Leibniz-Wolffian systems."[17] Through its prize competitions on timely philosophical problems, the Academy stimulated intellectual discourse.

Outside the Academy, the so-called popular philosophy became influential not only in Berlin but also in other places—among them, Göttingen. Representative thinkers were, among others, Friedrich Nicolai, Johann A. Eberhard, Christian Garve, Thomas Abbt, and Johann J. Engel. Popular philosophy was eclectic, based on common sense, practice-oriented, and nonsystematic. With their concern for the education of the public, the popular philosophers acted on the objective of the moral weeklies.

Apart from being spread through popular journals and treatises, enlightened ideas were also increasingly promulgated by the Protestant clergy. Whaley describes Protestant enlightenment as "primarily a utilitarian reform movement,"[18] dedicated to the welfare of society in the given political order. Friedrich strongly supported the Protestant church in such enterprises as historical-philological critique of the Bible, rationalistic criticism of Pietism, and refutations of French materialism and atheism.

17. Beck, *Early German Philosophy*, 316.
18. Joachim Whaley, "The Protestant Enlightenment in Germany," 117.

The Romantic Reaction

While the rule of reason spread further in Germany, and rationalistic thinking seemed to conquer public consciousness, voices began to make themselves heard that warned against the consequences of a triumph of abstract reason. They criticized rational religion, the optimism of Wolffian metaphysics, the rationalist moralistic view of art, and the acceptance of benevolent despotism by enlightened thinkers. The new movement set freedom against authority, subjectivity above norms, and faith above reason. In the realm of philosophy, the attempt was made to reformulate the concept of reason so as to incorporate aspects so far neglected—history, organic nature, feeling, and language. On the literary scene, the Sturm und Drang movement wrote the claims of subjectivity, freedom, and sentiment on its banner.

Pietism played an important role in the movement of "counter-enlightenment," as it was misleadingly called. Pietists traditionally had rejected rationalism, emphasizing instead subjectivity over established norms. Feeling, imagination, and faith were stressed as superior to reason. Apart from established Pietist groups, such as the one at the University of Halle, there always existed popular Pietistic movements. "Separatism" spread among the lower middle classes, especially among an emerging class of petty bourgeoisie, composed of dislocated former *Stadtbürger* (burghers), but also among villagers and the petty nobility, both oppressed by absolutist rulers.[19] These movements espoused utopian ideals that stemmed from popular forces defeated during the Peasants' Wars. The notions of universal priesthood and subjective religiosity contained an element of egalitarianism that questioned the hierarchical paternalism of the absolutist German states.

Almost all literary and philosophical figures of the following decades were "reared in Protestant households, invariably pious if not inveterately pietistic."[20] Philosophers of this movement, such as J. G.

---

19. Larry Vaughan, *The Historical Constellation of the Sturm und Drang*, 92–94.
20. Ibid., 108.

Hamann and J. G. Herder, did not hold back their political criticism. The writers of the Sturm und Drang—the young Goethe, J. M. R. Lenz, F. M. von Klinger, and H. L. Wagner—attacked the existing social order with the claim of liberty. They opposed the objectivity of the state with the subjectivity of the person, aesthetic rules with creative genius, and societal convention with a new, immediate feeling for nature.

Although these writers drew their inspiration from older literary figures, such as Friedrich G. Klopstock, A. von Haller, and Gotthold Ephraim Lessing, they produced a radically new kind of literature. The emphasis on emotions was nothing new. However, Lessing, for instance, had given priority to a rather passive feeling of sympathy. The goal of tragedy, in his opinion, was to arouse as much compassion in the audience as possible. He regarded this as a means to promote social virtue.[21] The undeserved sufferings of a tragic character were not supposed to create active protest against unjust social and political conditions. Rather, the audience was to dissolve in tears of compassion and then be exhausted but reconciled with the world. This passive sentimentality (*Empfindsamkeit*) can be contrasted to the active "sentiment" of Sturm und Drang. Cassirer sees their difference in the concept of freedom, which the latter contains but the former does not.[22] The concept of freedom is bound to that of radical subjectivity, as it was soon to be formulated by Kant. In Kant's view, the "true self" is spontaneously active, able to break out of the realm of natural causality. This concept of negative, anarchical freedom predominated in Sturm und Drang.

Kant had been strongly influenced by his reading of Rousseau, who had him convinced that there was an unchanging nature of man, which in its essence consisted of inner freedom. This idea of inner freedom is embodied in many characters of Sturm und Drang plays. All of its writers acknowledged their indebtedness to Rousseau.

---

21. It is probably not a mere coincidence that David Hume, too, saw "sympathy" as the source of morality. The concept of sympathy could provide a basis for morality, after traditional and rationalistic metaphysics had become unable to do so.

22. Ernst Cassirer, *Rousseau, Kant, Goethe. Two Essays,* 46.

In their radical subjectivity, their characters are alienated from the world as it is. Goethe's Werther kills himself. Lenz's "Private Tutor" castrates himself so he can fit into a world where there is no place for his personality and his passions. Karl Moor, in Schiller's *The Robbers*, breaks all the laws of society and religion until, realizing his guilt in that defiance, he submits to the forces of law. In doing so, he steps beyond the realm of negative freedom and thus of Sturm und Drang.

In the realm of philosophy, three writers have to be mentioned who effectively shaped the movement of counter-enlightenment—Johann Georg Hamann, Friedrich Heinrich Jacobi, and Johann Gottfried Herder. Hamann, the famous Magus of the North, was one of the main inspirers of Sturm und Drang. Together with Jacobi and Johann Kaspar Lavater, he was a leading figure of the so-called philosophy of faith (*Glaubensphilosophie*). The philosophers of faith sharply criticized the authority that reason possessed for rationalism. They utilized Hume's skeptical conclusions regarding the human faculty of knowledge in defending faith against reason.

Hamann criticized not only rationalist philosophy but also Kant's critical philosophy for its purism of reason, against which he set the "social and historical dimension of rationality,"[23] the necessary embodiment of reason. Hamann's theory of language—its divine origin and the closeness of poetical language to this origin—entailed a theory of art and the artistic genius in which art attains metaphysical significance. That is, art is believed to provide immediate insight into reality. This view not only strongly affected the Sturm und Drang movement but would also have great influence on Romanticism.

Jacobi—one of Reinhold's closest friends, by the way—carried the critique of rationality further. Against what he regarded as the consequences of rationalism—atheism and fatalism—he "took a *salto mortale*," a leap of faith.[24] For Jacobi, reason, or belief, is intuitive and immediate and renders knowledge of facts. The understanding functions indirectly on an intellectual level; it analyzes or synthesizes the

23. Frederick C. Beiser, *The Fate of Reason: German Philosophy from Kant to Fichte*, 16.
24. Beck, *Early German Philosophy*, 369.

given facts in a logical manner. On its own, it can conceive the world only as conditioned and final: "It can never arrive at the knowledge of the Unconditioned or God . . . thus . . . a logical, demonstrative philosophy must necessarily end in atheism and fatalism."[25] Jacobi's distinction between "reason" and "understanding" was to be an important one for Romanticism and German Idealism, discrediting the "understanding."

A most influential figure for Sturm und Drang and for the eighteenth century as a whole was Johann Gottfried Herder. Although he is sometimes considered a philosopher of faith, he did not perform a *salto mortale* as Jacobi did, but tried to synthesize "the one-sided philosophy of faith and feeling with the one-sidedness of the Enlightenment philosophy."[26] He did not despise rational understanding, but thought that both God and nature can be known by it. In opposition to the prevalent mechanical theories of nature, Herder developed a dynamic theory: nature is composed of "substantial or organic forces" and is created and sustained by God.[27]

Herder's "genetic" method could be applied to all expressions of human culture—religion, art, language, history, and science. It interpreted them, not by applying external standards, but by understanding them from within, by sympathizing with their creators' intentions. Thus allegedly universal rational standards were abandoned in favor of concrete, relative ones.

Herder's influence on Sturm und Drang was considerable. It was probably he who inspired Goethe's *Die Leiden des jungen Werthers* and *Götz von Berlichingen*. The former, an apotheosis of feeling, the description of a love so radical and solipsistic that it does not fit into society, created a huge public response. Not only were there many suicides; there occurred an "explosion of reading."[28] Whereas the writings of earlier enlightened authors had reached only the educated

---

25. Frederick H. Burkhardt, introduction to *God. Some Conversations*, by Johann Gottfried Herder, 20.
26. Beck, *Early German Philosophy*, 382.
27. Herder, *God. Some Conversations*, 2d conversation, 103.
28. Vaughan, *Historical Constellation of the Sturm und Drang*, 117.

classes, the literature of Sturm und Drang reached people in the lower classes as well. Reading societies and libraries sprang up, civic theater became popular, providing mostly sentimental and romantic trivializations of Sturm und Drang novels and plays, thereby meeting the needs of all the middle social strata that were socially and politically impotent in the absolutist state.

In the upper, better-educated bourgeoisie, reading materials and habits were different. During the last third of the eighteenth century, reading societies flourished, which acquired and lent books and periodicals to their members and organized conversations and discussions. These societies were solely for members of the upper middle classes, and were for males only. Their declared aims were mutual enlightenment, the improvement of morals, taste, study of the sciences, and, most important, human happiness. The offered reading materials possessed a rather academic as well as pragmatic character, consisting of lexica, political treatises, writings about enlightenment, travel books, and periodicals on such practical subjects as trade.

An important aspect of the societies was their ability to offer the "newest" publications. The attitude toward reading itself had changed. Instead of reading the same devotional text over and over in the family, people became interested in what was new. "Extensive" reading took the place of "intensive" reading.[29]

Self-Reflection: "True" and "False" Enlightenment

During the last third of the eighteenth century, several circumstances and events sparked public discussion of the enlightenment movement and, particularly, the concept of enlightenment itself. Among these circumstances and events were the heightened interest in public affairs and the spread of reading; questions raised by Herder, Hamann, and others about the authority of reason; an aggravated political situation with the Prussian Edict of Religion, tougher censorship, and the prohibition of Freemasons and Illuminati; the

---

29. Herbert G. Göpfert, "Lesegesellschaften im 18. Jahrhundert," 409.

advent of the French Revolution, which reinforced conservative tendencies; and the polarization of political discussion, each party claiming for itself the true ideal of enlightenment.

The discussion was initiated by the Prussian Academy, which in 1780 asked whether it was necessary to deceive the people,[30] thus problematizing the merit of popular enlightenment. Three years later, the discussion reached a new level when the *Berlinische Monatsschrift* asked the general question, "What is enlightenment?" The two most famous answers came from Mendelssohn and Kant. But many others wrote about the subject, among them Reinhold, who published his article "Gedanken über Aufklärung" (Thoughts on enlightenment) the next year.

Definitions of the concept were as numerous as the answers themselves. Enlightenment was said to consist in any knowledge in general, clear and distinct concepts (for example, Andreas Riem); freedom from tutelage (Johann B. Erhard, Kant); independent thought (Christoph M. Wieland); and practice-oriented, useful knowledge (Peter Villaume). H. B. Nisbet summarizes the views then shared by most enlightened thinkers: Enlightenment was thought of as "a process, or the result of a process, leading to some kind of improvement in the lot of mankind." The end of this process was the realization of "man's destiny," an important feature of which was the concept of freedom. Increased freedom, among other things, led to "the discovery of truth, or to increased knowledge." A majority of writers believed in "the redemptive value of knowledge." Knowledge made human beings more virtuous and "promote[d] morality." Some, in the tradition of Wolff, also thought that an increase in virtue was followed by an increase in happiness.[31]

In the course of the dispute, it became fashionable to claim "true enlightenment" for oneself and to dismiss adverse definitions as "false enlightenment." The latter concept provided a way of distancing

30. See Werner Schneiders, *Die wahre Aufklärung: Zum Selbstverständnis der deutschen Aufklärung,* 21. For this section, I rely heavily on his excellent presentation.
31. H. B. Nisbet, "'Was ist Aufklärung?' The Concept of Enlightenment in Eighteenth-Century Germany," 80–82.

oneself not only from views that deviated from one's own but also from undesirable, alleged consequences of enlightenment. Conservatives defended the old estates against claims for social equality by advancing a so-called relative enlightenment. This consisted in providing knowledge to people according to their traditional place in society—what was worth knowing by a nobleman was possibly dangerous for a simple peasant. It was the intention of the conservatives to affirm the political status quo while the lives of disadvantaged members of society were to be improved through instruction on practical—technical and moral—issues.

Others, like Christoph Martin Wieland, rejected any limitation of enlightenment. They thought that if enlightenment were identified with the knowledge of truth and falsehood, and of good and evil, any limitation of enlightenment would entail a restriction on knowing the good and the true. Consequently, enlightenment "relative" to people's social status was unacceptable, as was censorship of teachers, clergymen, or the press. In comparing enlightenment to the infinite perfection of which mankind was capable, Wieland—in his "Das Geheimniss des Kosmopoliten-Ordens" (The secret of the cosmopolitan order)—refused to set "unnatural limits" on enlightenment.

The "philosophers of faith," alleged proponents of counter-enlightenment, criticized certain concepts of enlightenment, but they did not in fact give up the concept itself. Hamann called contemporary enlightenment "a cold, infertile moonlight without enlightenment for the lazy understanding and without warmth for the cowardly will." He rejected Kant's notion of "self-incurred tutelage," pointing to actual power structures in society. Instead he made the "blindness of the guardians" responsible for the tutelage of their wards. Thus he held on to the concept of enlightenment by redefining it as "the release of an incompetent [*unmündig*] human being from the guardianship of which he is most guilty,"[32] referring to the release of the guardians and not the wards. In other words, he tied

---

32. Johann Georg Hamann, "Brief an Christian Jacob Kraus vom 18. Dezember 1784," 20–21. Kraus was a pupil of Kant's.

enlightenment to the political emancipation of all groups of society. In a similar attempt to broaden the narrow, purely rational concept of enlightenment, Herder described it as a "means in the service of life," making it part of man's education toward humanity, the "character of our species" that is "inborn only as a potential and has to be formed in us."[33]

The advent of the French Revolution brought about a new phase in the discussion of enlightenment. It was a widely accepted thesis that French enlightened ideas were responsible for the outbreak of the revolution as well as for the subsequent terror. Supporters of enlightenment in Germany used the ongoing debate about "true" and "false" enlightenment to distance themselves from the revolution, or at least from its aberrations, and they blamed "false" enlightenment. At the same time, the position of those who pleaded for limited enlightenment—relative to social status and needs—was strengthened. Instead of teaching people speculative ideas, practical knowledge should be spread, especially religious and professional knowledge.

By the end of the eighteenth century, the expectations connected with enlightening society waned. Reservations about the prospects for the process of enlightenment replaced the exuberant optimism of rationalistic enlightenment. People no longer claimed to live in the final stage of history, when the end of a rationally ordered society had been achieved. They were no longer convinced that with the increase of knowledge, people would also improve morally.[34] Whereas rationalistic optimism had long assumed that the education of the understanding—that is, for this kind of thinking, enlightenment—would entail the "education of the heart," or morality, this was not obvious to a thinker like Reinhold, as we will see.

Kant was cautious, too, when he characterized his age as not yet enlightened but in the process of enlightenment; he also called it an age of criticism. In his article on enlightenment, when he referred to the *Critique of Pure Reason* with its self-examination of reason,

33. Johann Gottfried Herder, *Briefe zur Beförderung der Humanität*, 27th letter, 38.
34. See Schneiders, *Wahre Aufklärung*, 27–28.

he tied his understanding of enlightenment to the surmounting of rationalism and its faith in the absolute power of reason. Therefore, Kant is seen by many as the one who was the culmination of the movement but who also transcended it. From a contemporary perspective, that was not true. Kant's interpretation of enlightenment was by no means as influential as is thought today. The debate on the concept did not stop with the publication of his article in 1783. Mendelssohn's definition—in his article from the same year—was more readily accepted.

The discussion about enlightenment continued until the turn of the century. An accord on some part of the concept on which all could have agreed was never reached.[35] However, Reinhold's *Fundamental Concepts* can be seen as a "systematic [summing up] of essential results of enlightenment."[36]

Since the focus thus far has been on enlightenment in the Protestant parts of Germany, some remarks on Catholic enlightenment and its difference from Protestant enlightenment are needed—especially in light of Reinhold's having been raised in Catholic Austria and having been a Catholic monk until his conversion.

Early Catholic enlightenment was basically a monastic movement in which members of the Benedictine and Augustinian orders were involved. Blanning characterizes it as generating an "intellectual revival," which centered on practical Christianity, anti-scholasticism, episcopalism (directed against the papacy), and rational natural law.[37] Jansenism, the Catholic reform movement that was particularly active in France and in Austria, shared the first two goals, though not the last two.

Catholic enlightenment was from the beginning directed against the Jesuits' strong influence in all parts of society. In Austria, many of Joseph II's reforms were designed to break Jesuit power by means of which the Roman Church—with its doctrines of papal infallibility,

---

35. Horst Stuke, "Aufklärung," 289.
36. Schneiders, *Wahre Aufklärung*, 181.
37. T. C. W. Blanning, "The Enlightenment in Catholic Germany," 119.

divine right of secular rulers, and so forth—enacted its political power in the real world. Most of the members of the Austrian clergy, having been educated by the Jesuits, opposed enlightened measures—as did many people of the lower classes of society. The latter, indubitably under the influence of the local clergy, still clung to superstition, belief in miracles, witchcraft, saints, the power of relics, and the devil, and were appalled when Joseph in his reforms attacked them all.

This opposition by the clergy and the lower classes is in vivid contrast to the situation in the Protestant parts of Germany, where it was the clergy, having been educated at universities where Leibnizian and Wolffian philosophy were taught, who spread enlightened ideas and actively contributed to the cause of enlightenment by educating their flocks in moral and practical matters.[38] In Austria, enlightenment was enacted exclusively from above by the absolutist ruler.

Since the Austrian Catholic enlightenment had to fight against ecclesiastical institutions that Protestant Germany had abandoned during the Reformation, many Protestants regarded it as "backward." An important factor contributing to this view was Pietism, which in Protestant regions had long questioned the authority of religious dogmas and furthered their disintegration. Early Catholic reform movements had not involved such questioning.[39]

The charge of backwardness was made, for example, by the popular philosopher Friedrich Nicolai in his *Beschreibung einer Reise durch Deutschland und die Schweiz im Jahre 1781* (Description of a journey through Germany and Switzerland in the year 1781), in which he argued against the idea of reuniting the Protestant and Catholic churches. His work contributed to a debate, known as the "Catholicism controversy," among philosophers over such a reunion. This debate had been initiated by an anonymous article in the *Berlinische Monatsschrift*,[40] which criticized the practice in some Prussian cities

38. See the section of this chapter entitled "The Rationalistic Phase."
39. Klaus Epstein, *The Genesis of German Conservatism*, 114.
40. Akatholicus Tolerans, "Falsche Toleranz einiger märkischen und Pommerschen Städte in Ansehung der Einräumung der protestantischen Kirchen zum katho-

of allowing Catholics to use Protestant churches as "misunderstood tolerance against an intolerant opponent."[41]

Reinhold, the former Catholic monk, took the side of Nicolai by pointing to the negative parts of Austrian enlightenment and reform Catholicism. He wrote about Nicolai's descriptions: "In almost every section of the work, one is made aware of the fine fetters with which the hierarchy ties a Catholic state in all its parts."[42]

Reinhold's Concept of True Enlightenment

His "Gedanken über Aufklärung"

In 1784, Reinhold published the article "Gedanken über Aufklärung" in Wieland's Der Teutsche Merkur. His main objectives in this article were to attack what he calls the "spirit of monasticism" and to defend Josephinism in Austria. These objectives can only be understood against the background of his biography.[43]

Reinhold was born in 1757 in Vienna.[44] His education was determined by a strong religious commitment, and he joined the Jesuit order as a novice in 1772. When the order was dissolved a year later, Reinhold became a Barnabite monk.[45] During the next six years, he studied theology and philosophy at the Barnabites' St. Martin College

---

lischen Gottesdienst," in Berlinische Monatsschrift 1 [1784]: 180–92. Norbert Hinske claims that Johann E. Biester "most probably" was the author (Hinske, Was ist Aufklärung? Beiträge aus der Berlinischen Monatsschrift).

41. Werner Sauer, Österreichische Philosophie zwischen Aufklärung und Restauration: Beiträge zur Geschichte des Frühkantianismus in der Donaumonarchie, 79.

42. Reinhold, "Ueber die neuesten patriotischen Lieblingsträume in Teutschland: Aus Veranlassung des 3. und 4ten Bandes von Hrn. Nicolai's Reisebeschreibung," 419.

43. The only biography written about Reinhold is the one by his son Ernst Reinhold. Unfortunately it is not very reliable and offers a eulogy rather than a critical assessment of Reinhold's life.

44. His son reports the birth date as October 16, 1758, which is corrected by the Korrespondenzausgabe, xi.

45. The Catholic order of the Barnabites had been founded in Milan in 1536 for the purpose of improving the education and morals of the Catholic clergy (see Ernst Reinhold, Reinhold's Leben und litterarisches Wirken, 13–14).

and St. Michael College in Vienna. Through one of his teachers, Paul Pepermann, he became acquainted with English enlightened thought, especially that of John Locke. Reinhold was a very successful student and was praised by his teachers. After the conclusion of his studies in 1780, he was not only ordained as a priest but also employed as a teacher of philosophy for the order. The subjects he had to teach were logic, metaphysics, ethics, religious rhetoric, mathematics, and physics. In 1782, he was appointed master of novices at St. Michael College in Vienna.

During his schooling, Reinhold got to know many people who played an important role in Vienna's intellectual and cultural life. Among his childhood friends were Johann Baptist von Alxinger, Gottlieb Leon, and Joseph Franz von Ratschky. Leon and Ratschky, together with the writer Aloys Blumauer, first published in 1777 the *Wiener Musenalmanach,* a collection of poetry. Reinhold shared their poetical inclinations. He became friends with the poet Johann Michael Kosmas Denis, who introduced him to the political writer and poet Joseph von Sonnenfels and the influential scientist, intellectual, and Freemason Ignaz von Born. Through these friends, whose circle later would be known as the "Wiener Freunde" (Viennese friends), Reinhold became acquainted with the ideas of Austrian enlightenment.

Under the rule of Maria Theresia and, from 1781 on, her son Joseph II, Austria was transformed into a centralized state, where the "particular interests of feudal aristocracy and the Church," which stood against that unification, were curbed.[46] Such a unification became necessary after the Austro-Prussian war, when Silesia was lost and Prussia became a great power. It became clear that the office of Holy Roman emperor, traditionally held by the Austrian king, had lost its function. "The complex edifice of the Austrian-Hungarian monarchy [could] only continue to exist within the framework of a modernized, centralized absolutist state."[47] Substantial reforms in

46. Sauer, *Österreichische Philosophie,* 23.
47. Leslie Bodi, *Tauwetter in Wien: Zur Prosa der österreichischen Aufklärung 1781–1795,* 32.

the realms of state administration, economy, society, military, education, and church were undertaken. The need for public servants loyal to such an enterprise made it necessary to free the educational system from clerical influence. Consequently, education in schools and universities was taken out of the hands of the Jesuits; curricula were modernized; Leibnizian and Wolffian thinking took the place of medieval scholasticism; modern natural law was taught and practically implemented; state power and church power were separated. By distinguishing between "internal and external religious service,"[48] Joseph was to some extent able to subject official Church institutions—"external religious service"—to the power of the state, leaving the internal aspect, or people's conscience, untouched. Eventually, he confiscated Church property, abolished religious orders like the Jesuits, dissolved their monasteries, canceled their vows, and in general did away with religious customs such as certain funeral rites and holy days. His policies were drastic and were often rejected by the populace, though many intellectuals and artists supported and admired him. The reform and partial abolition of censorship led to a literal "flood" of literature about all aspects of enlightenment. The so-called *Broschürenflut* (flood of brochures) has been well described by Bodi.

The "Viennese friends" supported Joseph's reforms enthusiastically. The Freemasonic lodge "Zur wahren Eintracht" (To Real Harmony), founded in 1781 and headed by Ignaz von Born, soon became their forum. They wanted to promote freedom of thought and conscience and to fight monasticism, seen as the archenemy of enlightenment. Reinhold became a member of the lodge in 1783; his joining was first kept a secret because of anticipated difficulties for the Catholic monk. During the same year he also joined the secret order of the Illuminati. By then, he had been writing for the Viennese *Realzeitung*, edited by his friend Blumauer, for one year. In a column entitled "*Theologie und Kirchenwesen*" (Theology and church), he wrote reviews of publications about religious matters. These reviews

48. Sauer, *Österreichische Philosophie*, 26.

already show his concern for the relation between true faith and superstition. Reinhold criticized monasticism and other Church institutions as supporting superstition and contradicting "sound reason." As Gliwitzky shows in his analysis of Reinhold's reviews, faith and reason were for Reinhold harmonious, because both were "sources of the love of God," though he did "not exactly determine how they were related."[49]

At the end of 1783, he fled Austria—first to Leipzig and then to Weimar. The reason for his flight is not known with certainty. Schiller mentions a girl whom Reinhold wanted to marry. In a letter to Blumauer, dated April 16, 1783, Reinhold described the discrepancy between his endeavor for self-cultivation (*Bildung*) and the ignorance required by his religious profession. Years later he wrote that a crisis in his religious beliefs, caused by his studies in speculative philosophy, made it impossible for him to continue as a monk: "It had become impossible for him to believe blindly, as he had done before."[50] This crisis was certainly deepened by enlightened critiques of Church orthodoxy and its institutions. Being a monk and at the same time criticizing the Church was probably an impossible task.

In Leipzig, Reinhold registered at the university and attended philosophical lectures. However, his whereabouts soon became known in Vienna. This in turn made impossible the attempt of von Born and other friends to have Reinhold released from his religious vows so that he could return to Austria without fear of persecution. Von Born advised him to leave Leipzig and go to Weimar, where some letters of recommendation helped him find a cordial reception at Wieland's home. After his arrival in Weimar in May 1784, Reinhold immediately broke with Catholicism and converted to Protestantism, with Herder as his pastor. Exactly one year later, he married Wieland's daughter Sophie.

---

49. Hans Gliwitzky, "Carl Leonhard Reinholds erster Standpunktwechsel," 32–33.
50. Reinhold, "Ueber die bisherigen Schicksale der kantischen Philosophie," preface to his *Versuch einer neuen Theorie des menschlichen Vorstellungsvermögens*, 53.

Wieland helped Reinhold during the following years to publish reviews and articles and thus gain a reputation as a writer on current debates. Decisive for Reinhold was his work for Wieland's journal *Der Teutsche Merkur*, of which he became co-publisher from 1786. Already in June 1784, one month after his arrival in Weimar, he became editor of the "Anzeiger des Teutschen Merkur." In *Der Teutsche Merkur*, Reinhold published his review of Herder's "Ideas of the Philosophy of History of Mankind" and his sharp critique of Kant's review of Herder's "Ideas." And here he published his *Letters on the Kantian Philosophy*—now all in favor of Kant—which helped found his reputation as one of the foremost philosophical thinkers in Germany. Of course, it took Reinhold some time to catch up with the current state of enlightened debate in the north of Germany. In his "Gedanken über Aufklärung," which he began publishing three months after his arrival in Weimar, he understandably still argues from the point of view of Josephinism, glorifying "Joseph and his wise men."[51]

In this article, Reinhold defines true enlightenment as popular enlightenment for "all classes."[52] It consists generally in the education of reason, and particularly in the correction of concepts important for everyday human life—as opposed to scholarly concepts—and whose clarification will lead to different, improved actions. Reinhold rejects any limitation of enlightenment, since he thinks every human being is capable of being rational.

Reinhold characterizes three false concepts of enlightenment, which are, according to him, the most common. The first is the misconception that enlightenment destroys religion and morality; the second is shared by those who think that popular enlightenment, in criticizing religious systems and showing their preposterousness, will lead to

---

51. Reinhold, "Gedanken über Aufklärung," 386. I refer to Batscha's pagination. The essay will be published in an English translation in James Schmidt, ed., *"What Is Enlightenment?" Eighteenth Century Answers and Twentieth Century Questions* (University of California Press, forthcoming). This essay represents Reinhold's early views on enlightenment; in *The Fundamental Concepts*, one finds his mature thoughts on the subject.

52. Reinhold, "Gedanken über Aufklärung," 355.

popular insurrection. These people come to the conclusion that enlightenment should be limited to a certain elite. The third concept judges the effects of enlightenment pessimistically: enlightenment only takes away "partly harmless, partly useful deceptions . . . without being able to provide anything better instead."[53]

Against these false conceptions, Reinhold poses the concept of "true" enlightenment in the broad sense as making "rational people out of ones who are capable of being rational." "Enlightenment in the narrow sense consists in the employment of those means which are given in nature in order to elucidate confused concepts into clear ones." Rational and thus enlightened persons are those who have at their disposal "a certain amount of clear concepts that are clear to a certain degree." And not any concepts will do—only those that "have considerable influence on human happiness."[54]

The concepts that are taught to people are "popular concepts" in contrast to "philosophical" ones. Popular concepts are clear, although they do not contain "logical and metaphysical definitions." They stem from a class of concepts that common people and philosophers share and that Reinhold describes as "communication-bridges." An example of such a concept is that of God as a wise father "who punishes only out of mercy." This concept mediates between the concept of divine justice as it is determined by distinct philosophical thought as "wisely distributed mercy," and the same concept as conceived by common people, namely, as the punishment of an implacable, even sadistic God.[55]

The Catholic Church is, for Reinhold, the worst enemy of enlightenment. He characterizes it as supporting "darkness of spirit" and "ignorance," and taking "incomprehensibility as the characteristic of the probability of any assumption of its infallible preachers." The "spirit of monasticism," a major target of Josephinism, consists for the former monk in "ignorance," "superstition," "ambition," and

---

53. Ibid., 366–70.
54. Ibid., 372–74.
55. Ibid., 378–80.

"greed."[56] He makes the secular interests of the Church responsible for its antipathy to the ideas of enlightenment.

Reinhold's concept of enlightenment, at this point, was within the Leibnizian and Wolffian tradition, proposing the clarification of concepts.[57] He was convinced that Joseph's reforms in legislation and education realized enlightened ideals, as far as that was possible under the given political circumstances. Reinhold regretted the effects of the *Broschürenflut* in Vienna after the relaxation of censorship, for it contributed to the confusion about the concept of enlightenment. However, at the same time he was convinced that the analysis of the concept was "infinite" and had to be completed by history. Reinhold construes the progress of enlightenment dialectically, as a desire for light produced by deepest spiritual darkness. "The bonzes of all nations had to do as much for the obscuration of human understanding as they actually did, before the sad effects could become obvious enough in order to force people to think."[58] Thus, he can judge the prospects of enlightenment optimistically.

In his "Gedanken über Aufklärung," Reinhold still believed that popular enlightenment basically happened from above, that it was a one-sided affair of the philosophers teaching the people. Reinhold did not share Kant's concept of enlightenment, which consisted in the individual's "competence" (*Mündigkeit*) in independent thought. Only after Reinhold had gained some distance from the situation in Austria did he start to think critically of Joseph's tyrannical absolutist measures, which he used to implement his policies. In his *Herzenserleichterung zweyer Menschenfreunde* (1785), he speaks of the "newest despotic principles" in Austrian politics.[59] A year later, he

---

56. Ibid., 362–63. Reinhold made an exception, though, in regard to his judgment on his former order (see Reinhold, *Ehrenrettung der Lutherischen Reformation gegen zwey Kapitel in des K. K. Hofraths Herrn J. M. Schmids Geschichte der Teutschen nebst einigen Bemerkungen über die gegenwärtige katholische Reformation im Oesterreichischen*, preface).

57. Sauer, *Österreichische Philosophie*, 68.

58. Reinhold, "Gedanken über Aufklärung," 370, 394.

59. Reinhold, *Herzenserleichterung zweyer Menschenfreunde, in vertraulichen Briefen über Johann Caspar Lavaters Glaubensbekentnis*, 25.

had "not only completely caught up with the state of enlightenment in Protestant Germany but had also thought it through."[60]

By then, he had studied Kant's critical philosophy and adopted the results of the critique of reason. His *Briefe über die Kantische Philosophie* (Letters on the Kantian philosophy), which he published from the middle of 1786 in *Der Teutsche Merkur*, made him instantly famous in Germany as the foremost interpreter of Kant's critical philosophy. In the first of the *Briefe*, he argues that a critique of reason is a necessity of the times. He shares the view of some of his contemporaries that religious enlightenment in Protestant Germany is actually declining instead of progressing. According to him, this decline is brought about by a growing "indifferentism," and even "hate and contempt" toward the employment of reason in religious matters. One symptom of this crisis of reason is the neglect of metaphysics. Referring to the romantic reaction against enlightenment, Reinhold blames "warm-headed enthusiasts" for the resurrection of superstition, that is, irrational faith. At the same time, he accuses their opponents, the deists, whom he calls "coldhearted sophists," of furthering the cause of atheism. The fight of these two groups perpetuates the "old antinomy of understanding and the heart," an antinomy that Reinhold finds unacceptable and that he wants to dissolve through the "mediation of reason."[61] Just at that time, the fight between these two positions was culminating in the famous pantheism controversy. Reinhold's *Briefe* presented an important contribution to that debate in offering a solution to the alleged antinomy of reason and faith.[62]

Another problem for enlightenment, as Reinhold sees it, is the "critical relationship between enlightenment and absolutism."[63] Although state churches and rulers had been freed by the Reformation from the hierarchical reign of the Roman Church, they now opposed

---

60. Alexander von Schönborn, *Karl Leonhard Reinhold: Eine annotierte Bibliographie*, 13.

61. Reinhold, *Briefe über die Kantische Philosophie*, new ed. Raymund Schmidt, 18–19.

62. See below, chap. 3.

63. Sauer, *Österreichische Philosophie*, 78.

further emancipatory progress: "As [reason] progresses and asserts principles which do not allow for the existence of clericalism [*Pfafferei*] and despotism, nothing is more certain than that both will try with all their might . . . to suppress the voice of their enemy [i.e., reason]."[64]

Having talked about the problems that enlightenment faces, Reinhold offers a surprising interpretation of the spirit of his age. Far from being pessimistic about the progress of enlightenment, he is convinced that the upheavals in all systems of thought, which are caused by basic misconceptions regarding the faculty of reason, will finally make people recognize the need for a critique of reason.

> The problem: What is the ability of reason? is prepared, assigned and made necessary by the present circumstances of the age. It would be a great merit of our age if the old misunderstanding of a reason that does not know itself . . . would be brought to light. However, this misunderstanding was an inevitable one on the long and troublesome path that the human spirit had to take leading to a scientific understanding of its power. The solution of this misunderstanding promises nothing less than universally valid first principles of our duties and rights, a universally valid argument in favor of our expectation of a future life, the end of all philosophical and theological heresies, and eternal peace in the sphere of speculative philosophy.[65]

Werner Sauer interprets Reinhold's concept of the necessary progress of reason as an "application of Kant's doctrine of antinomies in the sphere of philosophy of history or culture."[66] According to him, Reinhold applies the concept of an antinomy of reason, given in its very nature, to the historical development of reason. This results in the claim that this development—from dogmatism to skepticism and finally to the critique of reason—has been necessary and will in the end lead inevitably to the right, scientific conception of reason.

---

64. Reinhold, *Briefe*, 20.
65. Ibid., 90–91.
66. Sauer, *Österreichische Philosophie*, 82.

His Fundamental Concepts

By the time Reinhold published *The Fundamental Concepts*, he advocated a concept of enlightenment that encompassed the major aspects of the concept as it had been discussed during the period of its self-reflection. Since his book represented the outcome of years of discussions and consultations with friends and other like-minded people, it embodied the consensus of a number of supporters of the movement.

Another biographical remark is called for here. Until *The Fundamental Concepts* was published in 1798, Reinhold had undergone several transformations in his philosophical approach. After his study of Kant, he had adopted the critical standpoint, but had soon become convinced that Kant's critique of reason lacked a proper philosophical foundation. This he attempted to provide under the name of an *Elementarphilosophie* (fundamental philosophy),[67] which consisted in a new theory of the human faculty of representation. This theory initiated Fichte's *Wissenschaftslehre*. After intense discussions between the two, Reinhold himself temporarily converted to Fichte's philosophical system in 1797. Even though his theoretical ideas changed dramatically between 1784 and 1798, his practical philosophy was still basically Kantian. This premise has to guide the interpretation of *The Fundamental Concepts*.

The discussion of the concept of enlightenment takes up more than half of *The Fundamental Concepts*. Enlightenment in general still consists for Reinhold in the clarity and distinctness of concepts, with clarity referring to distinguishing the concept of one object from those of other objects, and distinctness referring to the conceptual differentiation of the parts within one object. Clarity and distinctness guarantee true and certain convictions. On the basis of this pair of concepts, he conceives of the distinction between extensive and intensive enlightenment: the former refers to the "number of different concepts that are compared," and the latter to the "precision and completeness of analysis of clear concepts" (article 126). "True"

---

67. First presented in his *Versuch einer neuen Theorie*, published in 1789.

enlightenment has to comprise both, if it is to combine knowledge with insight, that is, broad knowledge of the world, which all by itself would be superficial, and insight into individual subjects.

Another important distinction that he makes is between dead scholarliness, which relies solely on a thinker's ability to memorize, and autonomous thought, which is the very opposite of mechanical memorizing. It brings about a kind of insight that is qualitatively different from the insight produced by the precise and complete analysis of a concept, in that it can only be the result of a person's own thought.

As can be seen here already, Reinhold tried to integrate different concepts of enlightenment, as advocated by different people. Some had favored only quantitative, extensive knowledge; others, the ability to think analytically. Although the concepts of extensive and intensive knowledge were in Reinhold's early essay on enlightenment, the inclusion of "autonomous thought" was new and obviously a result of Kant's influence.

One substantial difference from his earlier concept of enlightenment is that Reinhold now gives priority to its moral aspect. Enlightenment in the narrow sense concerns people as free and rational beings, who are capable of free thought and free volition. The influence of the Kantian "primacy of practical reason" is obvious here. Reinhold's (and Kant's) rejection of eudaemonistic ethics, shared by many enlightened thinkers and all adherents of rationalistic enlightenment, represented a major objection to rationalistic enlightened thought.

In giving priority to practical reason, Reinhold had not shifted his emphasis completely. In his article on enlightenment, which he had written more than a decade earlier, the correctness of concepts had primarily to do with those that were important for people's lives. Then, he had derived this importance from material grounds—the relevance of the real world. Later, he emphasized "ethical, rightful and moral matters," because they concern the "proper self" of people, their "free and rational nature" (art. 150).

In addition to having a concept of "true" enlightenment, which automatically implies one of "false" enlightenment, Reinhold also distinguishes between "genuine" and "spurious" enlightenment. "Genuine enlightenment originates in the ethical. It is the obligatory effort to gain clear and distinct concepts about ethical matters" (art. 167). Thus it follows that the decision to fulfill one's duty—in other words, morality—is already a prerequisite for genuine enlightenment. Spurious enlightenment, on the other hand, is based on the drive for pleasure. Again, Reinhold's indebtedness to Kant is evident, since Kant sees moral conviction and attitude as the basis for morality. But Reinhold introduces a concept into the discussion about morality that Kant explicitly wanted excluded—that of sympathy, or the "heart." In itself it lacks the quality of morality (art. 100), but in connection with the moral feeling, taste, and the feeling of moral decency, it acquires "humanity of the heart" (art. 114), which Reinhold places above enlightenment of the understanding.

Reinhold, Kant, and Mendelssohn

If one thinks today of the famous question posed in 1783 by the *Berlinische Monatsschrift*: "What is enlightenment?," what comes to mind are the answers by Kant and Mendelssohn. Kant's definition of enlightenment is today regarded as authoritative. But Kant's use of the concept was actually different from that of most contemporaries. Stuke claims that it did not belong to the "central concepts of his critical philosophy," and that Kant developed it "not systematically," but "more casually and in a popular manner."[68]

If Kant did employ the notion differently, the reason is in his own philosophical outlook. In the preface to the first edition of his *Critique of Pure Reason*, Kant characterizes the epoch as "the age of criticism, and to criticism everything must submit."[69] At the end of his article on enlightenment, he refers to this characterization when he calls the age one of enlightenment. His concepts of enlightenment and criticism are closely linked. "Enlightenment is man's release from his self-incurred tutelage. Tutelage is man's inability to make use

68. Stuke, "Aufklärung," 265.
69. Kant, *Critique of Pure Reason*, A XIn.

of his understanding without direction from another."[70] Criticism consists in the "free and public examination," by means of reason, of such matters as religion and legislation.[71] Kant's *Critique* provides the basis for this criticism, as it determines the ability of reason to conceive concepts beyond the sphere of possible experience. In rejecting the possibility of having knowledge about God, freedom, the immortality of the soul, he deprived contemporary rational theology—that is, neology and deism—of its metaphysical basis.

Autonomous thought, then, is the employment of reason within its prescribed limits and the critique of all concepts according to this standard. And enlightenment is the conscious, voluntary decision of an individual to think independently, to "make use of his understanding without direction from another."[72] As such it has a moral quality.

In an article two years later, Kant defined autonomous thought as "to search the highest touchstone of truth in oneself (i.e. in *one's own* reason). . . . To use *one's own* reason means nothing but to ask oneself in regard to everything one is supposed to accept: Does one find it opportune to make the reason for assuming something or the rule which follows from the assumption a universal principle of the employment of reason."[73] Kant calls this principle "negative," since it does not add anything to positive knowledge. He stresses that enlightenment does not consist in any particular positive knowledge. This set him apart from many promoters of enlightenment who thought that it indeed meant the spread of useful knowledge.

The individual can decide to take the step away from tutelage and to think on his own. This step requires a transformation in the way of thinking and has to be accomplished again and again. For the public as a whole, enlightenment is easier, "if only freedom is granted." Once freedom exists in a state, "there will always be some independent thinkers . . . who . . . will disseminate the spirit of the rational

70. Kant, "What Is Enlightenment?" 90, 85.
71. Kant, *Critique of Pure Reason*, A XIn.
72. Kant, "What Is Enlightenment?" 85.
73. Kant, "Was heisst: Sich im Denken orientieren?" 283n; original emphasis.

appreciation of both their own worth and every man's vocation for thinking for himself."[74] Enlightenment thus is self-enlightenment of the individual and can be—but does not have to be—prompted or assisted by the example of others. An enlightened ruler, such as Friedrich II, could not do more for the case of enlightenment than remove any restrictions on the public use of reason.

Contrary to Stuke's claim, Kant's account of enlightenment is neither casual nor unsystematic. Centered on the claim of autonomous thought, his conclusions regarding individual and public enlightenment follow logically. His emphasis on "matters of religion" is most probably a result of contemporary discussions in Germany, particularly in Berlin. As Hinske points out, regular contributors to the *Berlinische Monatsschrift* had ongoing discussions on such topics as civil marriage, the relationship between faith and civil duty, and interconfessional toleration. In fact, the question "What is enlightenment?" had been a result of the debate on the merits of civil marriage. The enlightened theologian Johann F. Zöllner posed it at the end of his article "Ist es rathsam, das Ehebündniss nicht ferner durch die Religion zu sanciren?" (Is it advisable in the future not to sanctify marriage through religion?).[75] The overwhelming response showed the urgent need for an understanding of the basic concept.

For instance, it seems possible to trace Kant's distinction between the public and private use of reason to an anonymous article in the *Berlinische Monatsschrift*, which had appeared a few months earlier. There the author distinguishes between the "subordination" of a person as an officer or an official and the "freedom to think aloud."[76] In addition, a reference to Mendelssohn's position on this problem is obvious, according to Hinske. In his *Jerusalem* and in an article in the *Berlinische Monatsschrift* (1784),[77] Mendelssohn had claimed the incompatibility of faith and legal oaths. This would explain Kant's

74. Kant, "What Is Enlightenment?" 86.
75. In *Berlinische Monatsschrift* 2 [1783]: 508–17.
76. [Ernst Ferdinand Klein], "Ueber Denk- und Drukfreiheit," *Berlinische Monatsschrift* 3 (1784): 326; repr. in Hinske, *Was ist Aufklärung?* 403.
77. "Ueber die 39 Artikel der englischen Kirche und deren Beschwörung" (On the 39 articles of the English church and their conjuration).

emphasis on the situation of religious professions in his essay on enlightenment.

Another of Kant's concepts in that essay is "competence" (*Mündigkeit*), which he then employed for the first time in a published work. It can also be translated as 'being of age' and is still used in the sense of 'being an adult' (having reached the official age at which one is a legally, fully responsible person and does not need a guardian). Another denotation is 'being of sound mind' (in contrast to someone who is declared legally incompetent because of some mental incapacity). The modern sense, being a responsible, mature, socially and politically aware person, is certainly the result of its use by eighteenth-century enlightened thinkers. The term apparently also had a partially theological connotation. F. Lötzsch shows that it was used in Bible translations from early in the eighteenth century. Kant knew it probably through J. J. Spalding's *Die Bestimmung des Menschen*[78] and used it in his lectures before 1784. By the time he wrote the essay, the negative term "incompetent" was used by other writers as well.

In principle, Reinhold's concept of enlightenment in *The Fundamental Concepts* is in accord with Kant's. Reinhold views autonomous thought as the essence of general enlightenment. In adding the requirement of conceptual clarity and distinctness, he stresses a way of thinking that automatically follows from independent thought. An independent thinker will never accept a given concept, but will analyze its form and content, the relation to its object, and the relation to other concepts. Otherwise, he would be in danger of taking up prejudices, misconceptions, or mistakes. In Kant's words: "To think for oneself . . . is the maxim of unprejudiced thought." He also calls it "the maxim of the understanding."[79]

A difference in emphasis in Kant's and Reinhold's concepts of enlightenment can be noticed here. Kant understands "autonomous thought" as the activity of the understanding giving itself its own laws of thinking. He argues on the basis of his critique of theoretical

---

78. See Hinske, *Was ist Aufklärung?* 544–52.
79. Immanuel Kant, *Critique of Judgment*, par. 40, 136, 137.

reason. Only the decision to think autonomously is practical and concerns a human being's moral autonomy. The objects of thought do not matter. Reinhold, on the other hand, takes the primacy of practical reason further than Kant and demands that enlightenment, as the culture of intellectual power, must aim at the "ultimate end of humankind (practical cultivation)" (art. 139). Autonomous thought that is not subordinated to this purpose only "develop[s] the faculty of knowledge in general" (art. 147) and it remains theoretical. For Kant the decision to think autonomously is a moral one; Reinhold— apart from calling autonomous thought a "duty"—introduces morality as the subject of autonomous thought.

However, both philosophers' visions regarding the end of enlightened progress prove to be similar. Kant argues that it is a "crime against human nature" to inhibit the progress of enlightenment by installing "unceasing guardianship," since the "proper destiny" of mankind "lies precisely in this progress."[80] In his "Idea for a Universal History from a Cosmopolitan Point of View" (1784), Kant describes the teleological end of "continued enlightenment" as the "way of thought which can in time convert the coarse, natural disposition for moral discrimination into definite practical principles, and thereby change a society of men driven together by their natural feelings into a moral whole."[81] In other words, enlightenment aims at morality. In a later work, Kant pointed out that enlightenment in religious matters led to the concept of true religion and thus to principles of morality.[82]

Reinhold's conception of human destiny is similar to Kant's. Human destiny, for him, lies in "humanity," or "that which a human being ought to be and to become through freedom and rationality— hence, through the free exercise of his natural talents in conformity with reason" (art. 49). Their conceptions differ in that Reinhold

80. Kant, "What Is Enlightenment?" 89. Beck translates the German *Bestimmung* as 'destination'; I use the term 'destiny.'
81. Immanuel Kant, "Idea for a Universal History from a Cosmopolitan Point of View," 15.
82. Stuke, "Aufklärung," 271, who speaks about Kant's *Religion Within the Limits of Reason Alone.*

formulates the moral goal only for the individual, but Kant does so for both the individual and society. They also differ in that Kant does not deduce his emphasis on religious enlightenment from his concept of enlightenment. Morality follows incidentally. Although the decision to abandon tutelage and think autonomously is a moral one, Kant does not expand on this emancipative aspect of enlightenment and its possible effects on moral—and maybe political—autonomy. Reinhold, however, from the beginning defines his narrow concept of enlightenment as a moral one.

Moses Mendelssohn was the other famous philosopher who answered the question posed by the *Berlinische Monatsschrift*. His article was published as Kant was submitting his to the publisher, so they could not consider each other's views.

In his article Mendelssohn starts from the basic concepts of "education," "culture," and "enlightenment." As he points out, the three terms were relatively new in the German language, and he feels compelled to define them. "Education" (*Bildung*) was just then becoming a significant term in Germany.[83] For Mendelssohn it means the harmony between the "social state of a people in art and industry" and "the destiny of man." Mendelssohn divides it into "culture" and "enlightenment." "Culture" pertains to practical matters such as arts, crafts, social customs, and the subjective skills and inclinations that these require. Culture is possible only within society. "Enlightenment," on the other hand, is defined theoretically—as "rational knowledge (objective) and skillfulness (subjective) in rational reflection." Enlightenment takes place in society, and for the individual, for whom it is indispensable: *"A human being as a human being does not need culture; but he needs enlightenment."*[84]

At this point, I would stress that the concept of enlightenment is not really central to Mendelssohn's conception as a whole. It

83. Schneiders, *Wahre Aufklärung*, 44. Actually, the translation of *Bildung* as 'education' is an unfortunate choice in this context. *Bildung* here has more the meaning of 'forming' or 'developing.'
84. Moses Mendelssohn, "Über die Frage: Was heisst aufklären?" 4, 5; original emphasis.

would, therefore, be misleading to infer that his entire conception was a theoretical one. Rather, the concept of human destiny is at the center of his thought, a concept not treated in great depth in his essay because "of course contemporaries, especially the members of the *Mittwochsgesellschaft*, were more or less familiar" with it.[85] Nonetheless, that concept is crucial to an understanding of the essay. Stuke fails to trace the concept of human destiny in Mendelssohn's earlier writings and thus claims that it "remains open." As a consequence, he misunderstands the concept of *Bildung* and reads it in the modern sense, as state of education. He interprets Mendelssohn's approach to the entire complex of enlightenment as a theoretical one, missing the elements of autonomy and morality. Mendelssohn restricts enlightenment to "objects of human life according to their importance for and influence on the destiny of man."[86]

According to Alexander Altmann, human destiny, for Mendelssohn, means the "progressive unfolding and development of a human being's inner potential," a concept clearly influenced by Leibniz's monad.[87] All beings are endowed with such an inner potential. What is peculiar about humans is that they can perfect themselves through practice. "Life is the perpetual striving to unfold the abilities that are 'folded' into you [*eingewickelt*]." Like Lessing, Mendelssohn stresses the process more than the result of such striving, which is happiness through perfection. Human beings need resistance in their lives in order to grow, and they will continue growing in another, future life. In addition, the comparatively secondary role of theoretical enlightenment becomes clear once more in his insistence that destiny can be fulfilled without reason.[88]

In his enlightenment essay, Mendelssohn distinguishes between the destiny of human beings in general and the relative destiny of man as a member of society, his rights and duties according to his class.

85. Hinske, *Was ist Aufklärung?* 529.
86. Mendelssohn, "Was heisst aufklären?" 4.
87. Alexander Altmann, "Aufklärung und Kultur: Zur geistigen Gestalt Moses Mendelssohns," 277.
88. Mendelssohn, "Orakel, die Bestimmung des Menschen betreffend," 19, 23–24.

This distinction, together with his separating essential and accidental destiny, leads Mendelssohn to a concept of limited enlightenment: if essential and accidental human destiny clash, some prejudices will have to be tolerated for the sake of keeping truths that are linked to them. Practical culture, especially morality and religion, has precedence over purely theoretical truths.

Enlightenment for human beings in general differs from enlightenment for members of society: "That *enlightenment* which interests the human being as a human being is *common* without class difference; enlightenment for man as a member of society is modified according to *class* and *profession*."[89] However, he warns of the hypocritical abuse of this limitation. Modification by class and profession does not mean that enlightenment for human beings in general should be modified. It should be the same for everybody and will be supplemented by specialized knowledge and skills.

The only real problem arises if essential human and bourgeois destinies contradict each other. Mendelssohn abstains from suggesting a philosophical solution; he points instead to the naked power of the state.

The linking of both enlightenment and culture to the destiny of man, as a human being or as a member of society, makes these concepts real, giving them an immediate link to people's lives. Thus Mendelssohn's concept of popular enlightenment is similar to Reinhold's, but also more complicated in that it involves four elements: "1) . . . the volume of knowledge, 2) its importance, i.e. relation to the destiny a) of a human being and b) of a member of society, 3) its dissemination through all ranks, 4) according to professions."[90] Both thinkers are united in their stressing practice rather than theory. Reinhold emphasizes the primacy of practical, moral enlightenment, and Mendelssohn sees education (*Bildung*) as the continuous realization of human destiny and, thus, happiness.

89. Mendelssohn, "Was heisst aufklären?" 6.
90. Ibid.

Chapter 2

Reforming Morality

The Role of Morality in German Enlightenment

Reinhold was not the only enlightened thinker for whom morality had priority over all other goals of enlightenment. From the beginning, the moral improvement of people was one of the main objectives of German enlightenment. There were several reasons for this interest in morality: Schneiders claims that there existed "the need of laymen and members of the middle class for a moral reform of life that would complete the religious Reformation."[1] In other words, the Protestant Reformation, in its emphasis on otherworldliness, had failed to provide moral guidelines for secular life. Another reason is that the new middle class had to develop its own moral code in opposition to aristocratic values. A third reason lies in the historical situation of religious schism, the "plurality of conflicting religious claims to absoluteness," which brought about a "distancing from traditional religious systems of orientation."[2] These systems were also shaken by the growing awareness of other lands inhabited by non-Christians. It was an enlightened claim that they could possess their own moral integrity without being Christians. It followed that morality was independent of religious faith, since moral principles are not grounded in the acts or objects of religious commitment.

The process of detaching morality from religion began with the development of modern natural law in the seventeenth century. Samuel Pufendorf built a system of natural law that was strictly deduced from reason and thus independent of theology. He started from the

1. Werner Schneiders, preface to *Einleitung zur Sittenlehre*, by Christian Thomasius, unpaginated.
2. Hans E. Bödeker, "Menschheit, Humanität, Humanismus," 1076.

common "nature of man," as it was known from experience, and derived from that his supreme principle of the sociality (*socialitas*) of man,[3] a principle that would be influential up to Kant's time. Pufendorf characterized sociality as a person's benevolent disposition toward other human beings, or as "common love." The latter, or philanthropy, was to become a major component of enlightened ethics. It was clearly distinguished from Christian charity and so could function as the basis for a secular, this-worldly morality.

Thomasius employed the concept of philanthropy in his ethical doctrine of happiness. For him, human happiness was constituted by peace of mind, which was a product of the "rational love" for other people. In his *Einleitung zur Sittenlehre* (1692), Thomasius described the "nature of man" as consisting "in the virtuous love of other human beings."[4]

Another contribution to eighteenth-century ethical theory was Thomasius's distinction between a virtue of love, which was voluntary and thus not enforceable, and a virtue of justice, which was subject to external compulsion. He followed in this a distinction made by Grotius between enforceable and non-enforceable rights. This separation of ethics and natural law influenced natural-law theories in the eighteenth century and reappeared in Kant's distinction between 'legality' and 'morality' as well as in Reinhold's distinction between 'rightfulness' and 'the ethical'. Bloch sees the separation as appropriate for a politically weak middle class, which could then subscribe to an "oppositional individual ethics of intention."[5] This was solely a matter of inner conviction and was neither controllable nor enforceable by the state. This voluntaristic aspect of Thomasius's ethics became very important in eighteenth-century moral thought.

However, the idea of earthly happiness and how to achieve it—in other words, the concept of a utilitarian eudaemonism—represented Thomasius's greatest contribution to eighteenth-century ethics. Many

---

3. Samuel Pufendorf, *Acht Bücher vom Natur- und Völker-Rechte* (Frankfurt, 1711), 15.

4. Thomasius, *Sittenlehre*, 88.

5. Ernst Bloch, "Christian Thomasius, a German Scholar without Misery," 299.

supporters of enlightenment subscribed to doctrines of happiness. The moral weeklies explicitly limited their purpose to "the happiness of the present and temporal life."[6] Wolff and his followers advocated popular education in order to "contribute directly to the well-being and happiness of mankind."[7]

For Wolff, morality was independent of religion. In his speech "On the Practical Philosophy of the Chinese," he grounded morality in reason and used Chinese moral philosophy as an example of an ethics independent of religious faith. Philosophy, or world wisdom, was for him nothing but the "science of happiness."[8]

Individual moral improvement and happiness, common welfare and love, and their basis in human nature were major themes of German enlightenment and represented subjects for the moral weeklies, contemporary literature, and civic clubs and societies.

The stress on morality, on individual moral improvement, made sense only if people were morally accountable. And that accountability presupposes some degree of personal choice, or freedom. The concept of human freedom was indeed central during the first half of the eighteenth century. Christian Wolff and the Pietist Joachim Lange stood at the center of a debate on the possibility and correct interpretation of human freedom. Although the very possibility of freedom was unquestioned, problems arose about the relation of knowledge and faith, reason and revelation.[9] Leibniz and Thomasius had interpreted human freedom within the framework of religion. For Leibniz, human beings as parts of a contingent world needed divine assistance for morally good actions. But they were also free to reject divine grace, in which case their actions were morally evil. The problem in this theological construction of freedom was why God, who could foresee all human actions, did not prevent the evil

6. Die Discourse der Mahlern (1721–1722), pt. 1, quoted in Wolfgang Martens, *Die Botschaft der Tugend: Die Aufklärung im Spiegel der Deutschen Moralischen Wochenschriften*, 174.

7. Beck, *Early German Philosophy*, 261.

8. Christian Wolff, "Rede von der Sittenlehre der Sineser" (held in 1721 on the occasion of handing over the office of vice chancellor at the University of Halle), 178.

9. Norbert Hinske, "Wolffs Stellung in der deutschen Aufklärung," 312.

ones. In other words, how did those actions fit into the best of all possible worlds?

As we have seen, for Thomasius virtue—to be found in a person's internal attitude—was morally important, and external actions were morally rather indifferent. Agents needed a "willingness" for being virtuous, and thus they were accountable for their conduct. Barnard describes people in Thomasius's ethics as "self-directing agents," who can explain their actions and are "capable of determining the purposive direction of where [they] want to go."[10] He even brings the notion of autonomy into play, which might be going too far, given the Christian concept of the frailty of the human will. This concept still had a strong influence on Thomasius, especially in those periods of his life when he was closest to Pietist thought. The will could only seek divine grace and redemption from evil.

Wolff called the will free, but let it depend on the intellect for its motivation. His concept of freedom was still a relative one, since natural law as the law of moral actions was ultimately based in God. Only when internal freedom and spontaneity were united, did the concept of absolute freedom of the person result. According to Schmidt-Biggemann, this occurred for the first time in J. J. Spalding's *Die Bestimmung des Menschen* (1748), a work that had a huge public impact.[11]

With the publication of Spalding's book, the concept of the "destiny of man," of humanity, and its foundation in human nature became topics of wide-ranging discussion. What has been called the "anthropological revolution"[12] displaced the Christian concept of humankind by means of the concept of human beings as the creators of their own destiny. This completed what early enlightenment had started with its stress on this-worldliness in reference to Renaissance humanism. The Christian conviction of depraved

10. Frederick M. Barnard, "Rightful Decorum and Rational Accountability: A Forgotten Theory of Civil Life," 191.

11. Wilhelm Schmidt-Biggemann, *Theodizee und Tatsachen: Das philosophische Profil der deutschen Aufklärung*, 7–50.

12. See Bödeker, "Menschheit, Humanität, Humanismus," 1078–83.

human nature was replaced with the new notion of the dignity of human beings.

Humans were thought able to define and determine their own being autonomously. The moral weekly *Der Mensch* wrote: "In regard to his destiny, man is a rational, free being. He ought to get to know himself, the world, and God through his own reflection and through the naturally proper employment of his powers. He ought to act according to this knowledge and thus do his utmost to promote his happiness."[13] The idea of independent activity as the expression of human essence manifested itself in the positive attitude of the new middle class toward work. To work meant to assert one's being. Independent activity was thus the essence of education in the sense of self-cultivation (*Bildung*). This was in stark contrast to the aristocratic way of life, which excluded work and consisted mainly of the representation of social rank and power.

Since human nature was now seen as dynamic, the concept of history—individual and social—became important. People in teleological processes of personal development were aided by education, which would render them fully human and push them toward ever-increasing perfection. They were regarded as capable of emancipating themselves from natural and social restraints and of developing their talents. In the classic German *Bildungsroman* (novel of development), the narrative developed along with the hero's virtuous character, which happened in accordance with his inner possibilities.

Kant described human beings with regard to their rational, free character as ends in themselves and therefore as possessing dignity. The notion of autonomous self-determination became crucial for the concept of humanity.[14] Reinhold made use of it in his definition of 'humanity' in *The Fundamental Concepts*. "By humanity we mean that which a human being ought to be and to become through freedom and rationality—hence, through the free exercise of his

---

13. Der Mensch: Eine moralische Wochenschrift, pts. 1–12, quoted in Martens, *Botschaft der Tugend*, 231.
14. Bödeker, "Menschheit, Humanität, Humanismus," 1080.

natural talents in conformity with reason. . . . [H]umanity is human nature ennobled through freedom and reason" (art. 49).

Kant's and Reinhold's Concepts of Moral Autonomy

In contrast to many other enlightened thinkers, Kant and Reinhold did not subscribe to an ethics of happiness. They thought that notions of personal and societal happiness could only provide an empirical basis for human morality and thus could not properly ground a universal morality that would be absolutely binding for everybody.

It was Kant's intention to develop an ethical theory that rested on necessary and universal principles and would consequently be absolutely obligating. He thought that these principles had to be found in an intellectual realm, where human beings were seen as purely rational beings without material notions and feelings of happiness. In his *Critique of Pure Reason*, Kant distinguishes the realms of nature and of transcendental freedom. The laws of nature govern the first realm, and the second consists in the independence of rational beings from the causality of nature, in their "power of beginning a state *spontaneously*."[15]

This second realm seems to be one of lawlessness; since the laws of nature do not apply here, the cause of a free action lies outside the realm of experience. However, if actions are to be possible in this realm which do not have natural causes, if human beings are to be capable of acting freely, then a causality of freedom has to exist. According to Kant, "every efficient cause must have a *character*, that is, a law of its causality, without which it would not be a cause."[16] The problem, then, arises for Kant how to determine a kind of causality that does not involve heteronomy, as is the case with regard to nature, where every event is caused by some other, different event.

At that point, the idea of self-determination comes into play. On the basis of the transcendental idea of freedom—the "idea of a

15. Kant, *Critique of Pure Reason*, B 561.
16. Ibid., B 562, B 567.

spontaneity which can begin to act of itself"—practical freedom is described negatively as "choice's independence of coercion through sensuous impulses" and positively as the "power of self-determination," "the power of originating a series of events." It must be stressed here that practical freedom, at least in the Antinomies, is nothing but transcendental freedom "in the practical sense," seen from a practical viewpoint.[17] It would be misleading to construe a difference between the two, for example, to interpret practical freedom as merely comparative in contrast to absolute freedom.

Initially, freedom can only be described in a problematic way, as an idea—a conceivable though not knowable faculty, conceivable in the sense that it need not contradict nature. It cannot be described as factual, or real, because it then would belong to the realm of natural laws; we cannot even know its possibility. Although Kant is content to formulate a problematic concept of freedom within his theoretical philosophy, in his practical philosophy he needs "freedom as a real object."[18]

But Kant attempted to detect a special lawfulness belonging to freedom and to deduce from that moral law, and in this he failed. In the *Foundations of the Metaphysics of Morals*, his deducing the validity of the Categorical Imperative from freedom is marred by circularity. Only if he interprets freedom from the start as positive freedom in the sense of autonomy can he deduce the moral law. And only given "the already assumed importance of moral laws," does he arrive at that kind of freedom.[19]

Although Kant pretends to solve this "hidden circle" at the end of the *Foundations*, in his next great work on ethics he completely

17. Ibid., B 561, B 562, B 582, B 562. Kant uses the term *Willkür* (choice) for the negative kind of freedom he describes—"choice's independence of coercion through sensuous impulses" (B 562). I changed Kemp Smith's translation of *Willkür* from 'will' to 'choice.' It became more and more important throughout his ethical writings until he finally defined it in contrast to the concept of the will (*Wille*) in the *Metaphysics of Morals*.

18. Gerold Prauss, *Kant über Freiheit als Autonomie*, 64.

19. Immanuel Kant, *Foundations of the Metaphysics of Morals and What Is Enlightenment?* 68.

reverses the former line of argument. In the *Critique of Practical Reason*, he assumes the moral law as a "fact of reason" and infers the reality of freedom from it. He defends this assumption: "If there were no freedom, the moral law would never have been encountered in us." But we are "immediately conscious" of the moral law when we reflect on the "necessity with which reason prescribes [pure practical laws]" to the will.[20] Beck points out that this "immediate consciousness" should not be confused with some intuition or feeling. It is, rather, the "reflexive" knowledge that reason has of its own reality, "the fact that pure reason can be practical. . . . Only a law which is given by reason itself to reason itself could be known a priori by pure reason and be a fact for pure reason." The moral law expresses "nothing but the autonomy of reason."[21] It expresses itself in the call of duty of conscience.

Moral autonomy means to act in accordance with a law that reason prescribes itself, making practical reason self-legislating. The law it gives itself cannot contain any material elements, since that would lead to heteronomy, the dependence on natural causes. It has to consist in the formal aspect of a law as such. Kant formulates the moral law as the principle to act only from maxims that can be thought of as universal laws. A morally good will is a will that acts in accordance with this law only for the sake of duty, that is, not out of any inclinational motives, although they may of course be present. Only such a will is free, according to Kant; any other will is determined by heteronomous causes and does not belong to the sphere of practical reason.

One could question at this point, as Karl Ameriks does, whether an independent causality of freedom automatically leads to the formulation of the moral law as Kant provides it. In Ameriks's words, "There is nothing in the mere idea of transcendental freedom that requires it to be understood in such a particular way. There simply is no unique relation to morality."[22] This objection goes

20. Immanuel Kant, *Critique of Practical Reason*, 4n1, 29.
21. L. W. Beck, "The Fact of Reason: An Essay on Justification in Ethics," 211.
22. Karl Ameriks, "Kant's Deduction of Freedom and Morality," 74.

back to the problem of circularity, which Kant escapes, according to Ameriks, only by assuming the moral law in purely dogmatic fashion.

Reinhold generally follows Kant in his ethical theory. Since *The Fundamental Concepts* is written completely from the viewpoint of common sense and not from a philosophical standpoint, Reinhold treats his moral concepts as given through conscience. This procedure is justified on the basis of his theory of self-consciousness. In his theoretical philosophy, Reinhold had developed the concept of a self-consciousness that through its activity of representing produces "facts of inner experience," which are accessible to every human being. Among them are the moral concepts as he defines them. As it turns out, his definitions of fundamental concepts such as reason, freedom, and the will differ in some degree from Kant's. Reinhold redefines some of Kant's concepts in order to avoid certain problems that arise from Kant's construction.

In Kant's ethical theory, autonomy tends to be moral autonomy. In the *Critique of Practical Reason*, he identifies the two because he cannot find an argument for the reality of freedom, apart from assuming it for the sake of the reality of the moral law. This compels him to put "moral law and freedom in an analytical relationship" and ultimately to identify them.[23] "This fact [of the moral law] [is] inextricably bound up with the consciousness of freedom of the will, and actually [is] identical with it."[24] The moral law is the a priori product of pure practical reason, which Kant also equates with the free will. In the end, the concepts of freedom, free will, practical reason, and the moral law turn out to be interchangeable.

The will that acts morally for the sake of the moral law is free. This leaves Kant with the problem of accounting for a will that acts with the purpose of promoting the person's happiness. Can this will be free, or does the entire range of human actions performed for the

23. Prauss, *Kant über Freiheit*, 82.
24. Kant, *Critique of Practical Reason*, 43.

sake of happiness belong to the sphere of heteronomy? And what about immoral actions: "what of the will that rejects the moral law in its actions?"[25]

Kant remained ambiguous on this subject. In the *Foundations of the Metaphysics of Morals*, he concedes that a person is responsible for the influence that he allows his inclinations to have on his maxims of acting: "[Man] does ascribe to his will the indulgence which he may grant to them [inclinations and impulses] when he permits them an influence on his maxims to the detriment of the rational laws of his will." But in another place in the *Foundations*, he claims: "If the will seeks the law which is to determine it anywhere else than in the fitness of its maxims to its own universal legislation, and if it thus goes outside itself and seeks this law in the property of any of its objects, heteronomy always results."[26] At some places in the *Critique of Practical Reason*, Kant describes the striving for happiness as empirically determined. What determines the will in this case is the pleasure that a person expects from the reality of an object. Therefore, Kant concludes, the will depends on objects and is not free. In the same work, he contradicts this view when he describes the will that acts from desire as "pathologically affected (though not pathologically determined—and thus still free)."[27]

As Prauss correctly observes, it is the decision of the will to seek the law in the object: "For that it [the will] seeks the law in the object, cannot mean anything else than that the will itself intends it."[28] He calls this "self-determination to heteronomy." Thus, what Kant understands as heteronomy, clearly contains an element of autonomy—a fact of which, according to Prauss, Kant was not aware. Consequently, he determines all striving for happiness as heteronomous and allows for autonomy only in moral actions.

The quotations in which Kant speaks of the element of freedom in heteronomy contradict Prauss's claim that Kant was not aware of

25. John R. Silber, "The Ethical Significance of Kant's *Religion*," lxxxii.
26. Kant, *Foundations*, 77, 59.
27. Kant, *Critique of Practical Reason*, 20, 32.
28. Prauss, *Kant über Freiheit*, 59.

this. In my opinion, he was well aware of it, but could not reconcile it with his deduction of freedom from the moral law.

Reinhold makes a similar observation:

> Kant has too often and too expressly asserted that he also recognizes immoral actions as voluntary. This makes it impossible to contend that he limited freedom to the pure will, equated its positive aspect with practical reason, and regarded the will as nothing but causality of reason in desire. Yet he could [was justified to] and had to assume not only that the freedom of the will (the moral and the immoral one) was inconceivable without the consciousness of the moral law. But also that it could only be conceived under the condition that reason was practical in moral legislation. This assumption turns incorrect if one interprets it in the sense that a moral action is the exclusive effect of practical reason, that the freedom of the moral will consists merely in the spontaneity of this reason, and that practical reason not only gives the law, but also produces through itself the action that conforms to it.[29]

In the view of Henry Allison, Kant already in the first *Critique* and in the *Foundations* possessed the notion of the "spontaneity of the agent as rational deliberator," defined as "the capacity to determine oneself to act on the basis of objective (intersubjectively valid) rational norms and, in the light of these norms, to take (or reject) inclinations or desires as sufficient reasons for action." It follows from this that "even heteronomous or nonmorally based actions are free." Allison derives this view from Kant's analysis of actions on the basis of maxims as "self-imposed rules," of "acts of self-legislation." Such acts are possible only on the assumption of a "morally neutral conception of autonomy."[30]

Regarding this conception, I agree with Allison's reading of Kant. The first *Critique* contains more than enough textual support for it: "That our reason has causality, or that we at least represent it to ourselves as having causality, is evident from the *imperatives* which in all matters of conduct we impose as rules upon our active powers.

---

29. Reinhold, *Briefe*, 513.
30. Henry E. Allison, *Kant's Theory of Freedom*, 5, 6, 96.

'Ought' expresses a kind of necessity and of connection with grounds which is found nowhere else in the whole of nature."[31] Kant makes it clear that these imperatives are pragmatic as well as moral, and that reason in both cases acts spontaneously.

Of course, Allison is the first one to realize that this interpretation renders the very concept of heteronomy redundant: "All rational agency is 'autonomous' in this sense." Why was the "discovery" of autonomy so important, then, to Kant?[32] The ensuing question of how to understand the analytical relation here between autonomy and the moral law Allison answers by indicating that that relation can only refer to the positive concept of freedom defined as autonomy, not to that of freedom as a mere "causality of reason." Allison thinks that there is a crucial difference between practical spontaneity, as it appears in the first *Critique*, and autonomy of the will, the latter being defined as "that property of it by which it is a law to itself independently of any property of objects of volition."[33] Practical spontaneity refers to a rational being's capacity to act intentionally, guided by self-given maxims that "reflect the agent's needs as a sensuous being"; autonomy refers to an agent's independence from these needs, from "any *empirical* motivation."[34] Autonomy thus is identical with pure practical reason, and it renders the moral law itself.

A virtually automatic question is, Where does this moral kind of autonomy come from? And we are back at the problem of circularity, a problem Allison denies, since he accepts Kant's "reciprocity-thesis" about freedom and morality.

Followers as well as critics—among them Reinhold, Ulrich, and Schmid[35]—drew attention to the problem regarding amoral and immoral, evil actions that followed from Kant's near identification

31. Kant, *Critique of Pure Reason,* B 575; original emphasis.
32. Allison, *Kant's Theory of Freedom,* 96.
33. Kant, *Foundations,* 59.
34. Allison, *Kant's Theory of Freedom,* 97, 98. Allison follows Thomas Hill's interpretation.
35. See Johann A. H. Ulrich, *Eleutheriologie, oder über Freiheit und Notwendigkeit* (Jena, 1788); and Carl C. E. Schmid, *Wörterbuch zum leichteren Gebrauch der Kantischen Schriften,* 2d ed. (Jena, 1788).

of freedom, autonomy, and the moral law. Moreover, Kant himself recognized the difficulty and presented an attempted solution in the first part of his *Religion Within the Limits of Reason Alone*, which was published in 1792. In the same year, Reinhold published the second volume of his *Briefe über die Kantische Philosophie*, in which he also tried to solve the problem, though in a way different from Kant's.

In his *Religion*, Kant ascertains that "the source of evil" cannot lie in an object that determines a human being's choice through inclination, "nor yet in a natural impulse; it can lie only in a rule made by choice for the use of its freedom, that is, in a maxim." The choice of an evil maxim has to be free; otherwise, the person is not accountable. The "propensity to moral evil . . . must spring from freedom."[36] Finally Kant has arrived at what Prauss calls "autonomy to heteronomy."

However, this creates a new problem for him. If he still insists on the identity of autonomy and moral autonomy, of freedom and the moral law, the choice of an evil maxim cannot be explained. Kant therefore differentiates his concept of moral autonomy by ascribing a "disposition for the good" to all human beings. This disposition consists in nothing else but the "capacity for respect for the moral law."[37] Although every rational human being possesses this disposition, it is up to the individual to freely choose the law as the sole maxim of his actions. Freedom is thus released from its identification with the moral law.

The reason why the individual might not choose the good can be found in the "*natural* propensity in man to evil," which Kant also calls "the evil heart." Although this propensity belongs to the human genus, it is again a matter of individual choice. Kant describes three forms it can take on: first, the frailty of human nature; second, the mixing of immoral with moral incentives for acting, or impurity; and third, the viciousness of human nature. The last applies to human beings who choose evil maxims in order to defy the moral law, which

36. Kant, *Religion*, 17, 26. I changed the translation of *Willkür* from 'will' to 'choice.'
37. Ibid., 22–23.

makes them "devilish being[s]."[38] This is implausible, so Kant rejects this possibility of explaining evil.

He opts, rather, for an explanation that takes into account the dualism in human nature, namely, that human beings—apart from having a moral disposition—also are fond of their sensible incentives. Therefore, they tend to adopt maxims of both kinds, moral and sensible. Since one kind has to be subordinated to the other, they accept the moral law, intending to follow it only when it conforms to their inclinations. Thus they unintentionally "reverse the moral order of the incentives."[39]

The problem with this solution is that such an acceptance of the moral law is "hypocritical." As Kant himself realizes, his construction creates a *circulus vitiosus*, for "in this hypocrisy [he] already presupposes . . . the moral evil, whose possibility he first of all wants to explain."[40] Consequently, he admits that the rational origin of evil remains "impenetrable."

Reinhold takes a different route in explaining the origin of evil. In the preface to the second volume of the *Briefe über die Kantische Philosophie*, he criticizes as "completely undeveloped" Kant's previous definitions of the will, since they lead to misinterpretations concerning the possibility of morally evil actions. Realizing that Kant's identification of practical reason and freedom is at the root of the problem, Reinhold now separates the two. He defines practical reason as "independent spontaneity": "I call it a drive, insofar as it acts involuntarily, and possesses a determinate way of acting that is simply necessary, because it is the only possible way."[41] The fact that practical reason, according to Reinhold, generates the moral law with necessity represents a major difference from Kant's concept of practical reason, which identifies practical reason with autonomy, or positive freedom.

38. Ibid., 24, 30.
39. Ibid., 31.
40. Prauss, *Kant über Freiheit*, 98–99.
41. Reinhold, *Briefe*, 436.

Reinhold shifts the aspect of autonomy, or, better, of self-determination,[42] into his concept of the will, which he makes a third
concept between sensibility and reason. "Practical reason is not the
will, and the will is not practical reason, not even the pure will. Pure
volition is self-determination in satisfying or not satisfying [one's]
desire for the sake of the practical law."[43] The will is determined as
the opposite of an involuntary drive—as a "free faculty." It receives
the part of free choice between what Reinhold calls selfishly satisfying
one's desire and unselfishly acting for the sake of the moral law.

Thus, practical reason by itself is now absolutely necessary while
the will is free. The former establishes the moral law; the latter
decides for or against complying with it. Immoral actions can now be
explained as free decisions of the will in favor of desire and against the
moral law. Reinhold correctly observes that only voluntary actions
can be moral or immoral.

Prauss credits Reinhold with this insight, although he criticizes
the divorce of practical reason and free will. He accuses Reinhold of
sacrificing Kant's concept of autonomy as well as his fundamental,
new perception that moral action is possible only when a person acts
for the sake of a law he has freely imposed on himself. "With the
moral law of practical reason losing its autonomy to the freedom of
the will, yet preserving its necessity, this law changes into a kind of
higher heteronomy, just as Kant had discovered its essence to consist
in autonomy." Prauss also criticizes Reinhold for his "epistemological
carelessness," because he abandons Kant's "sole access" to freedom
through the fact of the moral law and presupposes the freedom of
the will without any attempt at a derivation.[44]

I do not share Prauss's criticisms and will add some qualifying
remarks. Reinhold does not completely separate practical reason from

42. Since the term *autonomy* means nothing but 'self-legislation,' which Reinhold
still ascribes to practical reason, it might be clearer to talk of 'self-determination'
of the will, a term he himself uses.
43. Reinhold, *Briefe*, 353.
44. Prauss, *Kant über Freiheit*, 89, 89–90.

freedom. He only determines as necessary the fact of the moral law and the formulation of its content. On the other hand, when the law is applied in an actual volition, the claim of the unselfish drive is free, "insofar as it determines to satisfy or not to satisfy the selfish drive . . . because only the will, which can comply with the practical law or transgress it, makes it the determining ground."[45]

I think what Reinhold has in mind with his definition of practical reason as necessary is the necessity of the fact and the content of the moral law. For Kant, too, the law is necessary in its reality and in its content as a fact of reason. It is with necessity that reason prescribes pure practical laws to the will. Whenever there exists a free, rational, and, at the same time, sensible being, the moral law will be present in it as a fact of its reason. It is not up to the individual to give himself the law or not or maybe choose a different one. And since it cannot involve any positive content, its single possible content is the pure form of a law as such. Therefore, since both the act of giving the law and its content are necessary, self-determination becomes for Reinhold an actual possibility only when the moral law, as a categorical imperative, applies to a human action. Only when the moral law as it exists with necessity in a rational being is confronted with the sensible side in a rational human being does the opportunity of choosing and thus determining oneself arise.

However, it cannot be denied that Reinhold changes Kant's definition of freedom by not allowing this property to absolute spontaneity. Freedom, for Reinhold, consists only in free choice. He thus reduces what had been a two-dimensional concept for Kant—self-determination through self-legislation and free choice—to a one-dimensional concept—the will as free choice. Only the execution of the moral law involves freedom; the self-legislation of practical reason does not. Consequently, only the execution can be called moral, not the legislation. However, Reinhold retains the concept of autonomy, which he describes as comprising self-legislation of reason and self-determination of the will.[46]

45. Reinhold, *Briefe*, 438.
46. Ibid., 502.

The fact that Reinhold assigns the aspect of self-determination to the will cannot prevent the conclusion that this self-determination now consists in the mere choice between two different laws, both generated by necessary drives. Moreover, the choice itself remains without its own causality, or lawfulness, and could therefore, according to Kant, not be conceived as effective. Without doubt, this is what Prauss means by a "form of higher heteronomy." However, the heteronomy of reason means that reason would be determined by something outside itself in its self-legislation. But that is not true. Reason gives the law with necessity, and to itself. Prauss's term is thus misleading. All he can claim is that the aspect of freedom is now missing from the act of self-legislation.

If this is a disadvantage in Reinhold's approach, there are also advantages. In contrast to Kant's, his solution allows him to account for the possibility of morally evil actions. But it also opens up the possibility of practical laws that are not moral, since the moral law is not identical with the law of practical reason.[47] Prauss calls for this possibility, but fails to realize that Reinhold's approach makes it possible.

Interestingly enough, Kant reacted in his later *Metaphysics of Morals* (1797) to Reinhold's criticisms. He vigorously rejects Reinhold's positive characterization of freedom as choice, accusing him of deriving an intelligible concept from experience.

> Freedom of will cannot be defined . . . as the capacity to choose to act for or against the law (*libertas indifferentiae*), as some people have tried to define it, even though as a phenomenon it provides frequent examples of this in experience. For freedom (as it first becomes known to us through the moral law) is known only as a negative property within us, the property of not being constrained to action by any sensible determining grounds. As a noumenon, however . . . freedom cannot by any means be theoretically described in its positive character as it constrains sensible will.[48]

47. Reinhold, "Einige Bemerkungen über die in der Einleitung zu den metaphysischen Anfangsgründen der Rechtslehre von I. Kant aufgestellten Begriffe von der Freiheit des Willens," 396–98.
48. Immanuel Kant, *The Metaphysical Elements of Justice*, 27–28.

Instead, Kant insists that freedom can only be positively described as the capacity of reason for inner legislation; the possibility of deviating from it he terms an "incapacity" (*Unvermögen*).

Kant might not have been completely unmoved by Reinhold's argumentation. His distinction between will (*Wille*) as legislative and choice (*Willkür*) as executive force—fully formulated for the first time in *The Metaphysics of Morals*—is somewhat reminiscent of Reinhold's distinction between legislative practical reason (the unselfish drive, which is necessary) and the will as free choice. For Kant, too, the will is now necessary and choice free: "The will, which relates to nothing but the law, cannot be called either free or unfree, for it relates, not to actions, but immediately to legislation for the maxims of action (and is therefore practical reason itself). Consequently, it is absolutely necessary and is itself incapable of constraint. Only choice can, therefore, be called free."[49]

Kant's accusation about Reinhold's deduction of freedom from mere experience follows from his rejection of Reinhold's theoretical assumptions. Prauss's criticism of Reinhold's "epistemological carelessness" refers to this point. However, it is not correct to claim that Reinhold simply assumes the reality of freedom without any attempt at a justification (as Prauss does) or that he derives it from experience (as Kant assumes). Reinhold holds that the reality of freedom depends on the consciousness of the moral law and on the faculty of self-determination. "Reason has a very real 'reason' to think of freedom as an absolute cause. The action of this faculty announces itself through self-consciousness as a fact. This justifies common sense in inferring the possibility of freedom from its reality."[50]

Of course, on a philosophical level, this will not be enough. Talking about the concepts of morality and the free will, Reinhold claims that "three different facts of consciousness" accompany each act of the will: "the distinction of the involuntary claim of the selfish drive from the also involuntary claim of the unselfish drive, and the

49. Ibid.
50. Reinhold, *Briefe*, 511.

distinction of both from the voluntary act of decision."[51] For Kant, there exists only a single fact of reason, known to reason through reflection on itself. From the fact of the moral law he infers the reality of freedom—you ought, therefore you can. Reinhold assumes the feeling of desire and the precept of the moral law as facts of consciousness and adds a third, free choice—you want to, you ought to, you can decide between the two. He explains these facts as expressions of three different, basic faculties of the mind—theoretical reason, practical reason, and freedom. They are "basic" in the sense that they cannot be deduced from anything outside of or different from themselves.

When Reinhold published the second volume of the *Briefe*, he had already a theory of the faculty of representation to prove the philosophical possibility of facts of consciousness. This theory rests on the concept of a self-consciousness that is the source of "facts of inner experience," or consciousness, the effects of our basic faculties. One of these facts is the inner experience of the moral law, from which philosophical reason can deduce the concept of freedom. Facts of consciousness are readily accessible to the human mind in an act of intellectual intuition, a concept whose possibility Kant denies. However, the transcendental task of determining the conditions of these facts' possibility is left to philosophical reason. Thus, contrary to Prauss's—and Kant's—accusation, Reinhold gives an epistemological reason for our conviction of freedom.[52]

In *The Fundamental Concepts*, Reinhold defines the moral concepts in the same way as in his *Briefe*. Here he provides the definitions without any further philosophical arguments. He can do so precisely for the reason that the facts of consciousness are given to common sense. Reason is characterized as determinate and necessary spontaneity, and the will as free and self-determining spontaneity (art. 18). The "self" in the concept of self-determination refers to

51. Reinhold, "Einige Bemerkungen," 585.
52. Reinhold, *Versuch einer neuen Theorie*, 89–94.

what Reinhold calls the proper self of a person, which consists of his rational and free nature. This nature is enacted through its self-determination. The will is the free choice between the options of acting for the sake of the moral law—or at least in conformity with it—and of acting contrary to the law. In regard to the reality of the free will, Reinhold describes it as given to every human being through conscience. "Of all the things that are certain through conscience, nothing can be more certain than the freedom of the will and the necessity with which reason makes demands on it. This freedom and this necessity, which are certain in themselves, represent the basis and essence of conscience" (art. 37).

Kant had argued in a similar fashion in the *Foundations of the Metaphysics of Morals*, claiming that human beings can act only under the assumption of their own freedom. He also argued from the standpoint of popular philosophy, or common sense. And Reinhold follows him in this, when he holds the natural conviction of freedom against the arguments of materialism, which try to reduce freedom and accountability to mere delusions (see art. 40).

Both Kant's and Reinhold's attempts to determine the origin and concept of evil are ultimately not completely successful. Reinhold half-empties Kant's concept of autonomy by reducing practical reason to a necessary drive. He thereby makes it possible to explain the source of morally evil actions and also opens up the possibility of practical laws of nonmoral actions. Kant, on the other hand, manages to explain the possibility of moral autonomy, although that means for him the impossibility of finding an explanation for human evil beyond the extremes of radical good and radical evil.

Morality as the Basis of Genuine Enlightenment

We have seen that Reinhold takes the primacy of practical reason further than Kant, claiming that genuine enlightenment originates in the practical and also demanding that enlightenment always aim at the practical. He thereby establishes a connection between morality and enlightenment that, in this explicit form, cannot be found in Kant's concepts.

As the obligatory effort to gain clear and distinct concepts about ethical matters, enlightenment depends on the decision to fulfill one's duty. On the other hand, morality presupposes enlightenment, because the attempt to execute one's duty depends not only on the good will but also on clear and distinct concepts, as they are produced by the understanding.

Reinhold's concept of enlightenment, then, rests on the foundation of an ethics that consists in the self-legislating activity of practical reason and in the freedom of the will. In contrast, that direction of enlightenment that he describes as having "the interest of sensibility . . . [as] the only incentive" is going to produce contradictions, just like an ethics based on the striving for happiness (art. 164). For the interests of different individuals or groups in a society vary so widely, people will champion different concepts of right, justice, or the state. Only if these concepts are based on enlightenment in ethical matters can they be defined in a rational, impartial manner, which is in the "true interest of humanity."

It is the character of spurious—in contrast to genuine—enlightenment to let the moral character of actions depend on judgments of pleasure and displeasure. These, in turn, determine how pleasure and displeasure follow from external circumstances, thus making morality completely heteronomous. Spurious enlightenment derives moral actions from correct judgments and immoral actions from ignorance. Therefore, human beings are not held accountable for immoral actions; people are thought to be naturally good. Reinhold rejects this account of human nature, which such philosophers as Rousseau and Helvetius propounded, for he thinks it deprives human beings of their innate autonomy and freedom.

Another consequence of an enlightenment determined by the striving for happiness, as Reinhold describes it, consists in the directedness toward external objects, which leads to the neglect of the internal experience of self-consciousness. It also promotes a spirit of materialism, which reduces human nature and human actions to their naturalistic base.

Kant's concept of enlightenment is not so clearly linked to morality. Nevertheless, the decision to think autonomously, to free oneself from tutelage, is itself an autonomous one. Since, for Kant, autonomy amounts to moral autonomy, the decision to think autonomously is a moral one. However, Kant does not specify the subject matter of autonomous thought.

Reinhold, on the other hand, gives autonomous thinking about ethical matters priority over autonomous thought in general. Enlightenment that focuses on the ultimate end of humankind is superior to a culture of skillfulness, which is supposed to serve merely as its instrument. Reinhold therefore limits his narrower concept of enlightenment to those human affairs that concern the rational, free "proper self" of human beings. These affairs encompass moral and rightful, and religious and political matters.

Chapter 3

Reforming Religion

Religious Movements in the 1600s and 1700s

The religious focus of the German enlightenment has to be seen against the long tradition of religious movements, which prepared the ground for religious enlightenment. The Protestant Reformation in the sixteenth century was against the degeneration of the structures of the Catholic Church. It claimed religious individualism against rigid religious institutions, the word of the Bible against papal bulls. Only a century later, Protestantism was a rigid religious doctrine itself and, in turn, was opposed by several theoretical and practical religious movements. Among the more important were rational theology, deism, Latitudinarianism, and Cambridge Platonism in England; Socinianism and Arminianism in the Netherlands; and neology and Pietism in Protestant Germany. In Catholic countries, religious movements also occurred—Jansenism, a Catholic reform movement in France and Austria, opposed the traditional Church.

In its negative view of human nature, its emphasis on original sin and radical corruption of the will, Reformation thinking had contradicted the contemporary ideals of Renaissance humanism. That humanism had first questioned Christianity's power over its believers and had emphasized the autonomy and dignity of human nature. These humanistic ideals were now brought forward again by the new religious movements. Some explicitly contradicted Augustinian dogma, its individual doctrines of original sin, predestination, damnation of heathens, Christ's vicarious satisfaction of human guilt, and the eternity of punishment,[1] which had strongly influenced Luther and Calvin. Other movements did not question

---

1. Allison, *Lessing and the Enlightenment*, 40.

these doctrines directly, but they criticized religious orthodoxy and ecclesiastical institutions, indirectly contributing to a situation more conducive to the transformation of old structures and beliefs. So they had a share in the development of the enlightenment, whether or not they supported enlightened ideals themselves. All these movements had goals in common: the reunification of the confessional churches in a single true religion, simple and reasonable piety, religious toleration, the fight against superstition and the reform of anachronistic cults, popular education, and the moral improvement of people.

The following sections contain brief descriptions of those religious movements that influenced German enlightenment and are therefore important for an understanding of Reinhold's position.[2] First I consider the original development of rational theology in England and on the Continent and the forms it took in German neology and deism, which played a major role in enlightened thinking during the second half of the eighteenth century. In the next section I contrast this rationalism in religion with Pietism, a movement that was irrational in its reliance on immediate religious feeling. Without knowledge of this movement, a proper understanding of German culture is virtually impossible. Last, I describe Jansenism, a Catholic reform movement that greatly influenced Austrian enlightenment, in order to elucidate the different conditions under which enlightenment developed in the Catholic parts of Germany.

Rational Theology and Natural Religion

Rational theology, developed first in England, represented the attempt to base religion solely on Scripture and on human reason. Thus would arise a "true Christianity," consisting in "those basic rational beliefs shared by all men in all ages."[3] Allison mentions Herbert of Cherbury and Baruch Spinoza as thinkers who laid the foundation

2. Reinhold's own biography could be interpreted as covering several centuries of religious development: He started out with the unconditional belief of a Catholic monk and ended with the enlightened, rational, but still personal belief of a Protestant married man. However, he never crossed the border to atheism.

3. Allison, *Lessing and the Enlightenment*, 4.

for natural religion. John Locke provided the epistemological basis for the difference between reason and faith, distinguishing propositions according to, above, and contrary to reason.[4] Faith was not to contradict reason, although it was considered above reason. Truths of faith were not deduced from reason, but were discovered through revelation, "upon the credit of the proposer, as coming from God."[5]

Reason's task was to examine the compatibility of revelation with reason. This "clearly implies the theologically dangerous proposition that revelation, or rather the proof that any particular doctrine is revealed, is always of a lower order of certainty than rational insight."[6]

It was only one step—but one "across an unbridgeable abyss"— from this to deism, represented by thinkers John Toland and Matthew Tindal. Deism denied the necessity of revelation, since it contradicted the rationality of Christianity. The idea that all those human beings who by accident had never heard of the Christian gospel should be condemned to eternal punishment was "morally offensive" to enlightened thought.[7] Another argument against revelation was its historical unreliability. Therefore, to follow the principles of natural religion—God's existence and providence—and of morality should be sufficient for anybody, Christian or not.

The enthusiasm for the new natural sciences had a great effect on people's beliefs: they came to think that truth was found in nature rather than in holy writings. Natural philosophy became the basis for natural religion and moral philosophy. As the deist Voltaire put it: "Natural law . . . which nature teaches all men" is that "upon which all religion is founded."[8]

The English ideas of rational theology reached Germany by the middle of the eighteenth century. The medium was translations

---

4. John Locke, *An Essay Concerning Human Understanding*, bk. 4, chap. 17 (Of reason), sec. 23, p. 279. These distinctions are already found in Aquinas.

5. Ibid., bk. 4, chap. 18 (Of faith and reason, and their distinct provinces), sec. 2, p. 281.

6. Allison, *Lessing and the Enlightenment*, 5.

7. Peter Gay, introduction to *Deism: An Anthology*, 12, 8.

8. Voltaire, *Oeuvres* (1883–1885), 25:39, 11:443, quoted in Carl L. Becker, *The Heavenly City of the Eighteenth-Century Philosophers*, 52; Becker's translation.

of works of English divines who refuted rational theology. These ideas gained considerable influence, for the ground was already well prepared. In the fifteenth century, Raimundus of Sabunde had promoted the formation of a rational, philosophical theology that was independent of traditional theology based on revelation. Nikolaus Cusanus—in his *De pace fidei*—called for a universal religion. This religion was Christianity, although its truths could also be found in other religions.

The German "school philosophy" was the next step in the development of an independent natural religion. During the second half of the seventeenth century, school philosophy and natural sciences became dominant in the Protestant parts of Germany. Together they produced a great increase in the number of physico-theological writings. According to Feiereis, school philosophy "prevented . . . that fateful break with theology that was so characteristic of the enlightenment in England and France." Instead, philosophy and theology entered a phase of intense discussion, at the end of which religion became the concern of rationalist philosophy only. Leibniz and Wolff initiated the process in which philosophy came to dominate theology. Both attempted to demonstrate philosophically the agreement of reason and revelation and so contributed to the development of an independent philosophy of religion and an "autonomous rational religion" in the second half of the eighteenth century.[9]

Leibniz still accepted the truth of Christian revelation. According to the distinction between that which is above and that which is contrary to reason, he accepted the truths of mysteries and miracles. They did not contradict reason, but were merely above it and thus incomprehensible for human understanding. Reason and revelation were in conformity.

Soon, though, the role of reason grew stronger. Wolff already tried to demonstrate "that the basic principles of his natural theology were found [in the Bible]." He also laid down criteria for the critical

---

9. Konrad Feiereis, *Die Umprägung der natürlichen Theologie in Religionsphilosophie: Ein Beitrag zur deutschen Geistesgeschichte des 18. Jahrhunderts*, 21.

examination of all revelation: It had to be necessary, and it could not contradict truths of reason and the laws of nature.[10]

The development of rationalistic criticism eventually led to the systematic rationalization of the content of Christian revelation, as, for example, by neologists. Deists went one step further, rejecting outright the validity of any revelation.

Neology was the most influential religious movement during the second half of the eighteenth century in Protestant Germany. It also exercised some influence in the Catholic parts of Germany. The adherents of the movement sought true Christianity, or natural religion, by way of historical-critical study of the Bible and critical examination of Christian doctrines. The rational, philosophical cognition of God was to be the basis not only of a theoretical rational theology but also of practical religiosity itself. Religious life was grounded on philosophy.

Important neologists were J. F. W. Jerusalem, J. J. Spalding, A. F. W. Sack, J. S. Semler, and J. A. Eberhard. Spalding's influential work *The Destiny of Man*, mentioned earlier, abandoned the traditional Christian concept of human beings as sinful and eternally damned and substituted a concept of human beings determining their own destinies. The destiny of human beings consisted in their happiness in *this* life and the next one. Spalding also treated nature as an image of divine perfection.

Neologists still accepted the fact of revelation and also defended its practical necessity. Supposedly, reason alone was not able to lead human beings to the truths of natural religion, at least not at that point in history—revelation was needed for that. If different revelations stood in the way of the unity of all religions, God was satisfied with the "agreement of attitudes and hearts."[11] People's internal religiosity, their adherence to the voice of conscience, gained priority over external confession.

10. Allison, *Lessing and the Enlightenment*, 35, 37.
11. J. J. Spalding, *Einigkeit in der Religion: Eine erweiterte Predigt* (1786), quoted in Feiereis, *Umprägung der natürlichen Theologie in Religionsphilosophie*, 41.

In contrast, deism declared that all revelation was superfluous and that reason by itself was sufficient to make the fundamental truths of religion known. Reimarus's *Apologie oder Schutzschrift für die vernünftigen Verehrer Gottes* was still an apology for the truths of religion against the claims of atheism, but at the same time it was a radical refutation of Christian revelation. Thus, it also was an "apology of reason," as Schmidt-Biggemann put it, that reduced the Messiah, the Son of God, to a merely human political revolutionary.

Only after rationalism in religion had reached its peak in a radical deism did people begin to develop some doubts concerning the scope of reason itself. These doubts were considerably spurred by Hume's skepticism, which exposed reason as incapable of dealing with questions concerning the existence and essence of God.

Pietism

Pietism was a very successful movement in the northern, southwestern, and central Protestant parts of Germany. It developed in reaction to denominational partition and oppression and the increasingly orthodox, dogmatic character of Protestantism itself, which occurred at the same time as the Thirty Years' War and which was incapable of dealing with the moral breakdown brought about by the war.

Pietism's roots, though, can be traced far back in "the tradition of zealous German reform Christianity . . . the Friends of God in the 14th, the Brethren of the Common Life in the 15th and the Anabaptists in the 16th century."[12] Part of its heritage was the mysticism of Jakob Böhme. The movement came to life in the late seventeenth century and maintained a great influence until the beginning of the nineteenth century.

Pietists rejected the ossified structures of scholastic doctrine and practice and emphasized the inner religious feeling. The individual was to be converted, reborn, regenerated in an experience of God's grace that did not need the external mediation of professional

---

12. Vaughan, *Historical Constellation of the Sturm und Drang*, 86.

preachers or established rituals. In this, Pietists were true followers of Luther's idea of an "invisible church." Other important features of Pietism were the demand for a practical, moral Christianity, a unified true church, and a universal priesthood. Its adherents were also concerned with popular education and charitable work.

The major Pietist ideas could be found in J. Arndt's prayerbook *Wahres Christentum* (True Christianity) from 1609. He said that man takes the "inward" path to Jesus Christ "when man goes into the depths of his heart, and in that very place perceives the Kingdom of God which is in us."[13] P. J. Spener's *Pia desideria* (1676), in which Spener followed Arndt's ideas, became a standard work. Spener called for "continual '*praxis pietatis*'," the individual's continual private communication with God, and self-examination "in order to better harken to the inner voice in preparation for a revelation of grace ['*Durchbruch der Gnade*'] and in anticipation of a resurrection of the spirit ['*innere Wiedergeburt*']."[14]

Spener and his pupil A. H. Francke co-founded the University of Halle, where Pietism gained great influence. It was on account of them that the rationalist Wolff was expelled from that university. Francke developed Pietism into a new dogma, and other Pietist groups, known as "separatists," rebelled, especially against its contempt for everything this-worldly. The new separatist movement retained strong elements of German mysticism and chiliasm, and consequently it possessed a much more sensuous character than Halle Pietism allowed. The separatist communities believed in the true church in which all the converted would be united in love.

In mainstream Pietism as well, meetings of meditation circles, or conventicles, stressed egalitarian togetherness. People from all strata of society could gather there, even members of the high nobility. "The original impulse [of the movement] was preserved especially among unprivileged strata," people who were being dislocated by

13. J. Arndt, *Sechs Bücher vom Wahren Christentum, nebst dessen Paradies-Gärtlein* (1856), quoted in Vaughan, *Historical Constellation of the Sturm und Drang*, 89; Vaughan's translation.
14. Vaughan, *Historical Constellation of the Sturm und Drang*, 88, 87.

social and economic change and for whom their faith represented a utopian hope.[15]

In the 1760s and 1770s, the proponents of the Sturm und Drang emerged from exactly these parts of society. They challenged the state of rationalistic enlightenment and, at the same time, contributed to the advancement of enlightenment by providing the missing element of feeling. Afterward, no one called for enlightenment of the understanding without emphasizing the importance of enlightenment of the heart. Reinhold's claim for the primacy of enlightenment of the heart was thus symptomatic of late enlightenment.

In regard to religion, the philosophers of faith, who inspired the Sturm und Drang, went back to a reliance on revelation. This was precisely the opposite of rational or natural religion, as it had been developed by neologists and deists. The critical philosophy of Kant—himself brought up in a Pietist household—would eventually present a third possibility beyond the mere alternative of reason or revelation.

Austrian Late Jansenism

The Jansenist movement originated in France, to defend the Augustinian dogma of grace and to revive the original Christian Church. Its ideas were employed by "reform Catholics" against Catholic orthodoxy. In France, the movement became very political; some of its members were involved in the French Revolution. In Austria, Jansenism gained the support of the state and eventually became the theological basis of Josephinist enlightenment.[16] The movement supported Joseph's absolutism and his transforming the Church into a state church, against the Jesuits, who had formerly held important positions in the Austrian state and had secured Rome's hegemony. Many Jansenists worked in the service of the state and contributed to the reforms introduced by Joseph II.

On a purely theological level, Jansenism stood for anti-Molinism, antiprobabilism, and antilaxism—in other words, rigorism. The Jesuit

15. Ibid., 91, 94.
16. For my account of Jansenism, see Peter Hersche, *Der Spätjansenismus in Österreich*, 43.

Molina had stressed the freedom of the human will, which, according to him, was not weakened by original sin. In contrast, Jansenius, the founder of Jansenism, adhered to the doctrine of original sin and the propensity to evil, from which the will could be saved only by divine grace. Probabilism, also a Jesuit doctrine, stated that when there were unresolvable doubts about the moral permissibility of actions, such actions were allowed. Laxism said that even a small probability of moral rectitude was sufficient, against a greater probability that the action was immoral. Rigorism, which contradicted probabilism and laxism, meant the Jansenists' strict moral attitude.[17] Jansenist theology, based on the Bible and the Early Fathers, advocated the return to the original Christian Church, the *ecclesia primitiva*. The Jansenist attitude toward life was puritan and ascetic.

In spite of all the differences that separated Jansenism from contemporary Austrian enlightenment, adherents of both movements shared many beliefs: hostility toward religious orders and monasticism; a rational cult, which included the rejection of Mariolatry and the worship of saints; anti-Roman feelings; rejection of scholasticism; claims for religious toleration; practical Christendom; an interest in popular education and charity; a general practice-orientation; democratization of church institutions; and the reunification of the churches. Therefore, many Jansenists were convinced that the *ecclesia primitiva* and enlightenment were compatible.

Differences between the two remained—for example, the Jansenists' concepts of corrupted human nature, of an ever-present punishing God, their defense of celibacy, and their otherworldliness. But these did not prevent the politicization of Jansenism, which became very influential. Its proponents held public office and published numerous popular books. During the period of Josephin rule, it was impossible not to come into contact with Jansenist ideas. Like other supporters of enlightenment, Jansenists participated in the controversy about true and false enlightenment, which in Austria determined the last stage of enlightenment. The Jansenists distinguished

17. Ibid., 25–26.

their concept of "true enlightenment" from the "false enlightenment" of French Materialists and atheists and of the German neologists and theological rationalists.[18] It can be regarded as certain that Reinhold, a Catholic monk and a promoter of enlightened ideals, was familiar with Jansenist ideas.

Religious Controversies of the 1770s and 1780s

Lessing was one of the first thinkers in Germany to express his discontent with the existing alternatives in the sphere of religion—rational religion or Pietistic inwardly, emotional religiosity. In his famous controversy with the pastor Goeze, Lessing argued from the standpoint of Lutheran nonconformity against the Protestant orthodoxy.[19] He denied, for instance, that the truth of the Bible was essential for Christianity and defended the right of a critical exegesis: "The letter is not the spirit, and the Bible is not religion, so that objections against the letter, or against the Bible, are not ipso facto objections against religion."[20] He rejected the exegesis carried out by neology and deism, because it assumed absolute, rational criteria for the critical assessment of revelation. Lessing thought that the inner truth of revelation could not be subjected to these criteria, but had to be sought in oral and written tradition and "reason enlightened through practice as it was lived in institutions,"[21] not through abstract reason.

Lessing criticized neology for giving up the distinction between faith and reason and thus abandoning the concept of faith altogether. Deism he criticized for deriving a universal religion solely from abstract reason and leaving open its relationship to the historically evolved forms of religion. By interpreting religious phenomena like

18. Ibid., 396.
19. See his "Anti-Goeze," a series of articles in response to Goeze's attacks on Lessing's Reimarus Fragments. These articles were published in 1778.
20. Lessing, "Gegensätze des Herausgebers" (Objections of the editor), in the Reimarus Fragments, in *Werke* (Munich: Hanser, 1977), 7:458; the translation follows Beiser's.
21. Willi Oelmüller, *Die unbefriedigte Aufklärung: Beiträge zu einer Theorie der Moderne von Lessing, Kant und Hegel,* 48.

miracles in their historical context, in light of their function for Christian believers or those to be converted at a certain time in history, he made the attempt to develop a concept of reason that incorporated the aspect of history.

He also opposed the kind of purely subjective, inwardly emotional faith that Pietism preached. He recognized the Pietists' critique of anachronistic church institutions, but he rejected their ahistorical approach to Christianity in its enthusiastic glorification of the early Church as its only valid form.

Lessing was the originator of still another debate, although indirectly, since it only commenced after his death. This debate, known as the "pantheism controversy," was sparked by the claim—made by Jacobi shortly after Lessing's death—that Lessing had been a Spinozist.[22] At that time, this represented a serious insult, because Spinozism was commonly equated with pantheism and, still worse, with atheism. It was no surprise that Moses Mendelssohn, who had been a close friend of Lessing's, reacted sharply to that claim. A public debate started that soon involved other famous thinkers as well—Kant, Herder, Goethe, and Hamann. Beiser calls it "the most significant intellectual event in late eighteenth-century Germany."[23] Reinhold's contribution to the controversy not only helped popularize Kant's critical philosophy but also made Reinhold famous.

Since the publication of his *Ethica* and *Tractatus theologicus-politicus*, Spinoza's thinking had been taken as proof for the thesis that philosophical rationalism led to atheism, fatalism, and nihilism. His "denial of providence, revelation, freedom of will, and a supernatural and personal God" was, for religious reasons, unacceptable. Moreover, Spinoza's critical reading of the Bible, his pantheism, his advocacy of religious toleration, "freedom of speech and conscience, democracy, a universal religion, and the separation of church and state" were dangerous to Lutheran orthodoxy and the state.[24]

---

22. In my account of this controversy, I rely on Beiser's excellent presentation in his *The Fate of Reason*.

23. Beiser, *The Fate of Reason*, 44.

24. Ibid., 49, 50.

Even before Spinoza formulated his philosophy, pantheism had been favored by those who adhered to the original claims of the Reformation, especially the radical notion of people's immediate relationship to God. The founders of the Protestant Counter-Reformation, Sebastian Franck and Valentin Weigel, already championed the same radical ideas of tolerance and democracy. Later, these ideas were also influential in Pietism.

Lessing had long been familiar with and sympathetic toward Spinoza's philosophy. But whether he was a Spinozist or not was merely the apparent cause of the debate, whereas the underlying issue was rationality and its effects, especially the relationship between reason and faith. As such, the controversy only helped continue a discussion that was already raging between adherents of a rational religion and enthusiasts for a purely emotional faith. That discussion had reached a sad climax: the philosopher of faith Johann Kaspar Lavater challenged the rationalist Mendelssohn either to refute his claims or to convert to Christianity—a most embarrassing incident in the eyes of all enlightened thinkers and most upsetting for Mendelssohn, who regarded Judaism as the rational religion per se.

Jacobi clearly fought on the side of "Lavaterism" in his promotion of irrational faith. He thought that reason "undermin[ed] all the essential truths of morality, religion, and common sense," that it questioned all fundamental human beliefs.[25] He was, for instance, concerned with Spinoza's denial of freedom and of final causes, which led, according to him, to "fatalism" in human actions. In his account of his conversation with Lessing about Spinozism, he described Spinoza's determinism:

> If there are only efficient and no final causes, the faculty of thinking only has the part of observing in the entire nature; its only business is to accompany the mechanism of efficient causes. We merely *believe* that we act from anger, love, magnanimity, or from a rational

---

25. Ibid., 46. Jacobi was greatly influenced by David Hume, although he did not share Hume's skepticism. Jacobi "grant[ed] an immediate certainty to the realm of faith" (ibid., 91).

decision. Nothing but illusion! In all these cases, it is really *a something* which moves us and which *does not know* anything of what it does.[26]

In other words, human beings did not determine their own actions. This led to fatalism and skepticism, which Jacobi intended to avoid by withdrawing from a "philosophy that [made] a complete skepticism necessary," namely, from all speculative philosophy and its universal application of the principle of sufficient reason. His alternative was a "leap of faith," a *salto mortale*, the headlong plunge into the positive faith in revelation. "His [the philosopher's] ultimate task is that which cannot be explained: the irresolvable, immediate, simple."[27] Lessing replied to this ironically by making up puns on Jacobi's *salto mortale*—how he would have to walk on his head—and confessing (also ironically?) to be a Spinozist himself.

By attacking Lessing, Jacobi was aiming at the whole movement of enlightenment, but especially at rationalist metaphysics with its proofs of God, freedom, and immortality. "Lessing's Spinozism was a symbol—a warning sign—for the dangerous consequences of all rational inquiry and criticism. Now it was this attack upon the claims of reason, and not merely the biographical sensation of Lessing's Spinozism, that really shocked Mendelssohn and the whole Berlin establishment."[28] Mendelssohn then drew up a defense of his own metaphysics; this was his major contribution to the controversy, his *Morgenstunden oder Vorlesungen über das Dasein Gottes*.[29] Having himself sympathies toward Spinozism, he tried to defend Lessing's position as a "purified pantheism." In order to achieve that objective, he offered an interpretation of Spinozism that was consistent with his own rationalist metaphysics in that he, for instance, upheld the distinction between understanding and will and thus was able to

26. Friedrich Heinrich Jacobi, "Ueber die Lehre des Spinoza, in Briefen an den Herrn Moses Mendelssohn," in *Die Hauptschriften zum Pantheismusstreit zwischen Jacobi und Mendelssohn*, ed. Heinrich Scholz (Berlin: Reuther und Reichard, 1916), 82.

27. Ibid., 88, 90.

28. Beiser, *The Fate of Reason*, 77.

29. Moses Mendelssohn, *Morgenstunden oder Vorlesungen über das Dasein Gottes*, pt. 1 (Berlin: Voss, 1785), excerpts in *Pantheismusstreit*.

retain the notion of a free will. He distinguished between an independent, infinite substance and a finite substance that existed for itself,
though not in absolute independence from the infinite. He could thus
maintain the notion of human existence apart from God. Within this
"purified Spinozism," "ethics and religion [were] saved."[30]

Eventually, other thinkers took part in the debate. Thomas Wizenmann, a friend of Jacobi's, pointed out similarities and differences in
Mendelssohn's and Jacobi's positions. He criticized Mendelssohn for
being inconsistent in his treatment of reason, which he sometimes
submitted to the guidance of common sense and sometimes not. If
reason was subordinated to common sense, "then there is indeed little
difference between his [Mendelssohn's] notion of common sense and
Jacobi's concept of faith." Wizenmann insisted that common sense
on its own was unreliable and had to be corrected by reason. In this,
he disagreed with Mendelssohn and Jacobi. However, he supported
Jacobi's practical concept of faith, which made no "claim to knowledge," but was a "demand of the heart."[31] Following a Kantian line
of argument, Wizenmann denied reason the ability to demonstrate
the existence of anything, including God. However, he allowed for a
part of knowledge in faith. Knowledge depended on experience; and
in the case of religion, this experience consisted in revelation: "Either
no religion or positive religion."[32] Thus, he championed the cause
of Christian faith in revelation and denied reason any part in it.

Kant was pressured by both parties in the controversy to enter
the debate. He did so with his article "Was heisst: Sich im Denken
orientieren?" (What does it mean to orient oneself in thinking?), first
published in the *Berlinische Monatsschrift* in October 1786. In this
essay, he argued for the defense of the authority of reason on the basis
of his second—not yet published—*Critique*. He took over from that
Critique the concept of the "need of reason," which made judgments

30. Mendelssohn, *Morgenstunden*, 28.
31. Beiser, *The Fate of Reason*, 111, 112.
32. Thomas Wizenmann, *Die Resultate der Jacobischen und Mendelssohnschen Philosophie von einem Freywilligen* (1786), quoted in Beiser, *The Fate of Reason*, 113; Beiser's translation.

necessary even in cases where no knowledge was available—as in the question of God's existence, in regard to which no intuition was possible. "Thus to take something as true on subjective grounds of the employment of reason still is of the greatest importance, when we lack objective grounds and, nevertheless, need to judge." A maxim was needed to guide these judgments on subjective grounds in order to avoid the dogmatic employment of reason, which led to enthusiasm.[33]

Practical reason had to postulate the existence of God as a guarantee for the reality of the highest good—of morality and happiness. Nevertheless, a postulate had to be limited to subjective use; it could not become knowledge. Kant called this "rational faith"—"one that is only based on data contained in *pure* reason,"[34] namely, on the concept of the moral law. Such a faith was the opposite of knowledge, though not of reason. "While Kant's rational faith is based on reason alone, Jacobi's *salto mortale* is contrary to reason." Kant had formulated an alternative to the dualism of faith and reason, as represented by philosophers of faith such as Jacobi, and instead contrasted faith with knowledge. At the same time, he appealed to all thinkers not to attack reason, owing to the danger of censorship. As Beiser points out, "the sad state of Frederick II's health and the imminent succession of Frederick Wilhelm II . . . [created] a great deal of anxiety in liberal circles in Berlin and Prussia at this time about whether freedom of the press would be maintained or new censorship imposed."[35] As further developments showed, this anxiety was fully justified.

It was this concept of rational faith that Reinhold presented in his *Briefe über die Kantische Philosophie* as the solution to the ongoing pantheism debate. The *Briefe* was the outcome of his reading of Kant's *Critique of Pure Reason* during the religious conflict between an enthusiastic faith à la Lavater on the one hand and neology and deism on the other. This crisis was most probably the cause for

33. Kant, "Was heisst: Sich im Denken orientieren?" 272n, 272–74.
34. Ibid., 276.
35. Beiser, *The Fate of Reason*, 116, 115.

his flight from Austria, which ended in Weimar. He conceived this dilemma as "the unfortunate alternative between superstition and unbelief."[36] Reinhold read the *Critique* in hopes of finding out about the possibility of a rational faith. He rejected neology and deism for neglecting the emotional element of religion, without which, for him, religion was incomplete. But he abhorred "Lavaterism," in which he saw nothing but a covert return to Catholicism and its superstitious, irrational kind of belief through "secret proselytization."[37] Some years later he described his situation:

> At the end of a period of many years, during which he had dealt with and abandoned the four major [metaphysical] systems, it became apparent to him that metaphysics offered him more than one plan to resign himself now to his intellect, now to his heart, but not one plan fit to meet the demands of both at the same time. [This] painful state of mind and the desire to rid himself of it . . . were the strongest incentives . . . to study the *Critique of Pure Reason.* . . . For over a year, he abstained from most other reading.[38]

From August 1786, Reinhold published the *Briefe* in *Der Teutsche Merkur*. They made Kant famous overnight and got Reinhold a position as assistant professor of philosophy. In April 1787, Reinhold received an appointment to the department at the University of Jena, where he remained until 1794.

In the *Briefe*, he represented Kant's concept of rational faith as a means between "irrational belief and rational disbelief." The rational justification for the belief in God, freedom, and immortality was no longer grounded on traditional metaphysics, on the speculative arguments of theoretical reason, but on "the secure, practical reason of the moral law."[39] The belief in God, freedom, and immortality was shown to be necessary on the basis of the necessity of the moral law. Thus, religious faith was now built on the foundation of morality.

---

36. Reinhold to Kant, October 12, 1787, in *Korrespondenzausgabe*, 272.
37. Reinhold, *Herzenserleichterung zweyer Menschenfreunde*, 141–42.
38. Reinhold, preface to *Versuch einer neuen Theorie*, 53–55.
39. Beiser, *The Fate of Reason*, 232.

The pantheism controversy—far from enforcing the contempt for Spinoza—led to widespread enthusiasm for Spinozism. Herder, Goethe, Schleiermacher, Schelling, and Hegel were much influenced by its pantheistic conception. Goethe, for instance, found in it the corroboration of his own holistic approach to nature. And in his *God. Some Conversations*, Herder took over Spinoza's concept of God, though he modified the abstract concept into one of a being whose reality was most evident as the immanent and active cause of nature and its laws.[40] This modification made the charge of Spinozist atheism obsolete and Spinozism acceptable in Germany.

Morality as a Basis of Religion

When the movement of enlightenment separated morality from religion, that did not mean that morality became indifferent toward religion. What happened was that the relationship was reversed: If religion had determined ethical norms, now morality came to serve as a basis of religion. Of course, this reversal took some time. The moral weeklies still assumed that Christian revelation was superior to this-worldly rational morality. Yet they admitted the superiority of reason for the purpose of popular education. The education in "natural religiosity," or "natural virtue"—in its emphasis on the human conscience as the "forum" for morality—was seen as a preparation for spiritual, Christian morality.[41] This educational goal rested on the assumptions that reason and revelation were in harmony, and that reason could provide proof for religious truths, assumptions shared by enlightened rationalist philosophers, neologists, and deists. Thinkers of the counter-enlightenment were first to attack these shared ideas.

Neology and deism already regarded morality as the essence of religion. Both assumed that it was possible rationally to prove the existence of God. Hume rejected this possibility in his *Dialogues Concerning Natural Religion*, and Kant followed Hume in this. In

---

40. Burkhardt, introduction to *God. Some Conversations*, 31.
41. Martens, *Botschaft der Tugend*, 182–83.

his *Critique of Pure Reason*, he denied the possibility of knowledge beyond the limits of possible experience. In other words, he denied that "we can know the existence of an original being through reason," as was claimed by rational theology. He also rejected natural theology for deriving God's existence "through analogy with nature, namely, as a being which, through understanding and freedom, contains in itself the ultimate ground of everything else."[42]

Kant took another route, building religion on the foundation of morality. From the absolute necessity of the moral law, he infers the practical postulate of the existence of a supreme being. Kant uses the "fact of pure reason,"[43] as he calls the moral law, not only to prove the reality of freedom as a practical, or moral, concept. He also employs it in order to transform the other ideas of pure theoretical reason—the ideas of the immortality of the soul and the existence of God—into "postulates" of practical reason. In Kant's ethics, the moral law requires the realization of the supreme good, a state in which moral attitudes are completely in accord with the moral law. Kant characterizes this appropriateness as "holiness." Since human beings are finite beings, burdened by their sensible nature, they are not capable of acting as holy, perfectly rational beings. In order to make the supreme good possible after all, as required by the necessity of the moral law, human beings have at least to be allowed to struggle infinitely for its realization. And that they can only do, if their souls are immortal.

Apart from moral virtue, the supreme good comprises yet another element—that of happiness. Kant's argumentation in regard to this second element eventually changed, until he dropped it completely. In the *Critique of Pure Reason*, he postulates that a higher moral being, God, has to exist who will guarantee the reward for virtuous conduct, so that happiness will be distributed according to worthiness. The worthiness to be happy is the "motive" (*Bewegungsgrund*) and "incentive" of the moral law.[44] Kant became aware that this

42. Kant, *Critique of Pure Reason*, B 659.
43. Kant, *Critique of Practical Reason*, 31.
44. Kant, *Critique of Pure Reason*, B 834, B 841.

argument carried the danger of moral heteronomy, and he weakened it in his second *Critique*. There he stresses the unselfishness of the subject, who assumes the existence of God as necessary for the possibility of the supreme good without using the incentive of happiness, relying instead solely on the representation of duty. Kant still uses the concept of happiness as a subjective end for human beings in his *Critique of Judgment*. In that work, he introduces the regulative employment of teleological principles. If human beings— as moral beings—are thought of as the ultimate ends of creation, determining their own destinies, then the world has to be conceived of as a system of ultimate ends, created by a rational, moral supreme cause. In other words, if morality is to be possible, nature has to permit this possibility. Nature has to be created in a certain way to allow for it: hence, nature must be the creation of God. This provides the basis for a teleological view of nature, where the ultimate ends of humanity can be realized. In his *Religion Within the Limits of Reason Alone*, Kant finally succeeded in presenting a proof of the existence of God that did not rely on the element of happiness. He makes the supreme good dependent on the foundation of a moral empire, whose "establishment can be only by the grace of God. Virtue is worthiness to this grace which now replaces worthiness to be happy."[45]

Kant describes the immortality of the soul and the existence of God as "postulates." The latter he defines as theoretical, subjectively true, and absolute hypotheses necessary for practical reason. A postulate claims "the possibility of an object (God and the immortality of the soul) from apodictic practical laws, but therefore only for the use of a practical reason."[46] It is morally necessary—that is, for the execution of the moral law.

Thus, Kant had built religion on the ground of morality. In his *Religion* he concludes: "Morality leads inevitably to religion." Moral obligation rests solely on the autonomy of reason. The existence of God is no longer the basis for moral obligation. On the contrary, the

---

45. L. W. Beck, *A Commentary on Kant's Critique of Practical Reason*, 273n35.
46. Kant, *Critique of Practical Reason*, 12n.

postulates of the immortality of the soul and the existence of God represent the result of ethical reasoning. Faith is only possible as pure rational faith, as the result of a moral attitude. Consequently, this God is described as a "moral ruler of the world," whose commands equal the human duties. He has to be able to look into the hearts of human beings, "in order to see into the innermost parts of the disposition of each individual, and, as is necessary in every commonwealth, to bring it about that each receives whatever his actions are worth."[47]

The moral commonwealth was Kant's answer to the question of human moral destiny. Although its perfection was unattainable for human beings, their duty was to do their utmost to come close to it in the earthly institution of the "visible church."

Even before he had discovered Kant, Reinhold was convinced that morality should provide the basis for religion. In his *Herzenserleichterung* (1785) he wrote: "It is known that religion has to be grounded in morality, not the other way around."[48] Sauer points out that this conviction was part of Viennese enlightenment thought and also of the ideology of the Illuminati, to whom Reinhold belonged. However, Reinhold lacked a theoretical justification for his conviction. His thinking consisted in a rather negative criticism of religious superstition, and did not provide a positive foundation for rational faith. He found this in Kant's critical philosophy. Later he wrote to Kant about his study of the *Critique*: "I anticipated, sought and found in it the means—not thought to be possible any longer—to be relieved from the unfortunate alternative between superstition and unbelief." He found in it the "moral epistemological basis for the fundamental truths of religion."[49] The *Briefe* resulted from his reading of Kant under this objective.

The first letter had the title "About a Need of Reason" when it was first published in *Der Teutsche Merkur*. Reinhold talked about the "spirit of the age" in regard to the state of religious enlightenment, the renewed struggle between superstition and unbelief, which

47. Kant, *Religion*, 7n, 91.
48. Reinhold, *Herzenserleichterung zweyer Menschenfreunde*, 13–14.
49. Reinhold to Kant, October 12, 1787, in *Korrespondenzausgabe*, 272–73.

implied for him the question, "Is a generally satisfying answer to the question regarding the existence of God possible? or rather . . . How is such an answer possible?" The answer could only be based on a critique of reason which determined its faculty and its limitations. Such a critique was required by the "present circumstances of the times."[50]

Accordingly, Reinhold answered the question regarding God's existence, freedom, and immortality on the basis of the Kantian critique of reason. In the second letter,[51] he argued in favor of Kant's proof that knowledge of God's existence was impossible, but that the assumption of his existence was necessary for practical reason. In regard to the conviction concerning God's existence, Reinhold remarked on the difference between philosophical reason and common human understanding, or common sense. According to him, the former analyzed the epistemological reason for that conviction, and the latter simply shared it. Philosophical reason expressed "through principles" those "motives" that had always provided the basis for that conviction.[52]

> When the sage sees himself compelled to assume a supreme being as the principle of moral and physical natural laws which is powerful and wise enough to determine and realize the happiness of rational beings as the necessary result of moral laws, then the common person feels himself forced to assume a being who in the future will reward and punish him for those deeds which his conscience approves or rejects (even against his own will).[53]

In *The Fundamental Concepts*, Reinhold argues solely from the viewpoint of common sense. He calls the conviction regarding the existence of God a "conviction of natural reason." That employment of reason which produces that conviction has to be transcendent, because its object is supernatural, but also grounded in the nature of

50. Reinhold, *Briefe*, 83, 90.
51. The second letter from 1786 equals the fourth letter in the enlarged edition of the *Briefe*. For the differences between these publications, see von Schönborn, *Bibliographie*.
52. Reinhold, *Briefe*, 100, 116–17.
53. Ibid., 120.

reason. It is the practical employment that reason makes of the freedom of the will "in prescribing the moral law to [freedom]. . . . This transcendent employment of reason immediately makes itself known to self-consciousness in and through conscience" (arts. 253, 255).

In the proof of God's existence, he seems to follow the line of argument Kant employed in his *Critique of Judgment*, although without introducing the teleological faculty of judgment, which would have meant a deviation from the viewpoint of common understanding. Reinhold introduces God not as the guarantor of happiness equivalent to virtuous attitude, but as the creator of a nature suited to the fulfillment of the moral law. Since the moral law is necessary, its fulfillment has to be thought possible. Its internal possibility is guaranteed through the freedom of the human will. However, the external possibility of its fulfillment, independent of the will of human beings, is possible only in a nature set up as an instrument for morality. "This character necessarily accrues to nature only insofar as it [nature] is conceived to be the effect of a cause which is infinite and free, and one which intends the fulfillment of the moral law as an ultimate end through nature. . . . Conscience believes nature to be the work of God" (art. 264). This belief is strengthened in the perception of the purposefulness of nature, as can be found in common experience.

With regard to the immortality of the soul, Reinhold again follows the Kantian argument on the infinity of the personality required by the necessity to fulfill the moral law, or by the necessity to transform our imperfect human will into a holy one.

All in all, *The Fundamental Concepts*, which attempts to provide universal principles and concepts in the realm of ethics, has to be seen as part of the enterprise Reinhold formulated in the *Briefe*, namely, to bring about a state of "perpetual peace" in speculative philosophy. This is to be achieved through a critique of reason which will remove all misunderstandings about the faculty of reason and which will allow for the formulation of "universally valid first principles of rights and duties . . . and a universally valid basis for our expectation of a future life." That would mean the "end of all philosophical and theological heresies. . . . The merits of our century could not be crowned more conspicuously, and Germany could not start the job of its noble calling as the future school of Europe in a more thorough and purposeful way."[54] *The Fundamental Concepts* contributes to that task by rendering universal concepts and principles on the basis of common sense. The religion established is a religion of the pure heart, of conscience based on the rational obligation of the moral law. Reinhold tries to salvage religious enlightenment by uniting reason and the heart in interpreting God as the rational moral law itself and by making true religion a moral religion (see arts. 277 and 295). "Blessed are those whose hearts are pure, for they shall see God" (art. 297).

In this quotation from Matthew, which also concludes the whole first section of the book, Reinhold merely hints at the harmony of the revealed Christian religion and moral, true religion. In his *Briefe* and still in the "Project," the second section of *The Fundamental Concepts*, he had argued that Jesus was the first teacher of true religion, the one who reconciled and united morality and religion. In a review of Kant's *Religion Within the Limits of Reason Alone*, Reinhold had determined the relationship between "church-faith," which was based on historical facts and Scripture, and "religious faith," which was purely moral and originated in pure reason: "It is completely impossible and contradicts the essence of morality to accept moral and, thus, religious convictions . . . for historical reasons. Religious faith, therefore, cannot be based on external facts, though it can be awakened by them insofar as they contain moral teachings and examples."[55] Jesus was, for Reinhold, the first to teach publicly the dependence of church-faith on religious faith, or the primacy of moral faith over faith in a revealed religion.

54. Ibid., 91.
55. Reinhold, "Ueber das Fundament der moralischen Religion," 343.

Chapter 4

Reforming Politics

The Holy Roman Empire of the German Nation officially still existed in the eighteenth century. But the German emperor was powerless, and there were more than three hundred secular and ecclesiastical rulers. The princes reigned as absolute monarchs in their principalities; only the ecclesiastical rulers were subject to Rome's power.

According to Vierhaus, absolutism as a form of government developed in Germany "when the older powers of political order (Empire, feudal system, system of estates) were no longer able to prevent territorial and social disintegration and to guarantee external security."[1] After the upheavals and devastations caused by the Peasants' Wars and the Thirty Years' War, all strata of society needed the protection of a strong government. The absolute monarch helped a weakened nobility against the demands of peasants and members of the newly developing middle class. At the same time, he granted opportunities to the educated middle class by employing its members as public servants, thereby creating a group of loyal supporters.

Absolutist rule was consolidated by centralizing the administration of state and society, weakening the power of the old estates and "increas[ing] . . . the prosperity and the number of the population in the interest of raising internal revenues."[2] Over time, however, the legitimization of absolutist monarchies changed. During the baroque period, it rested on the will of God. Later, during the time of enlightenment, absolutist princes based their right to power on rationality. For most of the eighteenth century, enlightenment and absolutism

---

1. Rudolf Vierhaus, "Absolutismus," 82.
2. Ibid., 80.

went hand in hand. Enlightenment was seen as originating at the top of society—with the enlightened monarch—and gradually, by way of the educated, filtering down toward the common people. Supposedly, the enlightened prince reformed society in the spirit of rationality for the benefit of his subjects.

Of course, this view favored the rulers, whose real (self-)interests were behind enlightened measures. Kant observed that the states were increasingly involved in competition for power. They could only survive if trade and craft within their country were thriving. This depended on civic freedom:

> At present, states are in such an artificial relation to each other that none of them can neglect its internal cultural development without losing power and influence among the others. Therefore the preservation of this natural end [culture], if not progress in it, is fairly well assured by the ambitions of states. Furthermore, civic freedom can hardly be infringed without the evil consequences being felt in all walks of life, especially in commerce, where the effect is loss of power of the state in its foreign relations.[3]

Absolutism both furthered and hindered the rise of the new middle class. The promotion of trade and manufacturing helped advance its economic situation, and the princely courts created some career opportunities for members of the economically weak German middle class. But political and social life was still defined by the old estates—nobility, burghers, peasants—and dominated by the nobility, the churches, and the courts.

Members of the middle class could participate in politics by working as state officials in the service of a prince. In those positions, they could be effective in their efforts at reform. They could also aspire to "ennoblement," which represented their only hope for social advancement. In turn, the absolutist courts were in need of educated employees who could carry out the reforms necessary for the centralization of power and other objectives of the absolutist state.

3. Kant, "Idea for a Universal History," 22.

This explains why absolutism and enlightenment were able to coexist and cooperate for such a long time in Germany. As state officials, the members of the middle class tended to be loyal to their princes and believed that enlightened reforms had to be administered from above. The common people were regarded as incapable of enlightening themselves. Consequently, the idea of a revolution from below was alien to most German adherents of enlightenment, and their trust in the effectiveness of gradual reforms was unlimited.

Only gradually did the middle class develop its own conception of life, its own set of social, moral, and political values. Beginning in the 1730s, the moral weeklies announced the new goal of a rational, virtuous, happy, and pious life. The noble style of life was characterized as formal and superficial, based on external representation and appearance. A good "patriot," on the other hand, did not emulate the extravagant appearance and idleness of noble life. He lived modestly, emphasized his private family life, avoided extremes of any kind, acquired more than he consumed, sought a good education, and was active in the community.

The new charitable, or "patriotic," societies helped advance these goals. Vierhaus stresses the importance of the concept of patriotism for the development of political consciousness in the middle class in Germany. "Those who had learned to regard themselves intellectually as citizens expressed in it [patriotism] the desire to overcome their private existence and their existence as passive subjects and to actively participate in the community." The "desire for a confirmation of their feeling of self-worth" was significant as well.[4] Indeed, all enlightened activity was seen as patriotic.

The concept of a patriot was connected to that of a "cosmopolitan," someone who believed in the equality and solidarity of all human beings. Cosmopolitans' concern for the welfare of mankind in general went beyond a national bias or political boundaries. As such, they represented the "universally valid specimen of the enlightened, autonomous human being who thinks and, whenever possible, acts

4. Rudolf Vierhaus, "Patriotismus," 101.

for the public welfare and who feels himself connected through a spirit of fraternity to all other human beings in other countries who share his endeavor."[5]

Besides the patriotic societies, the Freemasons' lodges, with their secret rituals and hierarchies, were another place where people could make up for their political exclusion and find "their identity [in the] discourse beyond the boundaries of the estates."[6] This was crucial in a society that was still dominated by the old estates, though they were slowly losing their power.

By the second half of the eighteenth century, a critical public had evolved out of the civic societies and clubs, using the press as its medium. The desire to be well informed about the world in general and one's own country in particular increased immensely. In the clubs and the reading societies and through correspondence, people discussed what they read, developing "common forms of thinking and a consensus of shared basic political convictions."[7] Public opinion claimed the right to pass final, rational judgment on all aspects of society and became more critical of the absolutist state. People believed that the public could put pressure on the authorities and "improve" them. The concepts of freedom, equality, law, and human rights became important beyond theoretical discussions—they were to limit absolutism. Human beings were not "mere machines"; they had their basic characteristic worth before they were subjects of a monarchy.[8] This humanness constituted itself through the family and the political and literary public. The latter was considered private, because it was still excluded from the state's authority. The middle class could not establish itself as a political estate. As Habermas observes, "The power of control over one's own capitalistically functioning

5. Rudolf Vierhaus, "Politisches Bewusstsein in Deutschland vor 1789," 183.

6. Richard van Dülmen, *Die Gesellschaft der Aufklärer: Zur bürgerlichen Emanzipation und aufklärerischen Kultur in Deutschland*, 15.

7. Hans E. Bödeker, "Zur Rezeption der französischen Menschen- und Bürgerrechtserklärung von 1789/1791 in der deutschen Aufklärungsgesellschaft," 260.

8. Bödeker, "Menschheit, Humanität, Humanismus," 1085. Bödeker refers to Friedrich Nicolai's *Das Leben und die Meinungen des Herrn Magisters Sebaldus Nothanker*.

property, being grounded in private law, was apolitical." The inward-looking style of bourgeois life was always intended to be public also, as demonstrated by the many letters written expressly for publication. The private was made political.[9]

John Locke gave expression to this development when he distinguished divine, civil, and philosophical, or moral, law. The last he also called the "Law of opinion or reputation," which arose in that "internal sphere of human conscience that Hobbes had excluded from the realm of state power." By passing judgment on the "Measure of Virtue and Vice," people determined what was moral: "Civic morality shifted . . . into the public sphere."[10] As subjects of a sovereign, people had no political power. However, their judgments as citizens possessed coercive power through the praise and the blame they expressed publicly; they acquired obligatory status. Morality became political. Therefore, Locke also used the term "the Law of private censure."

Publicly expressed convictions became more and more critical of traditional society. The claim that differences in social status should depend not on birth, but on ability and accomplishment, questioned the old estates as well as the enlightened absolute ruler. He had to prove his capability, if he wanted to retain power. In Prussia, the disenchantment with the philosopher-king was apparent—his war policies were too much at odds with his support for natural-law theory, and his paternalism was incompatible with freedom. In other states, the reality of absolutism and its incompatibility with enlightened ideals became obvious as well. Even before the outbreak of the French Revolution, political discussion in Germany became more radical.

The events in France in 1789 had a strong impact in Germany. Reactions ranged from enthusiastic support and hope for political change in one's own country to fear and rejection. The Ger-

9. Jürgen Habermas, *The Structural Transformation of the Public Sphere: An Inquiry into a Category of Bourgeois Society*, 28.
10. Reinhart Koselleck, *Kritik und Krise: Eine Studie zur Pathogenese der bürgerlichen Welt*, 42, 43.

man public changed its attitude with every phase of the revolution in France.

The first phase—from 1787 to 1792—involved the revolt of the French aristocracy against the absolute monarch. This revolt was supported by the third estate. At the same time, the peasants rebelled against the feudal system and the common people in the cities against high prices and unemployment. All this led to the founding of the National Assembly, the storming of the Bastille, the Declaration of the Rights of Man and Citizen, the enactment of a constitution, and the abolition of feudalism. With the help of parts of the first and second estates and the common people, the bourgeoisie came to political power.

These events evoked widespread sympathy in enlightened circles in Germany and were closely followed by newspapers and journals. Many writers—among them, Klopstock, Herder, Wieland, Schiller, and Kant—welcomed the revolution. At some universities prorevolutionary rallies took place. Nobles agreed with the measures against absolutism, as did some enlightened princes. Only a few members of the intellectual elite rejected the revolution from the start, among them the conservatives Justus Möser, A. W. Rehberg, and Ernst Brandes, not accidentally all of them active statesmen. They subscribed to a political empiricism influenced by Edmund Burke. It promoted political action on the basis of historical experience, not on the basis of a priori principles. Another prominent critic of the revolution was Johann Wolfgang von Goethe.

Although the events in France were for the most part favorably received in Germany, it was highly unlikely that they would be repeated there. The reasons included the enlightened thinkers' view that the French were now achieving what many Germans, living under the rule of enlightened princes, already enjoyed: freedom, rights of the individual, and religious toleration. They showed what Epstein calls a "spectator psychology,"[11] approving of radical policies

11. Epstein, *German Conservatism*, 434. Reinhold also uses *spectator* when he writes of the "political and scientific revolutions" of the age (see *The Fundamental Concepts*, preface).

in France without supporting their application at home. "Many Germans were proud of the parallelism which existed between the work of Friedrich the Great and the French Constituent Assembly in such matters as religious toleration, efficient administration, judicial reform, and explicit affirmation of the 'rights of man.' "[12] The Prussians felt they were already living in a state of law (*Rechtsstaat*). The Prussian Allgemeine Landrecht (general law of the state), as it was finally promulgated in 1794, was essentially different from the French constitution in maintaining the three estates. Still, it provided legal equality and security.

I must stress that the reception of the revolution described above was restricted to a small educated elite. Most people were illiterate and politically disinterested. Only a few peasant riots against feudal institutions occurred in response to the news from France. Germany's political partition and the dependence of the educated middle class on the absolutist courts prevented a repetition of the events in France, despite the hopes of German Jacobins. The belief in the effectiveness of gradual reform was deeply rooted and enforced by contemporary theories of evolutionary development.

Overall, then, the events in France during this first revolutionary phase were in agreement with enlightened ideals and could thus be received positively. However, this soon gave way to skepticism and even rejection as radicalism and violence increased dramatically. The common people, the fourth estate, had been gaining ground, as had young radicals of the bourgeoisie such as Marat and Danton, resulting in an uprising of the people and the provinces in August 1792. The king was arrested, and the republic announced. Sections of Paris organized themselves, starting a regime of terror for revenge against everybody who was suspected of betraying the people. The king's execution was but a step in the terror, which reached its peak during the second half of 1793 and the first half of 1794, until Robespierre's fall.

During this second phase of the revolution, new and more radical ideas were formulated and partly put into action: universal suffrage;

12. Epstein, *German Conservatism*, 437.

popular sovereignty; political, social, and economic equality. Although these ideas, expressed in the new project of a constitution, were never ratified, they influenced the daily practice of the politically active parts of society, the radical bourgeoisie and the *sans-culottes*.

Only German Jacobins continued to support the revolution, though most of them despised the terror and thus limited their support. For liberals and moderates, the execution of Louis XVI and Marie Antoinette was only the last proof that this was what Wieland called a "revolution without reason."[13] It prompted Klopstock, Schiller (both honorary citizens of the French Republic), and Herder to denounce the revolution. Like many contemporary moderates and elitists, they rejected popular sovereignty and condemned spontaneous actions by the common people as creating anarchy. Distrust of the "mob" was widespread among promoters of enlightenment.

As a result of the political radicalization in France, a wave of reaction swept through enlightened German states, doubtless from fear of similar changes. Providing the reactionaries with arguments against such developments was the conviction of many contemporaries that the revolution was "the triumph of philosophy and the consequence of enlightenment."[14] Censorship was reestablished or tightened, and real or alleged Jacobins were persecuted. Also contributing to this reaction were unfortunate successions in some German states, as well as the war between France and the Austrian-Prussian coalition in April 1792.

Finally, another important feature of German reaction to the French Revolution should be mentioned: the "conspiracy theory of the revolution," popular in conservative circles. In short, the French Revolution was the work of a small group of Freemasons and Illuminati, who spread their subversive ideas all over Europe. Its most important champion in Germany was the Lutheran pastor J. A. Starck. His thesis was that a "philosophic conspiracy," featuring

13. Quoted in Max Braubach, *Von der Französischen Revolution bis zum Wiener Kongress*, 12.
14. Vierhaus, "Politisches Bewusstsein," 193.

Voltaire, Rousseau, and the other Encyclopedists, had produced conditions for the revolution. The initial spark supposedly came from Bode and von dem Bussche, German Illuminati who had been on a mission to Paris in 1787. (Bode was a close friend of Reinhold's.) Starck called for rigid censorship, repression of secret societies, police spies, and similar measures against this dangerous threat.

For the Germans, the developments in France since 1792 seemed a mixture of irrationality, inhumane terror, and new despotism—in short, the complete breakdown of morality and loss of the heritage of enlightenment. The political interest kindled by the events during the first phase of the revolution gave way to a new moralization in public discourse. "The really old intention of enlightenment: to be critical theory with the purpose of moral practice is stressed more strongly. Morality, more than ever, is made a criterion for enlightenment."[15] Many contemporaries, in their disappointment, withdrew from political discussion into a world of pure ideas.

Theoretical Political Discussions in Germany

The development of political consciousness in Germany was supported by and itself supported theoretical discussions of natural law, constitutions, a constitutional state, and human rights. Diethelm Klippel distinguishes two tendencies in the theories of natural law. One, represented by Pufendorf, Thomasius, and Wolff, provided a political legitimation of absolutist rule. Leaving the sovereign in the state of nature and his subjects in the civil state, this theory placed the ruler outside the realm of civil laws. Although the sovereign was bound in principle by the rules of the state of nature, ultimately he was not, since the concepts of public welfare and happiness— that is, the purpose of the state—extended the sovereign's right of intervention.[16]

15. Schneiders, *Wahre Aufklärung*, 131.
16. Diethelm Klippel, "Naturrecht als politische Theorie: Zur politischen Bedeutung des deutschen Naturrechts im 18. und 19. Jahrhundert," 272.

Around the middle of the eighteenth century, the concept of "civil freedom" emerged. Monarchs were increasingly criticized for their abuses of power, which resulted in "unnecessary restriction of freedom."[17] What occurred, however, were appeals to the rulers to limit themselves.

The second tendency in German natural-law theories started with the philosophy of Kant. The new theories no longer provided a foundation for absolutism, but formulated fundamental human rights for a civil society. These were based on the concepts of humanness, freedom, and personality. Human rights referred to the civil state of human beings as the true state of nature, in which humans realized their own potential. These rights could no longer be given up. Any social contract that violated them was invalid from the beginning. Rousseau had emphasized in *The Social Contract* that human beings—contrary to Hobbes's claims—could not renounce their basic freedom, their rights and duties, because that would contradict their nature. The more important human rights were freedom of trade and industry, of ownership, of thought and expression, of the press, of religion, and the right to exist and to employ freely one's natural capacities.

The old concept of happiness as the purpose of the state was abandoned because of its incompatibility with civil freedom. Kant observed:

A government that would be built on the principle of benevolence towards the people, like a *father* towards his children, i.e. a *paternalistic government* (imperium paternale), where the subjects are treated as children who need tutelage and who are unable to distinguish between what is truly useful and what is harmful for them—, where the subjects are compelled to act passively in order to expect the way they *should* be happy to be shown merely by the judgment of the chief of the state and to expect from his mercy that he wants them to be happy—such a government is the greatest imaginable *despotism*

17. Johann Georg Heinrich Feder, *Grundlehren zur Kenntniss des menschlichen Willens und der natürlichen Gesetze des Rechtsverhaltens,* quoted in Klippel, "Naturrecht als politische Theorie," 272.

> (a constitution which removes all freedom of the subjects, who then
> have no rights at all).[18]

Under this new theory of natural law, the state had a merely passive role in guaranteeing the external freedom of its citizens—a role that an emerging political liberalism advocated.

Kant's theory of the state, based on his ethical system, was concerned with laws of freedom. Kant distinguished external and internal freedom, and accordingly he differentiated the lawfulness (*Legalität, Gesetzmässigkeit*)[19] of external actions—their external conformity to the moral law—and actions performed for the sake of the moral law. The former he called "juridical"; the latter, "moral."[20] Political theory referred only to external actions and their lawfulness, and it consisted in a theory of justice, or right.

In Kant's ethics, a moral subject is autonomous; he is his own legislator—that is, he himself prescribes the moral law. A people as a congregation of free and rational beings has to legislate its own constitution according to a common will. Kant characterizes the establishment of a civil constitution in an original social contract as an end in itself. It represents an absolute duty in "any external relationship of human beings in general which could not help getting into each other's radius of action." "*Right* is the restriction of everybody's freedom to the condition of its compatibility with everybody else's freedom, insofar as this condition is possible under a common law; and the *public right* is the essence of *external laws*."[21] In a civil society, free human beings live together under coercive laws, which are the product of pure, a priori reason.

However, Kant bases a civil society on the three principles: "1) The *freedom* of its members as *human beings.* 2) Their *equality* as *subjects.* 3) Their *autonomy* as *citizens.*"[22] While the first two

18. Immanuel Kant, "Über den Gemeinspruch: Das mag in der Theorie richtig sein, taugt aber nicht für die Praxis," 137.

19. Reinhold calls this *Rechtlichkeit*, which I have translated as 'rightfulness.'

20. Kant, *The Metaphysical Elements of Justice,* trans. John Ladd, 13. My translation of certain concepts differs from Ladd's.

21. Kant, "Über den Gemeinspruch," 136.

22. Ibid., 137.

principles apply to all members of a commonwealth, the third applies only to "citizens"[23] in a narrow sense of the word, those who are economically independent through something they own, including trade, craft, and artistic and scientific skills. Only they are supposed to participate in legislation. But this participation is merely fictive. The social contract is not a "fact." It is a "mere idea," a "rational principle" according to which a legislator gives "his laws in such a way that they *could* originate from the united will of an entire people" and regards "each subject insofar as he wants to be a citizen as if he had agreed to such a will."[24]

The theoretical discussion of natural-law theory became more practice-oriented when political events created questions about the German Empire. The first division of Poland, the attempt of Joseph II to exchange Belgium for Bavaria, and the subsequent founding of the Federation of Princes (Fürstenbund) in 1785 produced "the call for a reform of the constitution of the Empire."[25] Some people had become more critical of absolutism and the danger of despotism. Others discussed how the old liberties of the estates could be made effective again. Still others believed in absolutist rule as an instrument for modernizing society and the state, which could gradually be transformed into a rule of law.

The critical public followed closely political events abroad. The Declaration of the Rights of Man and Citizen sparked discussions about the right of a people to give themselves a new constitution. A debate on that subject was led in the Berlin Mittwochsgesellschaft, a "society of friends of the enlightenment." Among its members were Nicolai; Johann E. Biester, publisher of the *Berlinische Monatsschrift;* and Carl G. Svarez, main author of the Prussian Allgemeines Landrecht. It soon involved other thinkers, too. A major concern was the "relationship between the will to liberal reform and the traditional constitution of ownership." When in November 1789 the

---

23. *Staatsbürger* (citoyen), not *Stadtbürger* (bourgeois).
24. Kant, "Über den Gemeinspruch," 145.
25. Rudolf Vierhaus, " 'Sie und nicht wir': Deutsche Urteile über den Ausbruch der Französischen Revolution," 205.

French National Assembly decreed the nationalization of Church estates, the action was called a "sensational encroachment on the substance of traditional rights of ownership."[26] Many participants in the debate rejected the abolition of traditional rights—especially that of ownership—which so far had been questioned only in extreme cases. Under the old theory of natural law, *patientia* or *taciturnitas*—the fact that subjects did not protest against the state's political or societal institutions—was interpreted as a "tacit social contract." Some believed that sociopolitical and economic inequality institutionalized in the old estates was best for society. Rehberg justified his rejection of abolishing traditional rights by citing the elasticity of the principles of natural law, which were too weak a basis for legislation. With the same argument, Biester claimed the primacy of positive law over natural law. Others condoned the infringement of ownership. In his work *Freyheit und Eigenthum* (Freedom and ownership),[27] Ernst Ferdinand Klein presented the issue as an antagonism between rights of freedom and rights of ownership. He placed the right to personal freedom above that of ownership: "If a people cannot protect their personal freedom without encroachment on ownership, this is permitted."[28]

Kant rejected the right of a people to resist. Rebellion on the grounds of being deprived of happiness was not permitted, because happiness could not serve as a universal principle. He also denied the right to overthrow a tyrant who violated the original social contract. The conservation of the commonwealth, of a state of right, had primacy over any other concern, since it represented the ultimate end of the establishment of a state. Citizens had no right to question the way the head of state administered it: "For . . . who should decide whose side was right?"[29] In Kant's view, the right of resistance would make every rightful constitution insecure. It would lead to anarchy,

26. Günter Birtsch, "Freiheit und Eigentum: Zur Erörterung von Verfassungsfragen in der deutschen Publizistik im Zeichen der Französischen Revolution," 180, 181.
27. Ernst Ferdinand Klein, *Freyheit und Eigenthum, abgehandelt in acht Gesprächen über die Beschlüsse der Französischen Nationalversammlung* (Berlin, 1790).
28. Ibid., 116, quoted in Birtsch, "Freiheit und Eigentum," 185n22.
29. Kant, "Über den Gemeinspruch," 148.

and different parties would inflict injustice on each other. Freedom of speech was the only means of criticism permitted to a people.

Reinhold and the Democratic and Aristocratic Alternatives

Reinhold was a moderate in the realm of political thinking. He rejected all extreme, one-sided points of view and refused to subscribe to any party. In the preface to *The Fundamental Concepts*, he described the attitude of an "interested spectator" of the "political and scientific revolutions of our age," one who followed events but did not become active. He saw himself as a interested spectator, dissatisfied with the two existing political alternatives, as he and others saw them—democratic and aristocratic ideas.

In the terminology of that time, a "democrat" was anybody who fought for equality against privilege. The term was used in opposition to *aristocrat*, an adherent of aristocratic privilege (not necessarily a nobleman). The term *democrat* first appeared in several European languages in the early 1790s. It was associated with the French Jacobins and *sans-culottes* and thus with terror and anarchy. The older concept had designated direct democracy feasible for small communities, as Rousseau had described it in his *Social Contract.*

In his article "On the German Views of the French Revolution," Reinhold characterized the democratic standpoint as "political licentiousness" and the aristocratic view as "political thirst for power."[30] In his view, the French "democrats," the Jacobins, contradicted themselves by their actions. They replaced the ancien régime with their own brand of despotism. In order to support his criticism, he mentioned the events of August 10 and September 2, 1792, and January 21, 1793, the storming of the Tuileries and the arrest of the king, the so-called September Massacres, and the execution of the king.

---

30. Reinhold, "Ueber die teutschen Beurtheilungen der französischen Revolution. Ein Sendschreiben an den Herrn Hofrath Wieland. Im Februar, 1793," 69, first published in *Der neue Teutsche Merkur* (1793).

Reinhold contrasted the detested political bias with the cosmopolitan point of view of the independent thinker. An anecdote demonstrates his independence in everyday life. Reinhold refused to wear a wig like other people of his social status, not in order to show his sympathy for the French revolutionaries, but because life was just more practical without having to wear one.

In what follows, I relate Reinhold's views on some important contemporary political issues—the French Revolution, human rights, and constitutional reforms. A clear picture of his politics is necessary, because the literature does not yet offer a qualified evaluation. There exist two articles and one short section in a book that comment on Reinhold's political views. Zwi Batscha, in "Reinhold und die französische Revolution," accuses Reinhold of legitimizing the feudal estates system, of negating the concept of natural law, of denying the rights of the fourth estate, and of separating ethics from politics with a subsequent apotheosis of bourgeois inwardness. Reinhard Lauth, in "Nouvelles recherches sur Reinhold et l'Aufklaerung," ascribes to the Illuminatus Reinhold the role of indirect initiator of the French Revolution. And Renate Erhardt-Lucht, in *Die Ideen der Französischen Revolution in Schleswig-Holstein,* describes Reinhold as a fierce opponent of the French Revolution, a judgment that does not take seriously his differentiated comments regarding that event.

Reinhold welcomed the French Revolution because of the country's degenerated constitution and administration,[31] but he rejected Germany's copying the French upheaval. He based this rejection on the historical differences between the two countries. "The German constitution and state administration are different from the former French ones in every major respect. . . . The princes in Germany are compelled by their mutual interest to uphold the laws of the constitution, through which their sovereignty is limited in regard to its arbitrariness, but secured in regard to its essence and foundation."[32]

31. Reinhold, "Ueber die teutschen Beurtheilungen der französischen Revolution," 75–76.
32. Ibid., 83.

He also pointed to the political immaturity of the new German middle class as reason enough not to provide it political power.[33]

Although Reinhold felt sympathetic toward the German middle class, he objected to the abolition of noble privileges, because—like many of his contemporaries—he saw that as a violation of the right of ownership, contradicting "freedom and equality without which no sanctity of contracts, no right in general . . . could be conceived."[34] In *The Fundamental Concepts*, he ascribed a pivotal role to the right of ownership. Its recognition was equivalent to assenting to the general will, the basis of the commonwealth. Reinhold was here in agreement with Kant himself, who denied the right of a people to revolt, because such a revolution destroyed right in general. For both thinkers, gradual political reform was preferable to violent overthrow.

In contrast to some other Kantian thinkers, Reinhold rejected the direct application of abstract philosophical concepts to political reality on the grounds of an existing separation between philosophy and positive sciences. The latter depended on the close study of historical details; the former still had no secure foundation in ultimate principles. One of the reasons he cited for the errant development of the French Revolution was that political change was based on "shallow philosophy," which gained the acclamation of the "rabble," among whom Reinhold counted all people who did not think independently.

If philosophical concepts were to be applied to reality, they had to be adjusted to the particular historical and political circumstances. Reinhold criticized the French for trying to implement the theoretical doctrine of a "constitution as such" without specifying it. The consequence was, in his view, that concepts such as "freedom" and "equality" were defined by different political groups according to their own interests. The formulations of the French constitution, based on the declaration of human rights, were far too general and

33. Reinhold, *Briefe*, 618–19. This letter consists of his article "Die drey Stände: Ein Dialog," and its sequel "Die Weltbürger: Zur Fortsetzung des Dialogs, die drey Stände, im vorigen Monatsstück," both published in *Der neue Teutsche Merkur* (1792).

34. Reinhold, "Ueber die teutschen Beurtheilungen der französischen Revolution," 114.

indeterminate and thus open to misinterpretation and exploitation by "morally evil" elements of society, who used the political struggle for their self-interests. Those political groups in France who established the reign of terror after 1792 were those evil elements, and they thought "more about the humiliation of the nobility who provoked their envy than the relief of the common man, more about the possibility to rule in the name of the people than about the necessity to help the suppressed."[35]

His criticism of their immoral politics does not mean—as Batscha suggests—that he wanted to deny basic human rights to certain classes of society. His definition of "original right" states clearly that the rights of freedom and equality cannot be denied to any person: "The essence of the conditions on which the exercise of external freedom depends makes up original right. These conditions follow immediately from the character of personality. A person cannot be denied their employment without turning him into a mere thing" (art. 205).

It was essential to Reinhold that philosophy be based on a secure foundation, and then it could approach positive science again and eventually be applied.[36] In other words, he asked for systematic philosophical concepts that could be rendered specific in a particular historical situation without sacrificing their systematic character. His own project of a fundamental philosophy (*Elementarphilosophie*) was to provide these systematic concepts. How he arrived at this project needs to be examined more closely.

Reinhold, like Kant, based his political theory on his ethics. The concept of right encompasses both internal and external right, corresponding to the distinction between internal and external freedom. Internal right applies to actions in their moral or immoral intention. As such, they are subject to the moral law, the law of conscience. External right, on the other hand, refers to actions in their external rightfulness.[37] As such, they are subordinate to the juridical law,

---

35. Ibid., 77, 102.
36. Ibid., 80–81.
37. Usually rendered as "lawfulness" or "legality."

which demands the compatibility of one person's external, free actions and the actions of all persons. Juridical law enables people to perform freely external moral actions and to compel others to let them do so. Thus the concept of rightfulness originates in the moral law. Consequently, political concepts and principles arise for Reinhold on the basis of ethics. In this, his philosophy does not differ from Kant's.

When he wrote his articles on the French Revolution and on the three estates, he no longer believed that Kant's epistemological, ethical, and political theory rested on a firm foundation. Reinhold was convinced that a secure basis for epistemology as well as firm moral and rightful principles had yet to be found. Consequently, Reinhold rejected the application of practical concepts to contemporary reality on the grounds that "every concept of the moral law which has not been generally determined must lead to mysticism or libertinism by its nature."[38] He thought that his own fundamental philosophy would eventually provide the missing foundation and would thus make possible—after the necessary mediation—the application of philosophical concepts to reality.

Reinhold had a good reason for wanting to postpone political change and have it depend on a prior consensus among independent thinkers on principles on the basis of which that change was to occur. *The Fundamental Concepts* was meant to advance such a consensus. To accuse him of promoting reactionary inwardness, as Batscha does, is to slight Reinhold's theoretical and practical convictions.[39]

. For most political thinkers of the eighteenth century, rights of political participation were bound to a person's economic independence and education. Active political rights for the fourth estate represented a new idea and were only claimed by some radical French Jacobins and *sans-culottes*, not by the French bourgeoisie and not by German supporters of political enlightenment. Reinhold was even more conservative—he did not believe that the third estate was mature enough to share political power.

38. Reinhold, *Briefe*, 649.
39. Zwi Batscha, "Reinhold und die französische Revolution," 83.

He thought that the acquisition of wealth would help the new middle class to gain eventually rights of political participation. "The middle class is going to own more and more through trade, which will raise its demand to become a constituent part of the nation beyond doubt."[40] With the help of economic independence and intellectual autonomy, this class would bring freedom from tutelage to all other classes of society.

Reinhold's faith in the power of reforms was strong and remained unbroken. He did not belong to those critics of the French events whose initial unconditional enthusiasm changed to an equally unconditional rejection. From the start, his judgment was moderate. Nor did he subsequently embrace conservative claims against any political change. He saw clearly the danger of conservative reaction: "To me, the French Revolution seems dangerous to us not so much because of its attraction by which it was accompanied in the beginning, but because of its revolting and repulsive character which it has acquired since then."[41]

Reinhold was different in his political thinking from many contemporary thinkers. He distinguished himself through cautious judgments in which he avoided momentary enthusiasm for extremes and sought the safety of a true middle path. His insistence on the specification of abstract concepts according to historical circumstances shows his empirical-historical point of view, which makes him different from Kantians such as Fichte and Erhard and which brings him closer to Herder and Goethe with their ideas of organic political evolution. They believed that any change had to take into account the past and the present. Reinhold always described enlightenment as a real process and not as a theoretical concept.

Apart from Reinhold's empirical-historical outlook, his "peculiar philosophy of history" should be mentioned.[42] Timm describes it in

40. Reinhold, *Briefe*, 619.
41. Reinhold, "Ueber die teutschen Beurtheilungen der französischen Revolution," 91.
42. Hermann Timm, *Gott und die Freiheit: Studien zur Religionsphilosophie der Goethezeit*, 1:398.

reference to Reinhold's account of his original reading of Kant's *Critique of Pure Reason*. According to Timm, this reading was shaped by Reinhold's interpretation of his age as one of religious crisis. Probably influenced both by his strong religious background and the Spinozistic thinking of his new friends in Weimar,[43] he interpreted the crisis in terms of trinitarian eschatology—original unity (unbroken faith), strife of contradictory elements (the extreme positions of radical deism and enthusiastic "Lavaterism"), and subsequent reconciliation (in Kant's concept of rational faith), after the crisis had reached its climax. In his early article on enlightenment, he had already used the primitive (because mechanical) dialectical idea of a historical situation that had to reach its worst before it could change to the better. He described his great personal crisis, which transformed the Catholic monk into an adherent of the critical philosophy, with the help of the same model.[44] After Reinhold was no longer convinced that Kant's philosophy provided the desired reconciliation, he sought to develop the missing unification of opposites—of heart and reason, superstition and unbelief, phenomena and noumena—in his own fundamental philosophy.

The dialectical idea of the mediation of extremes by a middle path always accompanied him. It was also present in his political thinking. In his *Briefe*, he described history as the "natural course of events in the world," determined by the necessity of "destiny." "I regard nobility and clergy as the instruments of natural necessity, or rather of destiny which works through necessity, in the education of the middle class as that class of human beings in and through which humankind in Europe shall enter the state of freedom from tutelage."[45]

While, according to Reinhold, in France the democrats answered the coercive force of the old aristocratic system with new violence, exchanging one despotism for another, the new middle class in

---

43. Or maybe by historicizing the dialectic of Kant's Antinomy (see the section chap. 1 entitled "His 'Gedanken über Aufklärung' ").

44. See Reinhold, preface to *Versuch einer neuen Theorie*, 51–56.

45. Reinhold, *Briefe*, 620–21.

Germany was meant to develop a culture of the mind and the heart that—by means of "enlightenment and ennoblement"—would bring an end to all political despotism. "The true middle path is only possible, when both extremes are given, and the more determinate and obvious they appear, the faster they lead to the discovery of that path."[46]

Reading such passages, one is reminded of Hegel and Marx. It is not an overstatement to say that Reinhold's dialectical thinking stood at the beginning of German Idealism. Reinhold's "idea of mediation in his philosophy of history" separated him from Kant. His conception "open[ed] the byroad from Kant to Fichte and Hegel."[47]

46. Ibid., 620–21, 625.
47. Timm, *Gott und die Freiheit*, 411, 397.

Chapter 5

Reforming Freemasonry

Freemasonry was a product of the eighteenth century in Europe. In a sense, it represented a culmination of all aspects of the enlightenment movement. Lessing characterized it as an association of well-meaning people who share the concern for humanity: "Freemasonry . . . is something necessary, which is founded in the essence of man and of bourgeois society."[1] In addition, Reinhold's *Fundamental Concepts* was a direct result of a project of reforming German Freemasonry. Let us consider the main features of this historical phenomenon.

Freemasonry in Germany

Freemasonry was founded in England in 1717 and then spread to the Continent. The first German lodge was founded in Hamburg in 1737 by members of the wealthy bourgeoisie, which maintained close ties with England. Lodges soon existed all over Germany, even in the Catholic parts of the country, although the Church prohibited its members from joining the order. Freemasons' lodges were places where educated people from the nobility and the upper middle class could socialize and exchange ideas. The meetings were rigidly structured and included intricate rituals.

In the beginning, German lodges were hierarchically organized in accordance with the simple English system of apprentice, journeyman, and master—called "St. John Masonry"—which copied the guild system.[2] When French Freemasonry—"Scottish Masonry"—gained influence in Germany in the mid-eighteenth century, more

1. Lessing, "Ernst und Falk," 453.
2. Epstein, *German Conservatism*, 87.

elaborate structures "with extensive rituals and several high ranks" were introduced.[3] The so-called Strict Observance became even more important. Its members believed that they were successors of the old Templars. And finally, the "Swedish System" propagated a "gnostic-christophoric doctrine," which added more confusion to the collection of Freemasonic systems.[4] By then, Freemasonry as a whole comprised the most contradictory elements, ranging from the rational and enlightened to the irrational and esoteric.

Attempts were made to find a common basis, but they failed. At the Wilhelmsbad Convention in 1782, Strict Observance collapsed and the "rational wing" of Masonry gained ground again under the leadership of Johann J. C. Bode and Franz von Ditfurth. They founded the Eclectic Union in 1783, "which revived the three ranks of St. John Masonry and rejected playing at being knights."[5]

Some years before the Wilhelmsbad Convention, in 1776, another secret order had been founded, the order of the "Illuminati." During its relatively brief existence, it gathered a considerable number of members and supporters. Following a slow start in Bavaria, the order grew after the defeat of Strict Observance, integrating the progressive elements of Masonry. Conservatives went into Rosicrucianism.

The Illuminati were the first order with an explicitly political program. The Freemasons generally rejected interference with state and church, but the Illuminati wanted "through secret occupation of public offices, to establish a rationally and morally guided, authoritarian cosmopolitan republicanism, hence, to realize enlightenment in the political realm."[6] The order was officially forbidden in 1785, accused of causing the French Revolution and of being an instrument of Jacobinism. Its policy of radical secrecy helped its accusers claim a conspiracy against the state. Some former members, such as Bode, Reinhold, and von Knigge,[7] continued to work for its major goal,

3. Rudolf Vierhaus, "Aufklärung und Freimaurerei in Deutschland," 116.
4. Van Dülmen, *Die Gesellschaft der Aufklärer*, 61.
5. Ibid.
6. Richard Van Dülmen, *Der Geheimbund der Illuminaten: Darstellung, Analyse, Dokumentation*, 13.
7. Adolf Baron von Knigge wrote the famous *Über den Umgang mit Menschen* (On relations with other human beings), a book on manners, which was "intended

the establishment of the common rule of morality, and dedicated themselves to the reform of Masonry.

The order of the Rosicrucians, which was widespread in Germany during the second half of the eighteenth century, represented the counterpart of Illuminatism. Its ideology was deeply irrational, dominated by Neoplatonic mysticism and alchemistic belief in miracles. The order alleged that its origin was Moses and claimed to be in the possession of the philosophers' stone. Rosicrucianism was hostile toward enlightened ideals. During the 1780s and 1790s, some of its leading members gained considerable political influence in Prussia and, to a lesser degree, in Bavaria,[8] contributing to the crisis of enlightenment. Friedrich II's successor, Friedrich Wilhelm II, was influenced by the Rosicrucians.

Freemasonry continued to thrive in Germany well into the nineteenth century, despite setbacks during periods of political reaction, when it was prohibited in Austria, Bavaria, and Prussia.

Freemasonry and German Enlightenment

The movements of enlightenment and Freemasonry have often been called identical, as Vierhaus notes in his article "Aufklärung und Freimaurerei in Deutschland." He criticizes their simple identification, but affirms their intimate connection. As he points out, "The consensus of opinions that can be called European enlightenment . . . was broader than Freemasonry. It did not necessarily lead to the founding of Freemasonic lodges, as vice versa these lodges were threatened by completely unenlightened esoteric tendencies or a petty club mentality."[9] The diversity of Freemasonic orders and other secret societies shows that Freemasonry cannot be reduced to simply a part of the enlightenment. Orders such as the Rosicrucians supported the cause of anti-enlightenment. Nevertheless, Masonic

---

as a moral help for the bourgeoisie which became conscious of its importance" (van Dülmen, *Der Geheimbund der Illuminaten*, 43). It is still the most widely read book on manners in Germany.

8. Horst Möller, "Die Bruderschaft der Gold- und Rosenkreuzer: Struktur, Zielsetzung und Wirkung einer anti-aufklärerischen Geheimgesellschaft," 199.

9. Vierhaus, "Aufklärung und Freimaurerei," 119–20.

lodges offered the opportunity to promoters of enlightenment to meet and discuss their ideas. Moreover, many lodges expressed views in their publications that "can be read as typical manifestations of enlightened thought."[10]

Enlightened convictions were enacted in the lodges, where members addressed each other as "brother" regardless of social rank, where friendship was possible beyond social or confessional differences, and where the internal hierarchy depended on moral merit and not on social or economic standing in the outside world. Theoretically, the lodges were open to all classes of society, though in practice they attracted only educated people, those who came in touch with enlightened thought. The financial aspect also played a role, since membership was expensive. Thus, nobles and members of the upper middle class were able to become Freemasons. Exceptions occurred when craftsmen were admitted. More often, they, as well as students and women, were excluded.

The institution of Masonry was helped when enlightened dukes and princes—like Friedrich—joined. Also, many writers and philosophers were Freemasons—among them Lessing, Herder, and Goethe. In the orders dedicated to more conservative worldviews, the nobility often was in the majority, as was the case in Germany.

Morality and Politics

Morality—as the basis for an enlightened religion, as the essence of human personality—was a major issue of enlightened thought. The moral improvement and individual ennoblement of people were deemed more important than political change, which was beyond the power of the middle class anyway. The lodges were conceived by many as educational institutions. Their concentration on moral issues corresponded to their withdrawal from the public scene of official politics and religion. Debates on political and religious topics were strictly forbidden. The separation of morality and politics served to provide a neutral ground where the members of the lodges could

10. Ibid., 119.

discuss and partly live their enlightened ideas. Tolerance, freedom of thought and conscience, free inquiry, abolition of national, religious, and class barriers, and elimination of social injustice could only be promoted in a realm that was explicitly removed from the sphere of official absolutist politics.

The secrecy surrounding life in the lodges additionally enforced the separation from the public realm. This was in apparently complete contrast to the new phenomenon of the bourgeois public, which demanded openness and accessibility of all societal institutions to rational critique. Reinhart Koselleck finds the origin of this dualism in an essential feature of the absolutist state: "outer" and "inner," public and private, the citizen and the human being, whose inner identification with public law was not required.[11] This public-private split entailed a journey into man's own mental attitude (*Gesinnung*), which was, according to Hobbes, "in secret free."[12] Koselleck traces the public-private split back to Hobbes and the devastation caused by the religious wars all over Europe, which called for an absolutist power to guarantee an external order so the subjects could live in peace. The maintenance of public order became a political goal completely beyond moral justification. While political law dictated what was "legal," the morality of the private person became his or her own concern, as long as it did not interfere with public law.

According to Koselleck, this "moral inner space" was to cause trouble within the absolutist state. The promoters of enlightenment had to find a way to articulate their ideas in public, but still had to remain officially nonpolitical. The Freemasons' lodges were the ideal place for this. With their secrecy and declaredly exclusive interest in the moral improvement of individuals, their indirect power within the state influenced public opinion.

The order of the Illuminati intended to carry this hidden political potential further. Its members believed that enlightenment was the work of morality. They wanted to establish a "general rule of morality" (*allgemeines Sittenregiment*) that would naturally create virtuous

11. Koselleck, *Kritik und Krise*, 15.
12. Thomas Hobbes, *Leviathan*, 315.

conduct, fraternity, and self-determination. Adolf von Knigge, next to Weishaupt the most important leader of the order, pointed out that this would eventually change political institutions or even make them superfluous: "All artificial institutions, all constitutions, positive laws and the like" would be dispensable.[13] This "general rule of morality" was to be installed by infiltrating high political offices— not to overthrow governments, but to put highly moral persons into influential positions.

The order claimed knowledge of the " 'highest and most common ends' of mankind" and the ability to " 'determine the limits and concepts of right and wrong more precisely than others.' "[14] It was thus entitled to absolute moral superiority, which meant that simply and innocently promoting moral dispositions in people would cause unjust political orders and, indeed, any state in general to disappear automatically, leaving behind a perfectly virtuous, cosmopolitan community of human beings.

Weishaupt, the founder of the order, developed a philosophy of history that postulated three steps: the original state of nature, despotism, and the kingdom of reason and virtue.[15] He thought that secret societies were the necessary means to that ultimate end of nature, the state in which reason alone would prescribe the laws to humankind.

Weishaupt conceived of the order as an educational institution where people would be—more or less secretly—directed in their personal development from tutelage to moral autonomy. At the lowest rank, they would know nothing about the order's very existence, but would believe that they were simply members of some Freemasonic lodge. Higher-ranking Illuminati would guide them and regularly deliver assessments of their character. When their character was thought to be known completely and was deemed worthy, they

13. Adolf Freiherr Knigge, "Philo's endliche Erklärung und Antwort," 110.
14. *Gedanken über die Verfolgung der Illuminaten*, probably written by J. J. C. Bode (Frankfurt am Main, 1786), 27, quoted in Koselleck, *Kritik und Krise*, 78.
15. Adam Weishaupt, "Anrede an die neu aufzunehmenden Illuminatos dirigentes" (1782), in van Dülmen, *Der Geheimbund der Illuminaten*, doc. I, 7, pp. 166–94.

moved into the next rank of the "minerval," where they received a certain degree of information about the goals of the order.

At this stage, the order functioned as a kind of scholarly academy in which knowledge was collected and scientific research done. One of its major objectives was to develop a new, strongly empiricist concept of science, especially of the science of man. Knigge spoke of a "semiotics of the soul."[16] Finally, full knowledge of the order and its utopian political goals was accessible only to those in the highest ranks. Schindler calls the educational undertaking of the order "secret pedagogy."[17] According to him, the Illuminati represented the dualism between Masonic secrecy and the enlightened demand to make everything public.

Religion

At a time when the enlightened criticism of religion was strengthening, Freemasonry represented a sphere in which psychological needs for the irrational and the mystical could still be satisfied. All Freemasonic organizations contained some mysticism, even the most enlightened ones. Secrecy certainly was one such element. Ritual was another, giving people a temporal feeling of security formerly provided by the Church. The ritualized sessions in the lodge probably fulfilled a function similar to those in religious congregations.

More conservative orders, such as the Strict Observance or the Rosicrucians, were symptoms of the "increasing spread of mysticism, belief in miracles, and mysterious behavior, in short, of irrationalism, in the age of enlightenment."[18] They claimed to possess secret wisdom and knowledge of rituals of the Orient or of medieval alchemy. Their alleged descent from ancient or medieval orders—like the Templars—added to their aura. Within the Strict Observance, excessive development of the organizational hierarchy made the order's

16. Knigge, "Philo's endliche Erklärung und Antwort," 93.
17. Norbert Schindler, "Der Geheimbund der Illuminaten—Aufklärung, Geheimnis und Politik," 296.
18. Möller, "Die Bruderschaft der Gold- und Rosenkreuzer," 199.

leaders "invisible" and thus objects of various projections, which were comparable to those of certain religious groups or to utopian, eschatological beliefs. At the same time, they guaranteed absolute obedience to the order.

The Illuminati tried to use this myth after Strict Observance had collapsed. They substituted for the "invisible superiors" their own "vanished ones," who, apart from their mystical function, were used to secure submission within the hierarchy. Since any person could actually be a superior, an atmosphere of constant hidden surveillance existed for the lower ranks. The Illuminati in their rigid organizational structure and their requirement of absolute obedience resembled the Jesuits, whom they fought violently. Ironically, Weishaupt himself and several other members of the order, including Reinhold, were former Jesuits.

Masonic rituals had other functions than the obvious one of filling the mystical vacuum created by the rationalization of the Christian religion. Schindler thinks that the "ritualization of interaction within the lodges stabilize[d] subjective behavior that was set free from social pressures. . . . On the other hand, the ritualization neutralize[d] itself in the normative respect through its extremely formalized, ceremonial style and produce[d] a neutral ground for individual development as its proper goal." The rituals provided the opportunity to practice new ways of behavior. Thus, Freemasonry was an "esoteric balancing act between cultic devotion and autonomous self-formation."[19]

Ultimately, I would characterize the religious aspect of enlightened Freemasonry in the following way: It exchanged the Christian faith in a better life in the other world for the enlightened ideal of a more just, morally better life in this world. Elements of this were experimentally put into ritualistic practice in the lodges.

After the dissolution of the Illuminati, the publication of most of their secret documents sparked a huge debate in Germany about the merits and dangers of secret societies. A former Freemason, Ernst A.

19. Schindler, "Der Geheimbund der Illuminaten," 291, 292.

A. von Göchhausen, published *Exposure of the Cosmopolitan System* (1786), which addressed the problem of the relationship of a cosmopolitan to the authoritarian state.[20] His main points of criticism were that Masonry created a state within a state, that it promoted deism, and that cosmopolitanism was not a real possibility within an existing political state: "You are either a loyal subject or a rebel. There is no third possibility."[21] Another accusation was that of conspiracy, obviously pointing to the Illuminati. Reinhold in his review, "Revision des Buches: Enthüllung des Systems der Weltbürger-Republik" (Review of the book: Exposure of the cosmopolitan system), exposed the author's anti-enlightened, dogmatic mentality by simply quoting him at length. He then ridiculed Göchhausen's thesis that Freemasonry was only an unsuspecting instrument of the Jesuits, who, by way of promoting enlightened ideas, wanted to create anarchy, which would demonstrate the need for the truths of the Bible.

But one did not have to be a conservative to criticize secret organizations. Former Illuminati pointed out the despotism in the order's organizational structure, which seemed to contradict its enlightened goals. With regard to the "vanished ones," one author had written that no institution could be "more useful to watch subordinates, to make them more obedient toward the society."[22] Some—like Knigge—denounced its Jesuitism. Others decided that the secrecy of such organizations was dangerous because it made them liable to takeovers by irrational, irresponsible superiors.

Wieland, who had been particularly influential on Freemasonry and Illuminatism, in 1787 published "Das Geheimniss des Kosmopoliten-Ordens" (The secret of the cosmopolitan order), in which he responded to all the common criticisms of secret societies. He called on them to publish their secrets, which carried the danger of conspiracy. At the same time, he astutely stressed the difference of his

---

20. [Ernst A. A. von Göchhausen], *Enthüllung des Systems der Weltbürger-Republik: In Briefen aus der Verlassenschaft eines Freymaurers* (Rom [Leipzig], 1786).

21. [Göchhausen], *Enthüllung des Systems,* 177, quoted in Epstein, *German Conservatism,* 97; Epstein's translation.

22. *Gedanken über die Verfolgung der Illuminaten,* n.p., quoted in Koselleck, *Kritik und Krise,* 186n77.

cosmopolitan order and all the other orders: it never had a secret that could be given away. One did not have to hide simple truths. One either believed in cosmopolitanism and was therefore connected to all other cosmopolitans by natural sympathy, a spiritual tie, or one did not believe in it. Consequently, an organization was not necessary— so the danger of a "state within a state" or "hidden superiors" did not arise. Wieland assured his readers that every cosmopolitan, though he was far from having feelings of nationalistic patriotism, acknowledged the particular laws of his country. He would never disturb public order or call for violent political change. Nevertheless, the weapon of critique—reason—was at his disposal and could not legitimately be restricted by censorship.

Reinhold and Freemasonry

Reinhold was both a Freemason and an Illuminatus since his youth in Vienna. He belonged to the circle of "Wiener Freunde" (Viennese friends), which had its forum in the lodge "Zur wahren Eintracht" (To Real Harmony). The lodge was seen as *in nuce* an academy of arts and sciences, thus far lacking in Austria, that would educate its members and also influence the public by promoting freedom of conscience and thought and by fighting against monasticism. It fully supported Joseph's reforms.

Reinhold joined the order in 1783. He was proposed by Blumauer on April 16, voted for on April 28, and accepted on April 30.[23] In the summer of the same year, he became the speaker of the lodge.

During 1782 and 1783, the Viennese lodge kept close contact with the Illuminati. Weishaupt wrote in a letter dated January 11, 1783: "The ——— lodge in Vienna could join too."[24] Lauth interprets this as saying "est appelée une loge des Illuminés déjà existante" (is called a lodge of Illuminati that already exists), obviously an incorrect reading.[25] Von Born and Sonnenfels definitely were Illuminati. After

---

23. See *Korrespondenzausgabe*, 394.
24. Weishaupt to Zwack, January 11, 1783, quoted in van Dülmen, *Der Geheimbund der Illuminaten*, 285.
25. Reinhard Lauth, "Nouvelles recherches sur Reinhold et l'Aufklaerung," 609.

a rumor spread in Vienna in the fall of 1783 accusing Illuminati of endangering the state and the subsequent banning of the order in 1784, the lodge disbanded. Several sources prove that Reinhold was an Illuminatus. For example, in a letter to Reinhold dated August 16, 1786, Leon tells him about the decline of the order and addresses him as an older brother who knows much more about its goals than Leon, who had joined shortly before its dissolution in Austria.[26] In a letter to Reinhold dated September 15, 1815, Friedrich L. Schröder indicates that he possessed the list of members of the order in Vienna, which carries Reinhold as an *Illuminatus minor*.[27]

After his flight from Austria in the fall of 1783, Reinhold kept in close touch with his brothers in Vienna and continued his Freemasonic activities. Until he joined Wieland as the co-editor of *Der Teutsche Merkur*, he relied solely on the financial support of his Freemasonic brothers. He started to write for the periodical of the lodge "Zur wahren Eintracht" and continued to contribute to the *Wiener Realzeitung*.

Lauth's belief that Reinhold fled because he feared being revealed as an Illuminatus is not very convincing. Apparently, most of his friends in the lodge "Zur wahren Eintracht" were Illuminati too, but nobody else thought of leaving the country. Exactly how much Reinhold knew about the ultimate goals of Illuminatism cannot be determined. In Vienna, he was in the middle ranks as an *Illuminatus minor*. As such, he was not supposed to know the order's goals. That knowledge was reserved for the higher ranks, starting with the *Illuminatus maior*.[28]

But that might have changed after his flight. In Weimar, he made the acquaintance of Privy Councillor J. J. C. Bode, who was one of the most important members of the order. After its ban in Bavaria and subsequent disclosures of its goals, the two continued working for the order, although with the intention of reform. Lauth relates a story

---

26. *Korrespondenzausgabe*, 115.
27. Lauth, "Nouvelles recherches," 610, quotes from the unpublished letter (Bibliothek von Baden, Karlsruhe).
28. Van Dülmen, *Der Geheimbund der Illuminaten*, 122.

about Bode. In 1787, Bode and another Illuminatus, von der Bussche, visited Paris on a secret mission. Much has been made of this by adherents of the conservative conspiracy theory of the French Revolution. In his *Der Triumph der Philosophie im Achtzehnten Jahrhundert,* J. A. Starck claimed that the two managed to "explode the mine that had been deposited before by the Philosophes." Unfortunately, Lauth takes this conservative myth and goes so far as to conclude that Reinhold (of all people) had a part in the French Revolution: "One could say that Reinhold, as an intimate confidant of Bode, played a certain role as an initiator."[29]

According to Lauth, during the following years Reinhold advanced in the hierarchy and was initiated into the highest mysteries. Although he remained committed to the order, he also saw the problems of its secret organization. A letter dated 1791 indicates that he began to doubt the merit of secrecy and was aware that too many members could cause a secret organization to get out of hand. In the same letter, he mentioned the idea of a small group of people with similar convictions.[30] This idea he tried to realize during the next years.

The attempts by Bode to found a German federation of Freemasons in the Eclectic Union had faltered because of the external form of Masonry, which many now rejected. The early 1790s were the time of persecution of real or suspected Illuminati and Jacobins. Reinhold and several of his friends joined—after Bode's death in December 1793—in the project of a "federation of truth and friendship." The federation was conceived "without symbols and emblems, without special institutions and subordination" in order "to find out how much substance without particular form can achieve."[31]

The goals of the federation comprised mutual help in the fulfillment of one's duty and in the education of one's mind and heart, promotion of truth and virtue, guiding extant Masonic lodges toward these goals, and the fight against harmful secret societies

29. Lauth, "Nouvelles recherches," 621.
30. Ibid., 624n121.
31. See "Der 'moralische Bund' Reinhold's und der 'Einverstandenen': Beiträge zur Geschichte der maurerischen Reformbestrebungen in Deutschland, 1," 3.

and their "invisible superiors." The friends promised to correspond regularly about these issues, and Reinhold, who was to leave Jena and move to Kiel (in 1794), where he had accepted a position as professor of philosophy, agreed to work for the federation "in the north."[32] Important people—the law professor Hufeland, Schiller's and Goethe's friend Voigt, the philosophers Feder and Meiners—were contacted. But the project was a failure, because some friends had political objections to it.

Nevertheless, Reinhold planned another group together with two Masonic friends in Kiel, von Binzer and Jensen. They composed a scheme for a moral federation of consenting friends. The first of its thirty-two paragraphs stressed the apolitical, strictly moral character of the project. It would concern only "internal right or the morally good" and would aim at the moral ennoblement of the participants. At the same time, it insisted on the absolute autonomy of the moral sphere, with which the state could not interfere. The purpose of the state was the "safety of external right," which was guaranteed by the state's physical power.[33] Therefore, the state had no right to forbid a federation concerned only with internal right. On the other hand, the federation planned to influence public conviction, particularly those writers and teachers who professionally guided the public.

Subsequent paragraphs defined concepts essential to a moral project—freedom, right, humanity, and sound understanding. Some of the formulations resemble those in *The Fundamental Concepts*.

The final four paragraphs announced the goal of reforming Freemasonry. Its irrational elements—"mysticism, theosophy, theurgy, cabbala, and alchemy"—would be subject to independent investigation. Freemasonry, once purified of all alien ingredients, would become an "instrument of realizing and enlivening the spirit of humanity."[34]

Subsequently, all allusions to Freemasonry were erased from the proposal. Under the name "A project disclosing a consensus among

32. Ibid., 4.
33. Ibid., 7, 6–7.
34. Ibid., 15, 15–16.

well-meaning people about the principal elements of moral matters, as an attempt to contribute to the purification and consolidation of public convictions," and containing 50 paragraphs, a manuscript was printed in 1795 and distributed to friends. This was later published as section 2 of the *Verhandlungen*. In the preface to *The Fundamental Concepts*, Reinhold described the three friends' objective: "to express and conceptualize their favorite convictions, then put these convictions in writing." The last paragraphs explained the procedure and preconditions for joining the agreement. "One joins this consent by judging the content of the present scheme on the whole to be true, and by accepting the obligation to contribute, through oneself or others, to its improvement. . . . He [who is invited to join] declares whether he wants to be mentioned by name to the other consenting people."[35]

As the correspondence shows,[36] even this minimal requirement of consensus—public or not—was too much for some people. Most agreed with its principles, but rejected the proposed form of the federation. For some, it posed the danger of all secret societies— namely, of forming a state within a state or being taken over by invisible superiors. Others feared going public and being subjected to repression. One correspondent wrote that he would never join a federation that searched for a formula on which every member was supposed to agree. Reinhold's answer shows his concern for moral practice in society. He argued that acting morally was the ultimate end of all human beings. Moral actions presupposed "certain and determinate convictions," which had to be common in social interactions. These convictions had to be "universally valid," but not only that. In order to be effective, their validity also had to be actually universally accepted.[37] There was thus a need for an explicit consensus on principles.

35. Reinhold, *Verhandlungen*, 209.
36. The letters are published in part as section 3 of the *Verhandlungen* and contain reactions to both the "Proposal" and the "Project."
37. Reinhold, *Verhandlungen*, sec. 3, "Excerpts from the correspondence about the project," letter dated February 28, 1796 (author unknown), 236, 240 (answer).

In 1798, Reinhold published the improved and much enlarged version of the 1795 manuscript under his own name.[38] It had been planned from the beginning to improve the manuscript once a year and to print and publish it every three years. Reinhold was the author of this manuscript and the earlier federation plan, which contain formulations similar to those in his other works.

The first section of *The Fundamental Concepts* represented the final outcome of many years of discussions between Reinhold and his enlightened friends, correspondents, and Freemasonic brothers. It was the result of more than fifteen years of Reinhold's involvement with Freemasonry; it also presented the consequence of approximately six decades of evolving German Freemasonry. The proposed reform wanted Masonry to be an institution without secrecy and without symbols or emblems, since these would have undermined its purely moral purpose. The new form of association professed to be apolitical, far from any attempt to plot against the state. Nevertheless, as a moral institution, it claimed the right to influence public opinion and to act as a social force.

Reinhold remained a Freemason until the end of his life. In 1809, he joined the lodge "Amalia" in Weimar, to which his father-in-law Wieland belonged. In later years, he became the honorary member of several lodges. In 1820, he was elected Meister vom Stuhl of the lodge "Luise zur gekrönten Freundschaft" (Louise, to Crowned Friendship) in Kiel, which he himself had resurrected the same year. After his death in 1823, an obituary was composed, in which Reinhold's lifelong Masonic activities were honored: "He dedicated his entire earthly existence to the striving for and the teaching of truth. And he regarded it as the greatest happiness in his life that in this respect his profession was in harmony with his innermost inclination."[39]

---

38. Sec. 1, "An attempt to present the manner of thought of common and sound understanding regarding some principal points about ethical matters" (*The Fundamental Concepts*).

39. A. H. Baggesen, "Reinholds Todtenfeier, den 5. August 1823: Ein maurerisches Denkmal," 108.

Chapter 6

Reforming Philosophy

German "Popular Philosophy" and Scottish Common Sense Philosophy

Reinhold's *Fundamental Concepts* is conceived from the standpoint of "common sense," a concept at the heart of his version of "popular philosophy." This version is fundamentally different from the movement of German "popular philosophy" of his day. Proponents of this movement popularized the exoteric content of Leibniz's and Wolff's doctrines for the sake of educating the general public and succeeded in "making them part of the public consciousness." At the same time, they introduced French and British enlightened thought to Germany, translating the works of Locke, Hume, Reid, Oswald, Beattie, and the French philosophes. Beiser points out that "although almost all of the *Popularphilosophen* were influenced by Leibniz and Wolff, some of them were empiricists and more loyal to the tradition of Locke, while others were rationalists and more true to the tradition of Wolff."[1] Their major point of disagreement concerned the possibility of justifying a priori ideas, a disagreement that would eventually lead to different reactions to Kant's critical philosophy. Somewhat in contrast to Beiser, Kuehn emphasizes the "more empiricistic approach" and the "new appreciation of British science and philosophy" in combination with a "distaste" for the Leibniz-Wolffian method.[2]

Nevertheless, the popular philosophers did not subscribe to any particular doctrine. They "were indeed self-conscious eclectics,"[3] who

1. Beiser, *The Fate of Reason*, 166, 169.
2. Manfred Kuehn, *Scottish Common Sense in Germany, 1768–1800: A Contribution to the History of Critical Philosophy*, 37–38.
3. Beiser, *The Fate of Reason*, 166.

combined elements of completely different philosophical theories into a "philosophy for the world." The criteria for selecting these elements were their "popularity" and their basis in common sense and applicability to human life. The concept of eclectic thinking had not yet acquired the stigma of superficial and random borrowing from different sources that it has today. On the contrary, it was associated with autonomous thought. One should remember that eclectic philosophy had flourished during the period of early enlightenment before Wolff gained influence. It started in the seventeenth century with a change in the relation between *inventio* and *judicium*. Selective judgment independent of tradition or authority became more important than having all available knowledge. Thomasius called all excellent philosophers eclectic. In his *Introductio ad philosophicam aulicam* . . . , he characterized eclectic philosophy as necessary (regarding the infinity of available knowledge), useful (in the search for truth), tolerant, unbiased, and irenic (preventing unrest and confusion in church and state).[4]

The Göttingen popular philosophers characterized their position in terms of their opposition to Wolff. Samuel Christian Hollmann's critique of Wolffian philosophy rejected any metaphysics that worked on the basis of speculative principles. In the field of logic, he based philosophical thought on human psychology, following the example of British philosophers.[5]

J. G. H. Feder followed Hollmann's conception of philosophy, basing his logic on psychology. For him, the starting point for the study of logic lay in everybody's "inner experience." Its execution was guided by "common sense," a faculty not separable from reason itself. Basic epistemological concepts—'representation', 'thought', 'concept', and 'idea'—were defined on the basis of inner sensation, but their "quasi-empirical foundation . . . remain[ed] unexplained."[6]

4. Helmut Holzhey, "Philosophie als Eklektik."
5. Walther Ch. Zimmerli, " 'Schwere Rüstung' des Dogmatismus und 'anwendbare Eklektik': J. G. H. Feder und die Göttinger Philosophie im ausgehenden 18. Jahrhundert," 63.
6. Ibid., 64.

Truth, morality, and beauty were determined in accordance with the "inner sense," which supposedly was the same in all human beings.

Feder stated: "1) What all human beings cannot think other than in this certain way *is true*. 2) What to all human beings appears *beautiful* in a natural way, is really beautiful. 3) What to all human beings by virtue of their natural drives and sensations seems continuously *right* or *wrong*, is really right or wrong."[7] Metaphysics, in Feder's sense, dealt with the most general truths of reason and laws of nature. He did not aim at constructing a metaphysical system. His practical philosophy was based on the psychology of the drive for pleasure.

Concepts such as 'inner sense' and 'inner experience' indicate that the German popular philosophers were influenced by British empiricists, mainly Locke and Bacon. The Scottish philosophy of common sense—with its rejection of idealism and skepticism—was widely known and appreciated by such diverse thinkers as Garve, Feder, Lichtenberg, Mendelssohn, Hamann, Herder, and Tetens.[8]

Scottish philosophers Thomas Reid, James Beattie, James Oswald, and Dugald Stewart were deeply influenced by the empiricism of Locke and Hume.[9] Yet they rejected what they called the "theory of ideas," the epistemological conception of representation. In short, this conception limited human knowledge of the external world to "ideas" in the mind, which represented external objects to the mind and were the mind's only access to the world. In reducing everything in the world to mere representations in the human mind, Hume faced a radical skepticism, from which, according to him, human beings were saved only by their natural beliefs. These beliefs, represented in common sense, enabled them to lead their lives. Common sense comprised mathematical and empirical reasoning, epistemological beliefs, and moral judgments.

---

7. J. G. H. Feder, *Logik und Metaphysik*, quoted in Zimmerli, " 'Schwere Rüstung' des Dogmatismus," 65; original emphasis.

8. Manfred Kuehn, "The Early Reception of Reid, Oswald, and Beattie in Germany: 1768–1800."

9. For my representation of Scottish common sense philosophy, I rely on S. A. Grave, *The Scottish Philosophy of Common Sense*, and on Kuehn, *Scottish Common Sense*.

Despite Hume's emphasis on the importance of common sense, his Scottish critics thought that his representational theory led to complete absurdities—for instance, that there were no known external objects, only conglomerations of impressions, or that there existed no personal identity, only a series of momentary sense impressions. Reid rejected Locke's concept of the mind as a *tabula rasa.* He assumed instead that human nature instilled certain first principles of common sense in the human mind.

In contrast to a view that considered sense "as the power by which we receive certain ideas or impressions from objects," Reid started from the meaning of *sense:* "In common language, sense always implies judgment. A man of sense is a man of judgment. Good sense is good judgment. Nonsense is what is evidently contrary to right judgment. Common sense is that degree of judgment which is common to men with whom we can converse and transact business."[10]

The principles of common sense could not be proven deductively, since that would require "premises more obviously true than the truths of common sense, and there are none."[11] They were thought to be intuitively self-evident and to have an irresistible authority over the human mind. One task of common sense philosophy was to help regain for these principles common acceptance in practical life despite skepticism. (I shall not investigate here whether skepticism had really questioned the importance of common sense beliefs.)

Reid was convinced that his philosophy of common sense defended common sense beliefs as well as philosophy by revealing possible sources of philosophical errors. These mistakes arose, for him, out of erroneous methods. To reform method was the objective of his new philosophy of the mind. The working of the mind was to be studied through introspection, that is, the "accurate reflection upon the operations of our own minds,"[12] the common features of all languages, and human conduct. The data from these empirical studies would lead to the development of firm principles, and the

10. Thomas Reid, *Essays on the Intellectual Powers of Man,* essay 6, chap. 2, p. 557.
11. Grave, *The Scottish Philosophy of Common Sense,* 83.
12. Reid, *Essays on the Intellectual Powers of Man,* essay 1, chap. 5, p. 54.

new philosophy of mind would attain the status of a science and could serve as the ground of other sciences. Reid intended to construct a theory of the human mind which was analogous to modern natural science, as conceived by Newton and his predecessors. Reid's philosophy of mind is especially interesting in light of Reinhold's project of construing a philosophy of mind—or consciousness—that could serve as a scientific basis for all other knowledge.

Kuehn states that "Scottish common sense was a formative force at the University of Göttingen" for popular philosophers Feder and Meiners. Philosophers J. C. Lossius, Ernst Platner, and Dietrich Tiedemann used Reid's theory of sensation in their search for a material basis of sensation in human physiology. But it was also appreciated by some Berlin rationalists—among them, Eberhard and Mendelssohn. The latter used common sense as a "means of orientation" in metaphysics.[13] Kuehn mentions some "independent critical empiricists," such as Garve and Tetens (who was important in Kant's development), who were influenced by common sense philosophy. For Tetens, "the cognitions of common sense are the ground to be worked in speculative philosophy."[14] The philosophy of common sense was highly controversial, even in the eyes of those who found positive elements in it.

Kant's Critique of Common Sense Philosophy

Kant's critical project was a threat to all common sense philosophy. It provided the very examination of the faculties and limitations of reason that popular philosophy lacked (since it deemed this examination impossible). The first review of his *Critique of Pure Reason*, written by a famous popular philosopher, identified Kant's transcendental idealism with that of Berkeley, one of the main targets of Scottish criticism.[15] Kant's sharp attack accused the

13. Kuehn, "Early Reception," 483, 484.
14. Johann Nicolaus Tetens, *Über die allgemeine speculativische Philosophie* (Bützow and Wismar, 1775), 17, quoted in Kuehn, "Early Reception," 484; Kuehn's translation.
15. The review was originally written by Garve, but distorted by its editor Feder, who added the comparison between Kant's and Berkeley's idealism, seeing "Kant's idealism through the eyes of Thomas Reid" (Beiser, *The Fate of Reason*, 173).

reviewer of completely misunderstanding the *Critique*. However, the review—which stood out from the silence that greeted the *Critique*—prompted Kant to compose the *Prolegomena to Any Future Metaphysics*, in which he tried to present his critique of pure reason in a more accessible fashion. He also reworked the chapter on the deduction of pure concepts of understanding in the *Critique* and added an extra chapter on the refutation of idealism. In contrast to Berkeley, Kant claimed to prove that experience was real and not illusory, since it involved appearances of things-in-themselves whose existence was undoubted.

In his refutation of idealism, Kant's argument was similar to Reid's.[16] He attacked the theory of representation and its epistemic priority of inner experience. Reid had claimed that outer experience was as immediate as inner, but Kant claimed: "The required proof [for the existence of external objects] must, therefore, show that we have *experience*, and not merely imagination of outer things; and this, it would seem, cannot be achieved save by proof that even our inner experience, which for Descartes is indubitable, is possible only on the assumption of outer experience."[17] Outer experience was more important than inner.

Kant has often been interpreted as a fierce critic of common sense philosophy. And he did write a few derogatory remarks about it. The one at the end of his first *Critique* is often quoted: Sound reason is "mere misology, reduced to principles."[18] Referring to Scottish philosophy as "naturalism," Kant criticizes it for evading the justification of concepts and judgments in knowledge claims. Thus, raising "metaphysics to the level of a science" is impossible.[19]

Kant distinguished sharply between the common and the metaphysical, speculative employment of understanding. Sound understanding applied rules correctly in concrete circumstances. Concrete examples were necessary to understand its own rules. "Common

16. For this interpretation of Kant, see Manfred Kuehn, "Kant and the Refutations of Idealism in the Eighteenth Century."
17. Kant, *Critique of Pure Reason*, B 275.
18. Ibid., B 883.
19. Kuehn, *Scottish Common Sense*, 173.

sense, therefore, is only of use so far as it can see its rules (though they actually are a priori) confirmed by experience."[20] Speculative understanding had the task of comprehending these rules a priori, independent of experience, and thus belonged to metaphysics. The realms of common understanding and metaphysics should not be mixed, according to Kant. Common sense was incapable of providing metaphysical principles. Kant rejected the appeal to common human understanding with the help of which common sense philosophy tried to avoid justifying the truth of metaphysical propositions.

In other places, Kant characterized common sense more favorably. A recent claim is that common sense was more important for Kant than commentators have realized. Kuehn attempts to show that the Scottish philosophers, and Beattie in particular, played a crucial role in the development of Kant's thought. He quotes a remark by the historian of philosophy Wilhelm Windelband that Kant "begins at the point at which the Scots had stopped."[21] In Kuehn's view, Beattie's "analysis of the human faculties" started in "a very rough fashion" what Kant would do later. Another similarity can be found in the role of synthetic a priori elements in their respective theories of knowledge.[22]

Reason and common sense are not opposed; they spring from the same root. In the theoretical realm rational thought has to check the claims of common sense, but in the practical realm things might be the other way around. The decisive role of common sense—in the form of the human conscience—for the Categorical Imperative and for other ethical concepts could, of course, never have been doubted by anybody: "No doubt the concept of 'right', in its common-sense usage, contains all that the subtlest speculation can develop out of it, though in its ordinary and practical use we are not conscious of the manifold representations comprised in this thought."[23] In

20. Immanuel Kant, *Prolegomena to Any Future Metaphysics*, 118.
21. Wilhelm Windelband, *Geschichte der neueren Philosophie*, vol. 2, quoted in Kuehn, *Scottish Common Sense*, 175.
22. Kuehn, *Scottish Common Sense*, 185, 175.
23. Kant, *Critique of Pure Reason*, B 61.

spite of this positive role, it was basically Kant's negative account of common sense that influenced contemporary thought. Toward the end of his philosophical career, Kant "appears to have realized that he had even less in common with his many friends and 'followers' than with the common-sense philosophers."[24] In 1799 he published an open letter with the aim of clarifying his relationship to his self-appointed heirs Beck and Fichte: "Since some reviewers maintain that the *Critique* is not to be taken literally in what it says about sensibility . . . I therefore declare again that the *Critique* is to be understood by considering exactly what it says and that it requires only the common standpoint that any cultivated mind will bring to such abstract investigations."[25]

Kant criticized not only common sense philosophy but other important contemporary philosophies as well. He blamed rationalistic metaphysics for claiming to have knowledge that transcended the possibility of experience. Kant determined that the conditions of knowledge were sensibility and understanding. Therefore, all knowledge had to involve immediate intuition and mediating concepts. As in the case of knowledge of God's existence—traditionally demonstrated by the ontological, cosmological, and physicotheological proofs—such intuition was impossible. Kant denied the very possibility of such knowledge.

Although Kant refuted speculative metaphysics, he did not follow Hume's empiricist skepticism, which denied the very possibility of metaphysics. The goal of his critical enterprise was to establish metaphysics as a science. It was unacceptable to Kant that skepticism, though it allowed for epistemological beliefs (as, for example, in causality), thereby destroyed the objectivity of scientific knowledge, for which the objective validity of principles (such as causality) had to be guaranteed. Hume's denial of the possibility of synthetic a priori judgments that were objectively necessary, not merely logically necessary, led Kant to the question how these judgments were possible. Mathematics and natural science demonstrated that possibility. The

24. Kuehn, "Early Reception," 487.
25. Immanuel Kant, *Philosophical Correspondence 1759–1799*, 254.

problem was not to prove that the concept of causality was indispens-able, "for this Hume had never doubted; but whether that concept could be thought by reason a priori and consequently whether it possessed an inner truth, independent of all experience."[26] This quotation occurs during Kant's critique of Reid, Oswald, Beattie, and their critic Priestley, who all misunderstood Hume. They conse-quently assumed without proof what he had doubted—the justifiable application of a priori concepts—and tried to prove what he never had questioned—the indispensability of those concepts.

In his *Critique of Pure Reason*, Kant investigates the nature and limits of knowledge. In claiming two sources of knowledge, sensi-bility and understanding, Kant not only criticizes rationalism, which makes the intellect the sole source of knowledge. He also criticizes empiricism for accepting only sensibility as a source of knowledge. Kant traces the intellectual element in all theoretical knowledge, and at the same time he maintains that all knowledge comes from experience and cannot arise from concepts alone: "Thoughts without content are empty, intuitions without concepts are blind."[27] L. W. Beck characterizes the enterprise: "His question was: How not to be dogmatists in metaphysics without being skeptics in our knowledge of nature."[28]

The *Critique of Pure Reason* determines what can be known from pure reason without transcending the limits of possible experience. This amounts to the transcendental question regarding the possibility of a priori truths. These truths, though given a priori to experience, do not transcend experience, but make it possible as objective. The *Critique* studies the faculty of reason with regard to this pure knowl-edge. "Metaphysics" consists of "the system of pure reason, that is, the science which exhibits in systematic connection the whole body (true as well as illusory) of philosophical knowledge arising out of pure reason."[29]

26. Kant, *Prolegomena*, 6–7.
27. Kant, *Critique of Pure Reason*, B 75.
28. L. W. Beck, "Kant's Strategy," 14.
29. Kant, *Critique of Pure Reason*, B 869.

With the highest principle of objective knowledge, which claims that "the conditions of the *possibility of experience* in general are likewise conditions of the *possibility of the objects of experience*,"[30] Kant initiates a complete revolution, one that substitutes epistemology for ontology. In upsetting traditional definitions of true cognition, the principle guarantees that the a priori forms of intuition and a priori concepts of pure understanding that Kant deduces apply to reality.

The price Kant has to pay for this solution to objective knowledge is that he has to distinguish two aspects of the same object of cognition—the object as appearance, as it appears to human beings, and the object in itself, independent of being experienced by humans. The same object belongs to the phenomenal world and the intelligible world, depending on the way it is viewed.

The theory of two worlds proved advantageous for Kant's ethical theory. The concept of an intelligible world allows for a concept of freedom whose idea is at least not contradictory and thus thinkable, though its reality cannot be theoretically proved.

> Morality does not, indeed, require that freedom should be understood, but only that it should not contradict itself, and so should at least allow of being thought, and that as thus thought it should place no obstacle in the way of a free act (viewed in another relation) likewise conforming to the mechanism of nature. The doctrine of morality and the doctrine of nature may each, therefore, make good its position. This, however, is only possible in so far as criticism has previously established our unavoidable ignorance of things in themselves, and has limited all that we can theoretically *know* to mere appearances.[31]

Reactions to Kant's critical philosophy were as diverse as the people who formulated them. Beiser categorizes them according to the two great philosophical camps at that time, the Lockeans and the Wolffians. Apart from the accusation of idealism, the Lockeans' main points of criticism centered on the problem of apriority. Kant's a priori

30. Ibid., B 197.
31. Ibid., B XXIX.

method of epistemology was unacceptable to them; they advocated a naturalistic epistemology. The Wolffians' criticisms were in part the same as the Lockeans', though for different reasons. They accused Kant of skepticism, of denying the possibility of knowledge. In other words, like the Lockeans, they identified his idealism with that of Berkeley. They criticized as useless his distinction between analytic and synthetic propositions. Instead, the distinction had to be logical. According to them, both kinds of propositions could be derived from purely rational principles. Interestingly enough, though, some of his critics thought that Kant did not offer anything beyond what the Scottish common sense philosophers had attempted.[32]

Reinhold's Fundamental Philosophy and Kant's Critique of Reason

The publication of Kant's *Critique of Pure Reason* was followed by years of almost complete silence, on which Kant sarcastically commented in his *Prolegomena*. This was certainly a result of the immense difficulty of the work. Even when reviews finally started to appear, many showed serious misunderstandings of Kant's intentions. So Kant was very thankful when Reinhold started to publish his *Briefe über die Kantische Philosophie* in *Der Teutsche Merkur* in 1786. He praised them in his first letter to Reinhold: "My admirable and amiable fellow, I have read the beautiful letters with which you have honored my philosophy and which were unsurpassed in their graceful thoroughness. They did not fail to have every desired effect in our region."[33] In the January issue of *Der Teutsche Merkur*, Kant officially declared that the *Briefe* gave the correct interpretation of his critical philosophy. The letters quickly made his philosophy popular.

Thus, Reinhold became the official interpreter of the Kantian philosophy. As a reward for his *Briefe*, he received a professorship in philosophy at the respected University of Jena. There, he proved that he not only possessed an astute philosophical mind but also

---

32. Kuehn, *Scottish Common Sense*, 209–13.
33. Kant to Reinhold, December 18, 1787, in *Korrespondenzausgabe*, 298.

was an excellent teacher. He attracted students from all over Germany. Toward the end of his years in Jena, he had approximately 600 students[34] (out of 860 university students).[35] In 1794, Reinhold moved to Kiel, where he had been offered a post as a full university professor. Although Kiel was not the cultural and intellectual center that Weimar and Jena were, Reinhold found at the university an enthusiastic welcome. He became "*the* great teacher of the Kantian philosophy" in that region;[36] participated in the discussions of many circles, liberal (for instance, the Reimarus circle) as well as conservative (the Reventlow circle in Emkendorf); and became active in Freemasonry and in other (for instance, charitable) societies.

Reinhold did not remain solely a popularizer of Kant's philosophy. He perceived a general crisis in enlightenment, a "hatred of reason," that made rational argumentation difficult. He became convinced that it was a "need of the time" to secure safe principles for all important aspects of societal life and especially morality. It was the goal of philosophy to "enlighten about rights and duties."[37] These principles would have to be generally valid and accepted in order to have the necessary impact.

Kant's philosophy was a case of a theory that did not gain general acceptance because it rested on unclear premises.[38] Kant had promised that his critical study of the conditions of knowledge would examine all presuppositions. But he relied on some assumptions that he thought were safe to make because the skeptic Hume had relied on them too. These included the passive receptivity of the senses and the awareness of our selves. From these assumptions, Kant derived necessary propositions about the a priori conditions of knowledge "in the absence of knowledge of which we could not know

34. E. Reinhold, *Reinhold's Leben und litterarisches Wirken*, 48–49, 66.
35. Kurt Röttgers, "Die Kritik der reinen Vernunft und K. L. Reinhold: Fallstudie zur Theoriepragmatik in Schulbildungsprozessen," 800.
36. Renate Erhardt-Lucht, *Die Ideen der Französischen Revolution in Schleswig-Holstein*, 107.
37. Reinhold, *Briefe*, 102.
38. See Wolfgang Schrader, "Systemphilosophie als Aufklärung: Zum Philosophiebegriff K. L. Reinholds," 78.

even these Humean presuppositions to be true." Beck describes this method, with which Kant begins in his *Critique of Pure Reason*, as analytical.[39] Only after Kant had thereby proven his presuppositions did he turn to the synthetic method, which he himself claimed to use in the *Critique*.

Reinhold thought that Kant fell short of his own ideals of a critique and a science of philosophy by proceeding analytically from unproven presuppositions. A science, according to Kant, had to be grounded systematically upon one idea—"the concept provided by reason—of the form of a whole—in so far as the concept determines *a priori* not only the scope of its manifold content, but also the positions which the parts occupy relatively to one another."[40] Reinhold claimed that a synthetic method had to start from one principle and deduce from this all its propositions. This principle was to be self-evident, so that no unproven assumptions entered the system.

Reinhold set out to revise transcendental philosophy according to the ideals of critique and science. In his search for a fundamental principle, he came upon the concept of representation, a concept Kant had not sufficiently defined, although it was fundamental for his *Critique*. Intuitions, concepts, and ideas were different kinds of representation. The concept of representation also was at the basis of Kant's conception of knowledge.

> Every reader of the critique of reason knows that the forms of representations, as they are laid down by the critique, are not traced back to a universally accepted principle. They also know that the work neither mentions a first principle of the science of the faculty of knowledge nor a first principle of philosophy in general. This principle shall directly ground Fundamental Philosophy [*Elementarphilosophie*] and indirectly ground theoretical and practical philosophy, which are derived from Fundamental Philosophy.[41]

39. L. W. Beck, "Toward a Meta-Critique of Pure Reason," 23.
40. Kant, *Critique of Pure Reason*, B 860.
41. Reinhold, "Ueber das Verhältniss der Theorie des Vorstellungsvermögens, zur Kritik der reinen Vernunft," 264. He presented his Fundamental Philosophy in the two volumes of his *Beyträge zur Berichtigung bisheriger Missverständnisse der*

In 1789, Reinhold published the *Versuch einer neuen Theorie des menschlichen Vorstellungsvermögens* (Attempt of a new theory of the human faculty of representation), his first attempted formulation of a basis from which to derive the results of Kant's critical philosophy. He developed in this work the concept of "representation in general," lack of analysis of which, in his opinion, had provoked most misunderstandings of the *Critique of Pure Reason.* The foundation of his new theory is consciousness, which "works in all human beings in accordance with the same fundamental laws." From this foundation, Reinhold claims to derive all other propositions of the critique of reason without relying on any presuppositions. "In the whole treatise, no proposition that was stated in the critique of reason was allowed to be taken as proven or even as probable . . . the author had to secure the universal validity of his theory by not assuming anything as universally valid that was not actually universally accepted."[42] The fact of consciousness is the starting point that cannot be doubted and has to be accepted by everybody, even the fiercest skeptic. "Compelled by consciousness, one agrees that there pertains a representing subject and a represented object to every representation. Both have to be distinguished from the representation to which they belong."[43]

Thus, at the basis of Reinhold's fundamental philosophy lies the proposition of consciousness: "In consciousness, the subject distinguishes the representation from the subject and the object and relates it to them both."[44] This proposition is, according to Reinhold, a description of what is happening in consciousness, that is, of the "fact of consciousness" (*Thatsache des Bewusstseins*). This fact implies that human beings possess the "faculty of representation," whose possibility Reinhold deduces in his "science of the faculty of representation." He shows that the a priori forms of sensibility, understanding, and

---

Philosophen (1790, 1794), *Über das Fundament des philosophischen Wissens* (1791), and the second volume of the *Briefe über die Kantische Philosophie* (1792).

42. Reinhold, "Ueber die bisherigen Schicksale der kantischen Philosophie," preface to *Versuch einer neuen Theorie*, 64, 66.

43. Reinhold, *Versuch einer neuen Theorie*, 200.

44. Reinhold, "Neue Darstellung der Hauptmomente der Elementarphilosophie," in *Beyträge zur Berichtigung*, 1:167.

reason originate in the nature of representations in general: "Space and time, the twelve categories, and the three forms of ideas are originally nothing but properties of mere representations."[45]

In the last, short section of his *Versuch*, Reinhold develops a theory of the faculty of desire. He assigns the faculty of desire an even more fundamental role than the faculty of representation, a move that some commentators have interpreted as an attempt to save Kant's primacy of practical reason. Alfred Klemmt quotes, for instance, Nicolai Hartmann's *Die Philosophie des deutschen Idealismus*.[46] Distinguishing between possible and actual representations, Reinhold lets actual representations be produced by a representing force, which the faculty of desire allows. The mere possibility of representations is grounded in the faculty of representation. He calls the relationship between the representing power and its faculty the "drive" for representation: "To be determined through the drive to produce a representation, is called desire, and the faculty to be determined through a drive, [is called] faculty of desire in a broader sense."[47]

This drive encompasses a "drive for matter" and a "drive for form." The drive for matter is purely receptive, "satisfied with the given" and is called "selfish" by Reinhold. The drive for form is spontaneous, satisfied by acting and thus "unselfish." It is capable of being determined by pure reason and so includes a free will. The will is a person's faculty to determine himself to action; volition is "the actual, consciously performed self-determination to an act of the drive"; and morality is "the realization—intended for its own sake—of the way of acting of pure reason."[48]

Where Kant has sensibility and understanding as the two different stems of human knowledge, Reinhold starts from their common root, representation in general, which precedes all consciousness. From a single highest principle, the proposition of consciousness, he wants

---

45. Reinhold, *Über das Fundament des philosophischen Wissens*, 72–73.
46. Alfred Klemmt, *Karl Leonhard Reinholds Elementarphilosophie: Eine Studie über den Ursprung des spekulativen deutschen Idealismus*, 119–20.
47. Reinhold, *Versuch einer neuen Theorie*, 561.
48. Ibid., 567, 570.

to construct "the entire theory of representations, knowledge, and also reason, and ultimately even of desire and volition." His theory of self-consciousness, part of that of consciousness, was the first one that set out to explain the problem of "self-relatedness in self-consciousness."[49]

I give but a brief description of Reinhold's philosophical development after the phase in which he formulated his fundamental philosophy. For a short time, he supported Johann Gottlieb Fichte's theory of scientific knowledge.[50] Fichte was a great admirer of Kant and Reinhold; his theory of scientific knowledge was the outcome of his reading of Reinhold's fundamental philosophy. Initially influenced by Schulze's critique of Reinhold in his *Aenesidemus*, Fichte did not accept Reinhold's principle of consciousness as the first principle of philosophy, granting it that status only for theoretical philosophy. He called for a more encompassing principle that was itself absolutely unconditioned, that is, free. Only a free act could "serve as the foundation for *all* philosophy, practical as well as theoretical."[51] Fichte chose absolute autonomy, a principle that determines itself in a kind of "absolute self-relation."[52] He substituted Reinhold's "fact" (*Thatsache*) of consciousness with his own "act" (*Thathandlung*) of the I that posits itself. Klemmt thinks it possible that

> Fichte felt reinforced by the statements at the beginning of Reinhold's 'theory of the faculty of desire' [last section of the *Versuch*] in his decision to unfold the entire critical philosophy anew by starting out

49. Dieter Henrich, *Konstellationen. Probleme und Debatten am Ursprung der idealistischen Philosophie (1789–1795)*, 240, 222.

50. In a recent publication, Dieter Henrich hints at an additional change of system that Reinhold underwent in 1792 following a major critique of his fundamental philosophy by the *Repetent* Diez from Tübingen (Henrich, *Konstellationen*, 224, 242). A new work about this subject, one of whose authors is Marcelo Stamm, had not been published when this manuscript went to press.

51. Daniel Breazeale, "Between Kant and Fichte: Karl Leonhard Reinhold's 'Elementary Philosophy,'" 810–11, 811n52. I translate *Elementarphilosophie* as fundamental philosophy; Breazeale translates it as elementary philosophy.

52. Jürgen Stolzenberg, *Fichtes Begriff der intellektuellen Anschauung: Die Entwicklung in den Wissenschaftslehren von 1793/94 bis 1801/02*, 8–9.

from Kant's primacy of practical reason, and that he understood it as the confirmation of his own philosophical will.[53]

After extensive discussions with his critic Fichte, Reinhold officially "converted" to Fichte's theory of scientific knowledge in 1797. He acknowledged that his own fundamental philosophy had failed in its objective of providing an ultimate principle for all philosophy. It was still based on presuppositions that were outside the subject and could not be deduced from a single principle. "I realized that my Fundamental Philosophy presupposed the empirical for the sake of the possibility of the transcendental and vice versa without giving a higher common cause of both, and that it could only break out of this circle through a *salto mortale* into the realm of the transcendent." He then admitted that only Fichte's theory of scientific knowledge succeeded in transforming philosophy into a strict science. Fichte's "pure I" was different from his own subject of consciousness in that the latter presupposed an object of consciousness and so was an empirical subject. Fichte's I, on the other hand, was "original activity that, to the reflecting self-consciousness, declares itself as positing itself through itself, that is, as subject and object at the same time."[54]

However, this conversion "did not solve all the problems" for Reinhold, as Reinhard Lauth observes. The theory of scientific knowledge "create[d] paradoxes for natural thought (which includes the standpoint of conscience)."[55] The relation of philosophical knowledge, morality, and faith proved precarious. "The finite spirit that abstracts from all reality for the sake of pure knowledge, also rises above his own reality. . . . He cannot believe in a God, and he cannot act in regard to the real in experience."[56] Speculative knowledge, whose progress is infinite, can never be applied to reality, because it is never

53. Klemmt, *Elementarphilosophie*, 120.
54. Reinhold, preface, in *Auswahl vermischter Schriften*, 2:ix, x.
55. Reinhard Lauth, "Fichtes und Reinholds Verhältnis vom Anfange ihrer Bekanntschaft bis zu Reinholds Beitritt zum Standpunkt der Wissenschaftslehre Anfang 1797," 154–55. "Theory of scientific knowledge" refers to Fichte's *Wissenschaftslehre*.
56. Reinhold, *Ueber die Paradoxien der neuesten Philosophie*, 107.

complete. "Thus, a complete contradiction between speculation and life comes about."[57] Although Reinhold could at first avoid these paradoxes by strictly separating philosophizing reason from common sense—as in *The Fundamental Concepts*—and scientific philosophy from living faith, he soon broke with Fichte's system. Contributing to his decision were his friend Jacobi's philosophy of faith, his criticism of all speculative philosophy, and his thesis that Fichte's idealism was Spinozism in reverse.

When in 1799 Reinhold became acquainted with the thinking of Christoph Gottfried Bardili, he subscribed to and officially promoted Bardili's "logical realism." Bardili's philosophy, resting on a "dualistic metaphysical presupposition," seemed to provide an alternative to Fichte's speculative philosophy. Intellect and world remained separate; they were not identified as in Fichte's system. This appealed to Reinhold, who through all his philosophical changes remained a realist.

Bardili contrasted his logic to that of the transcendental philosophers. His was "transsubjective," possessing independent ontological being. Reinhold wrote that this logic "declared the character of all subjectivity in general to be representation and, thus, non-thinking, and pointed out—through a thinking purified of subjectivity and freed from confusion with representing—the absolute in itself in its manifestation as the original truth in all truth and the manifestation of truth through original truth."[58] The absolute in itself became for Reinhold the realm where faith and knowledge could be reconciled.

In his final philosophical phase, Reinhold developed a philosophy of language, in which he tried to determine the role of language in mediating between thought and reality. Reinhold had always been aware of the necessity of determinate concepts in philosophy which called for a precise terminology. In the essay "Ueber den Begriff der Philosophie," he wrote about the concept of philosophy: "The

57. Lauth, "Fichtes und Reinholds Verhältnis," 157.
58. Reinhold, "Rechenschaft über mein Systemwechseln," in *Beyträge zur leichtern Uebersicht des Zustandes der Philosophie beym Anfange des 19. Jahrhunderts*, no. 5, 39. These *Beyträge* are not to be confused with his earlier *Beyträge zur Berichtigung.*

determinate concept and the determinate meaning of the term 'philosophy' are really one and the same. This is true of all philosophical concepts and the meanings of their signs."[59] Later he called for "philosophy as a critique of language—in the sense of a meta-critique of reason," which would continue the transcendental project by revealing the transcendental function of language. Cloeren interprets Reinhold's critique of language as a precursor of twentieth-century logical positivism in its claim to end metaphysical illusions and misunderstandings by eradicating inaccurate terminology.[60] However, this interpretation is misleading, since Cloeren accords to Reinhold the same hostility toward metaphysics as positivism displays. But Reinhold's endeavor was to make metaphysics possible as a science by means of a thorough critique and clarification of philosophical language.

Reinhold's Version of a Popular Philosophy

When Reinhold worked at his project of a systematic foundation of philosophy, he pursued not merely theoretical interests. He was also guided by practical reasons connected to his enlightened ideals. Already in his early essay "Thoughts on Enlightenment," he had argued in favor of popular enlightenment, which would be advanced by a mediation between theory and practice. When he read Kant for the first time, he did so because he was concerned about the contemporary crisis in religious beliefs. After having become a Kantian, Reinhold adopted Kant's conviction of the primacy of practical reason, a conviction he never gave up, though his philosophical system later changed.

Consequently, one of the major objectives of his fundamental philosophy was to provide a universally accepted first principle: "A universally accepted proposition must be possible as a first principle,

59. Reinhold, "Ueber den Begriff der Philosophie," in *Beyträge zur Berichtigung*, 1:8–9.
60. Hermann-Josef Cloeren, "Philosophie als Sprachkritik bei K. L. Reinhold: Interpretative Bemerkungen zu seiner Spätphilosophie," 228.

or philosophy as a science is impossible. Then the reasons for our moral duties and rights, and consequently these duties and rights themselves, must be left undecided forever. And chance will eternally maintain its role in the guidance of human affairs—a role that belongs to reason."[61]

However, Reinhold's fundamental philosophy was formulated in a highly theoretical fashion. This clashed with his old ideal of popular enlightenment. It also clashed with contemporary criticism of a purely rational enlightenment, as formulated by the philosophers of faith and the Sturm und Drang movement. Reinhold sought a different way to provide a basis for the moral improvement of humankind. He offered a new kind of "popular philosophy," which had only the name in common with the "popular philosophy" of Feder, Garve, and Nicolai. The name itself had by the early 1790s become a term of abuse. So this was another one of Reinhold's attempts of salvaging.

The Fundamental Concepts was an example of Reinhold's version of popular philosophy. It was written from the standpoint of common, sound understanding, a faculty common to all human beings and whose cultivation for Reinhold involved not only enlightenment of the understanding but also education of the heart.

Reinhold's concept of common understanding is considerably different from the concept of common sense, as employed by Scottish common sense philosophers or German popular philosophers. For them, common sense is the sole source of the basic principles of philosophy, which are found with the help of empirical introspection and which themselves cannot be justified. For Reinhold, on the other hand, common sense and philosophy belong to completely different realms, the former being empirical, the latter being transcendental. He rejected "popular philosophy" precisely because it refused to justify its ultimate principles.

Reinhold's philosophy of consciousness determines the representing activity of the mind through mere reflection on the concept

---

61. Reinhold, *Über das Fundament des philosophischen Wissens*, 367.

of a representation in general, excluding any empirical reference. Philosophizing reason proceeds to the transcendental causes of the activity of representing which must be present a priori in the subject. It searches for the ultimate causes of experience beyond the empirical level. Those ultimate causes are comprehensible "whose immediate effects occur in experience . . . these causes are none other than the conditions of experience given within the subject, sofar as experience depends on the subject and not on external objects."[62] Ultimate causes outside the subject as well as those whose effects are not immediately given in experience are beyond the limits of knowledge.

In contrast to philosophizing reason, common sense, for Reinhold, deals only with facts and their immediate causes in experience. Common sense as understanding has access to outer experience through sensible representation, but as reason, it has access to so-called facts of inner experience, or self-consciousness. This proves decisive for the problem of morality and how to ground it in something other than human psychology. Like Kant, who relies on the concept of a moral law given as a "fact of reason," Reinhold starts from "facts" of moral consciousness, or conscience. But he provides a philosophical basis different from Kant's.

As we have seen, Reinhold's fundamental philosophy rested on the proposition of consciousness. While Kant developed his critique of reason in constant reference to the facticity of experience, Reinhold set consciousness in its place.[63] He distinguishes three different kinds of consciousness: of representation, of the object, and of the subject. The last he calls self-consciousness. Empirical self-consciousness refers to the subject in connection with the body, and pure self-consciousness belongs to the subject as a separate entity. In pure self-consciousness, the representing subject represents itself as representing. The "facts of inner experience," of which it becomes

62. Reinhold, "Ueber den Unterschied zwischen dem gesunden Verstande und der philosophierenden Vernunft in Rücksicht auf die Fundamente des durch beyde möglichen Wissens," in *Beyträge zur Berichtigung*, 2:14–15.
63. See Alfred P. König, *Denkformen in der Erkenntnis: Die Urteilstafel Immanuel Kants in der Kritik der reinen Vernunft und in Karl Leonhard Reinholds "Versuch einer neuen Theorie des menschlichen Vorstellungsvermögens,"* 75.

aware during this process, are completely nonempirical. They are the product of an intellectual intuition, which reason makes possible. This went far beyond critical philosophy, which did not allow for intellectual intuition.

Reinhold distinguishes sharply between "real experience" of outer objects (among which he counts the empirical subject) and "mere inner experience" of transcendental objects. "Inner experience is independent of outer experience insofar as it contains facts whose determinate concepts must be completely removed from external impressions and the conditions of the organism." It depends solely on the representing subject. "Reason, through which alone the mere subject of experience (neither in space nor in time, thus neither as something represented to be outside of us, nor as change within us) can be immediately represented—reason makes inner experience as such possible, insofar as one understands it not merely as a state of thoughtless feelings, but as the essence of the facts of self-consciousness."[64]

The facts of inner experience are the immediate effects of the "transcendental laws of reason," which lie within the subject—the same way the facts of outer experience are the immediate effects of transcendental laws of the understanding. Making these facts possible, reason plays a special role in "examining itself and all the other faculties of the mind." Kant had always been criticized for his reliance on faculties of the mind which he did not further derive as conditions of the possibility of experience. Reinhold now makes these conditions accessible to the representing subject. "The completely sufficient, therefore ultimate, causes of experience, insofar as experience depends on the subject, must be given within the subject a priori to all real experience. Their immediate effects, on the other hand, must occur through facts of experience, insofar as these depend immediately on the subject, that is, they must occur through facts of inner experience as such." Or put differently: "If, indeed, inner experience as such can lead to ultimate causes, then this is only

64. Reinhold, "Ueber den Unterschied," 58, 25–26.

possible insofar as the faculty of representation in its effects can become the object of inner experience. And these effects are none other than those representations which belong to the mere subject, that is, representations in regard to that which makes them mere representations."[65]

The a priori forms of intuition, the categories and the ideas, as the *Critique of Pure Reason* presents them, are such facts of inner experience, and the immediate transcendental causes are the faculties of sensibility, understanding, and reason. The faculties are accessible only to philosophizing reason but are nevertheless effective in common sense: "[They] have always been the cause of the unchangeable, of pure truth, which were contained in human knowledge, through all changes, imperfections and errors." On account of this unconscious effectiveness of the transcendental laws, sound common sense is endowed with a kind of instinct for truth, which makes it superior to that philosophizing reason that has not yet ascertained knowledge of those laws. "The understanding as such cannot err."[66] Only its employment can lead to error, since it depends on external and internal circumstances—physical, psychological, and moral conditions. The moral condition here refers to the freedom of the will, of the decisions people make and the influence they allow their inclinations to have on them.

Since it was Reinhold's conviction when he wrote *The Fundamental Concepts* that philosophizing reason had not yet determined an ultimate principle for practical philosophy, he based his argument on facts of conscience. Conscience, for him, represents a particular kind of self-consciousness in which pure and empirical self-consciousness are combined. A person is conscious of an "ought"—the moral law—which is the demand that reason imposes on the empirical subject, that is, to act in conformity with reason. In order for the person to be able to comply with the law, he must possess a free will. Thus the person cannot be a solely empirical subject; he must be thought of as a pure, intelligible subject as well. "In the practical respect, the subject

65. Ibid., 25, 8, 63.
66. Ibid., 16, 19.

is independent of the difference from and inter-connectedness with his body through his freedom, which is certain because of the moral law. Although he is not independent of it in his existence, he is in his acting."[67]

The Fundamental Concepts starts from commonly experienced facts, as they are provided by conscience. Reinhold describes human conscience as a feature that indisputably belongs to all human beings and that represents the "most certain" kind of consciousness (art. 35). It is the source of natural moral truths. The goal of *The Fundamental Concepts* is to consolidate and further develop these moral truths, badly needed at a time when political revolution, war, and religious and philosophical crises shook the foundations of traditional norms. The truths have to be presented in their character as common convictions, so that they will be recognized as "universally valid" and "universally accepted" as such, which, for Reinhold, is a prerequisite for the ultimate end of humankind—acting morally. In thus mediating between philosophical, political, and religious parties, Reinhold resumed the eclectic tradition of "irenic" philosophy.

According to Reinhold, there exists a "natural content" of moral convictions—the facts of moral consciousness—whose discovery is not bound to scholarly investigation or historical research, but can be directly found in conscience (art. 10). It is the task of common sense to judge these convictions by analyzing their content and determining their form.

As we have seen, Reinhold distinguishes between the natural and the philosophical employment of reason. Natural reason, or understanding, is limited to the realm of experience. Natural convictions are lawful and necessary, though they do not comprehend the underlying laws. Philosophical reason, on the other hand, scientifically deduces its convictions from laws. However, the content of the convictions is the same; natural and philosophical convictions cannot contradict each other. "Since the results of true philosophy are

---

67. Reinhold, "Ueber den gegenwärtigen Zustand der Metaphysik und der transcendentalen Philosophie überhaupt," in *Auswahl vermischter Schriften*, 2:273.

nothing but purified and completed natural convictions, they must be conceivable by such concepts and expressable by such propositions as can be understood and found to be true through mere natural reasoning" (art. 90).

For Reinhold, natural convictions involve feelings as well as concepts. Cultivating those convictions requires both "education of the heart" and "enlightenment of the understanding." The latter means the clear and distinct thinking of concepts and, thus, of convictions. It also emphasizes the importance of autonomous thought. Reinhold combines in this concept of enlightenment in general the major ideas of rationalistic and critical enlightenment.

By also treating the education of feeling, he includes an element that had been missing during the height of rationalistic enlightenment and that various critics of the movement had since called for. The concept of humanity of the heart comprises the disposition to humaneness, or sympathy, and its relationship to the selfish drive, which is reminiscent of Kant's concept of the "unsociable sociability" of man. It also contains the moral feeling—the pleasure a person feels in the presence of moral lawfulness—taste, and propriety. Reinhold's concept of moral feeling must not be confused with Kant's concept of respect for the moral law, which, apart from pleasure caused by absolute necessity, also involves displeasure that arises from the compulsion that the law imposes on sensibility. The pleasure of the moral feeling exists in a person's free decision to act for the sake of the law. Taste, on the other hand, includes for Reinhold the feeling of the beautiful and of the sublime. The connection of feeling to morality through the moral feeling guarantees that sentiment does not become merely sentimental, but is linked to a person's rational, free self.

In subsuming enlightenment of the understanding under the education of the heart, Reinhold changed the emphasis of enlightenment, which had rested on reasoning and knowledge. His more holistic view integrated all aspects of a person's development, the cultivation of all his faculties, into a whole self. He had come a long way from his earlier concept of popular enlightenment, according to which philosophers taught clear and distinct concepts to the people.

His new version of popular philosophy combined different aspects of enlightenment thinking on a strictly popular basis, that is, on the basis of common sense. And it responded to criticisms of the counter-enlightenment by incorporating more subjective aspects of ethical and aesthetic sentiment into enlightened thought.

Conclusion

Reinhold was an exemplary representative of the movement of enlightenment. His biography shows his many struggles for enlightenment. He was well read—he was acquainted with the relevant German texts, as well as English and French philosophical, political, and literary writings. He was an excellent teacher, and his concern for his students transcended the boundaries of university seminars. He was in personal contact—or, when that was not possible, corresponded—with many important German thinkers about all subjects regarding enlightenment. As a member of several discussion groups, he disregarded ideological divisions, meeting with liberal-minded people (the Reimarus circle) and conservatives (the Reventlow circle). Reinhold participated in the written public discourse not only through his philosophical publications but also through being an editor and a reviewer. As a lifelong Freemason, he worked for the goal of a common rule of morality, a goal that was also at the heart of his philosophical work. Von Schönborn characterizes Reinhold as an "important node in the communication network of the educated, through which enlightenment constituted itself."[1]

As a theoretical thinker, Reinhold was representative in his great stress on the concepts of morality and faith, which were at the center of German enlightened thought. In assigning primacy to ethical enlightenment, he went beyond enlightened rationalism, which had emphasized conceptual clarity and distinctness. He also went further than Kant, who had based enlightenment on the moral decision to think autonomously. Reinhold determined that ethical concepts were the most important content of autonomous thought.

Reinhold was also representative of enlightenment thought in making morality the basis of religion. Precritical enlightened philosophers

---

1. Von Schönborn, *Bibliographie*, 17.

had grounded religious claims in speculative metaphysics. Kant's critique of reason shattered these claims. Instead, Kant grounded faith in God on the necessity of the moral law, as it was given to reason and immediately known through conscience. In *The Fundamental Concepts*, Reinhold followed Kant's popular derivation of the moral law from conscience. From the possibility of executing the moral law, he then derived the necessary ideas of God's existence and the immortality of the soul.

One important idea of enlightenment was to educate the public. For this purpose, philosophical concepts were "popularized," made more accessible, by the "popular philosophers." Reinhold provided a different kind of popular philosophy. He attempted to formulate concepts that were generally acceptable to all human beings on the basis of their conscience, which they supposedly had in common. And he hoped that he would thus overcome all the theoretical differences regarding ethical concepts which prevented the development of publicly shared convictions in "moral, rightful, political, and religious affairs." His goal was the improvement of the individual and of society as a whole.

In his formulation of moral and political concepts, Reinhold—like Kant—clearly departed from those based on material definitions of human pleasure and happiness. Reinhold's were merely formal—the moral law required the lawful character of maxims of actions; the state legislated and enforced external right and provided its citizens with an external framework in which they could enact their freedom in ways compatible with the freedom of other citizens. Reinhold's political philosophy can thus be characterized as liberal.

By the end of the century, the optimistic view of the prospects for human happiness had given way to a more pessimistic frame of mind. Hopes for the possibility of enlightenment from above had disappeared. Instead, absolutist rule came under increasing criticism. And the direction the French Revolution had taken contributed to that political pessimism. Hope was now turned inward and attached to individual moral improvement, a trend well expressed by Reinhold's concept of individual ennoblement.

Perhaps Reinhold's most important contribution to enlightenment thought was that he considered the criticisms of "counter-enlightenment" and incorporated its claims into the concept of enlightenment itself. He wrote at a time when the Sturm und Drang had made its mark and when romanticism was on the rise. Reinhold subordinated the enlightenment of "cold" theoretical understanding to the enlightenment of the "heart" and practical deliberation. It was reason that still provided the guiding principle in human ennoblement. Reinhold was not a romantic; he did not lose faith in reason. The physical and emotive elements of human personality formed part of the concept of "humanity," which encompassed cultivating these elements toward a morality of the whole person. Reinhold's definition of human destiny as the development of people's humanity was basically the same as the concept of "education" or "self-cultivation" (*Bildung*), which was crucial for critics of rationalistic enlightenment, such as Herder and Goethe. It was at the basis of a new literary genre, the classic *Bildungsroman* (novel of development), as developed by Wieland and Goethe. From Reinhold's concept of humanity, it was only one step further to Schiller's concept of beauty, which symbolized the natural harmony of sensibility and reason in a human being.

While Reinhold, the Catholic monk who had converted to Protestantism, defended rational faith, some romanticists converted to Catholicism as the more sensuous and irrational faith. *The Fundamental Concepts* might well be interpreted as an attempt to save enlightenment and the primacy of reason from such romanticist thought. His work allows a place for aesthetic feelings in the education of the heart, but assigns them a role subordinate to theoretical and practical reason. Imagination has to be disciplined, so that it can work for truth and morality. This was clearly a denunciation of romantic tendencies to set the imagination loose and seek truth in the realm of aesthetics.

Reinhold stood between two ages. He "systematically summed up essential results of enlightenment."[2] His concept of enlightenment

2. Schneiders, *Wahre Aufklärung*, 181.

encompassed conceptual clarity and distinctness as well as autonomous thought. He formulated a concept of humanity that was characteristic of the German classical age. In his emphasis on individual ennoblement and his rejection of any political practice that was not securely based on universally accepted concepts, he was a typical representative of German enlightenment. Writing at the end of the age of enlightenment, he reacted to tendencies of thought as formulated by enlightenment's critics. He accounted for valid criticisms by incorporating elements of new thought in *The Fundamental Concepts*. Still, he stood firmly on the ground of enlightenment, at least in regard to his conception of morality.

However, when he wrote *The Fundamental Concepts*, his theoretical thought was developing beyond the boundaries of critical philosophy, which had been the culmination of enlightened philosophy. His construction of philosophy on the basis of one principle represented a significant deviation from Kant's method. And in dealing with the new philosophies of Fichte and Bardili, Reinhold called for an "even higher starting point" in philosophy, consisting in the "relationlessness of the absolute."[3] Together with his dialectical method of thought, these two ideas had a decisive influence on the philosophies of the German Idealists.

3. Reinhard Lauth, "Reinholds Vorwurf des Subjektivismus gegen die Wissenschaftslehre," 276.

II. Translation

The Fundamental Concepts and Principles of Ethics

Deliberations of Sound Common Sense, for the Purpose of Evaluating Moral, Rightful, Political and Religious Matters

Published by

C. L. Reinhold, Professor in Kiel

Volume 1
Lübeck and Leipzig
Friedrich Bohn, 1798

Preface

The longer the political and scientific revolutions of our age continue, and the further their influence extends, the less will a member of the educated public as a spectator be able to refrain from participating in one or another noteworthy event. Although the majority of this public is not able or willing to defend or fight against the new structures, it is nevertheless interested in this struggle. For what is at stake is nothing less than the institutions which are the basis of both the rightful status quo and the convictions which underlie moral actions.

As long as this controversy remains unresolved, the interested spectator loses, whether or not he supports one of the quarreling parties. Either he perceives improprieties and injustices on both sides, or he adheres to the way of thinking of one or another party. In one case, he will fear with equal anxiety both alternatives, the continuation or the end of a conflict in which two equally destructive evils limit each other because they both compete for absolute power. In the other case, his unconscious self-love will cause him to embrace the biased and exaggerated elements of one party the more strongly the more he anticipates human welfare or misery to result from the victory or defeat of this party. And anything that feeds his hopes and fears will reinforce and multiply prejudices, so he becomes more unjust or more discontent, and antagonizes or infects his neighbors.

Of a completely different kind are those spectators who are interested in the entire disturbance of constitutions and doctrines only because it is an entertaining spectacle. Their own hearth seems too far removed from the scene of political disturbances for them to fear for life and property. Gaining and enjoying wealth are the only serious matters in their lives. The content of moral and religious convictions is not close enough to their hearts for them to care about innovations in the form of these convictions. Nevertheless, they cannot help noticing the struggle developing around these innovations—if only to satisfy their curiosity. Their curiosity may have been triggered by the notoriety of the debate, or the desire to be able to converse about it in public, or to take delight in the wit and sagacity of the combatants. The more complicated the controversy and the more superficial their knowledge of it, the more obvious it seems to them that the subject of the dispute, which in fact becomes more controversial upon closer study, cannot be made out. They regard their previous indifference as a mark of the soundness of their understanding. Therefore, they congratulate themselves and are proud of it.

All the more confidently they now reject questions concerning accountability, God and immortality, raised from time to time by the voice of conscience. They regard these questions as broodings over chimeras and residues of the effects of those prejudices which were indispensable and unavoidable during the childhood of mankind. These same prejudices are maintained by their guardians,[1] partly out of prudence, partly out of their own naïveté, partly for the sake of easier guidance of those who need tutelage, and partly for the sake of perpetuating tutelage.

Meanwhile, there are at least a few scholars—of which there are so many these days—who feel compelled by their professional duties to consider moral, rightful and religious matters and the status of the systematic concepts in their fields. But few among them have the ability, the courage, or the time to penetrate the meaning of the latest system.[2] In regard to its content, this system was originally the masterpiece of a philosophizing reason. It was supported by the rarest originality of genius and the most extensive and deep insight into the existing systems. As far as its form is concerned, it became controversial among those who knew it best and admired it most. The majority of scholars who declared themselves for or against the critical system in fact accepted or rejected it owing to

1. The modern term *guardian* is a narrow legal term that refers to "the person responsible for rearing a child or somebody who is mentally unfit to take care of himself." I use it nevertheless as the translation for the German *Vormund*, since the latter carries the same connotation and was employed by Kant, Reinhold, and others for those who kept others in tutelage.

2. Reinhold refers to Kant's critical philosophy.

misconception. The concepts that these scholars presented to the people became more abstract, subtle and speculative, regardless of whether they wanted the general public to participate in the benefits of the new doctrine, or to save them from its pernicious influence. However, sophistry in moral concepts could not occur at a more critical time, since horrible public acts of injustice threaten to numb the moral feeling and make good faith more and more suspect. Injustice threatens convictions about what humankind should and can do far more strongly in the hearts, than such convictions could be shaken by all the intellectual speculative struggles. Through these horrible acts the mighty use force under the banner of civic freedom or civic order to dominate the world.

The less that ethical conviction,[3] which is so necessary for rightful and moral actions, can resort to external support, the more such conviction is compelled to rely on the inner sanctuary of moral self-consciousness. Civil constitutions, church dogmas, and philosophical doctrines, which at other times could offer such external support, are now wavering themselves. Therefore, ethical conviction seeks certainty in conscience and protects itself through its own strength against the exhausting, obscuring confusions which threaten it from all sides. Ethical conviction requires that the truth of its concepts be as independent as possible from political fate, which is determined by chance through ruse or violence. It has to remain aloof from scientific disputations, which produce a new conflict for each one that is settled. It elevates these concepts to the utmost clarity and distinctness by reflecting on the moral, vivid feeling, and abstracting from all doctrines and external events. The only means to easily and certainly attain this ethical conviction without really transcending its own boundaries lies in actual consultation with several conscientious persons.

It is from this point of view that the present attempt has been undertaken; from any other it would be misunderstood by its critics.

---

3. Here and in the following sentences Reinhold personifies "moral conviction." Although this seems an odd construction, I decided to retain the original.

Section 1 contains the elaboration and correction of the project provided in Section 2, in which three friends, living in one place, tried to express and conceptualize their favorite convictions, then put these convictions in writing, and gave the printed manuscript to several friends for scrutiny. Section 3 presents the beginning of the correspondence emerging from that effort.

Kiel, 26 March 1798.

Contents

Section 1.

An attempt to present the manner of thought of common and sound understanding regarding some principal points about ethical matters.

Part 1

Intention of this project

1. Convictions—decided and definite convictions that is—are presuppositions for ethics in general, and thus for rightfulness and morality of action. The immediate conditions of rightful and moral actions are called the fundamental truths of ethics.

2. As ethics is the common ultimate end of all human beings; and as ethics is expected from everybody who is able to use his reason; and as the essential rights and duties are the same for all human beings; and finally, as certain duties of one human being correspond to certain rights of another, the fundamental truths of ethics must be universally valid, and the convictions of which they are part must be held in common.

3. If these fundamental truths, in their character as shared convictions, are to be recognized and asserted, then one must be able to capture them in concepts and express them in terms that are suited to be understood and found to be true at least by those who are concerned about ethics more than usual and who therefore reflect on it more than usual. Thus, fundamental concepts and principles must be conceivable which are universally valid in themselves. Therefore, should they not actually be accepted as universally valid among the experts in ethical affairs, it is not because the concepts are flawed.

4. As these fundamental truths, in their absolute purity, cannot be attained completely by any concept and expression, the already existing fundamental concepts and principles can never be absolutely universally valid. For exactly that reason, there is the possibility and the need to elevate these concepts to ever-higher levels of purity and universal validity through continuous purification and more precise definition.

5. This need becomes more evident if one takes into consideration the increasingly obvious discrepancy between the different ways of

thinking about ethical matters among teachers, and the discord about the fundamental concepts and principles of ethics even among the foremost experts and keepers of jurisprudence, moral philosophy and theology. This discrepancy and this discord, in their entire extension and character, can hardly be found healthy and harmless, much less inevitable and indispensable, by any unbiased though not indifferent observer.

6. The lack of consensus about the fundamental truths of ethics among the leaders of public conviction must become more precarious in direct proportion to:

the development of appetites and the prevalence of selfish prudence through the multiplication, refinement and spread of luxury and its artificial needs;

the spread of reading among all classes of the public, and the reduction of the influence of the few good authors by the immensely increasing number of mediocre and bad ones;

the retreat of the increasingly controversial knowledge of ethical nature behind the progress of the secure insights into physical nature;

the increasing shakiness of the foundations of all the sciences and public convictions referring to ethical, political and religious matters; and the spread and confusion of the fight to conserve the old structures or introduce new structures;

the increasing impact, under the current circumstances, of different ways of thinking on the common welfare and on the ennoblement of the nation—and the growing difficulty in the struggle of reason against haphazardness—brought about by ignorance and passion—especially since reason is at odds with itself in the few isolated sincere independent thinkers.

7. It cannot be surprising that the rights and duties of mankind seem foolish to so many businessmen and men of the world, and annoying to so many pious zealots. It is not a surprise if one realizes that the fundamental concepts of right and duty in general, and especially the specific characteristics through which the moral law is distinguished from the positive laws and laws of nature, are still controversial among the keepers and teachers of the ethical sciences.

The true opponents and the alleged friends of natural law and rational religion fight over old and new prejudices, which are supported by ignorance and passion. They already have many partisans who fight solely for absolute power because these prejudices concern existing institutions and habits the continuance or suspension of which will hurt the selfish interests of one party and benefit the selfish interests of the other.

Meanwhile, the few who are able and willing to fight for truth and right against delusion and selfishness are preoccupied with refuting one another. Divided by their fundamental concepts, they challenge one another more strongly than they could be challenged by the united power of their external adversaries.

Therefore, they have been the weakest party until now, not because the others are superior to them in number and eagerness, but because they weaken each other through their quarrels. One always destroys what the other has built and what only an independent thinker could destroy and build. They certainly know, through unanimous feelings, the good cause of humankind, which they fight for and through which they should and could be the more powerful ones. But they misjudge it through discordant concepts.

8. If the legislators and rulers do not themselves belong to one of the fighting parties, there is nothing more natural for them than to disregard the controversial rights and duties of mankind and not consider them.

On the other hand, if they are undecided about those parties, they set up laws and institutions that contradict each other—for instance, they abolish the death penalty and replace it with cruelties against mankind that are worse. They allow for and take away the external freedom of conscience simultaneously, and sacrifice the rights of the single citizen out of eagerness for the common good.

But if they belong to one of those fighting parties, whichever it may be, they enforce its doctrinal claims through public measures with all their might, and are considered despots and tyrants in the eyes of the opposing party.

9. As long as only mere opinions, and indeed contradictory opinions, are stated even by the sincere independent thinkers about

ethical, political and religious fundamental truths, and especially about the difference and the connectedness between them, reason works against itself in its advocates. People from all classes are confused by their own teachers with regard to their most important convictions. The teaching profession is depriving itself more and more of reputation and influence in the other classes. Any firm and true public conviction is suffocated, and the holiest interest of humankind is surrendered to the advocates of superstition and infidelity, of slavery and licentiousness, to the unbidden instructors of enlightenment and the appointed and paid instructors who obscure the common understanding.

10. The quest for universal validity of ethical fundamental concepts and principles must neither be left exclusively to the speculations of philosophers, nor altogether to the thoughtlessness of the crowd. In their fight for different systematic concepts about the scholarly and artificial forms of ethical convictions, the scientific authors often lose sight of the natural content of these convictions. The practical expert of ethics draws this content neither from the systematic concepts of the school philosophy[1] nor from the morals of the world, but immediately from conscience.

11. Concerted attempts by independent and sincere men to agree on the natural content of those convictions seem, therefore, to be a necessity of our time. These convictions must spring from within their conscience and are coupled with a desire to find a way of thinking and a language for the fundamental truths of ethics that continuously approaches the expressions of natural, sound understanding. This is the more urgent, the more our authors who treat rightful and moral matters either exclusively write for philosophy and philosophers or merely popularize the principles and doctrinal claims of one or another of the philosophical doctrines that themselves are still controversial among philosophers.

12. And misunderstandings occur that are partly caused by the indeterminateness and ambiguity of the careless and uneducated (vul-

---

1. That is, the Wolffian philosophy.

gar) use of language, and partly by the bias of the different specific (particular) linguistic customs of the philosophical sects. These misunderstandings can only be corrected by the discovery, recognition and propagation of that linguistic usage that is independent of the thoughtlessness of the big crowd as well as of the quarrels of philosophical parties. That language must be the instrument and result of natural and sound understanding and therefore is entitled to universal validity. Only concerted efforts, being made intentionally for the sake of this ultimate end, can bring this usage of language closer.

13. The endeavor of the participants to support each other in thoughtfulness, candor and moderation, and to adopt the true middle course of right and morality in their studies and undertakings, cannot be separated from these efforts. This endeavor becomes more desirable as the zeitgeist tends toward exaggeration and bias and is subject to aroused passion and hair-splitting speculation. The spirit of this age is torn between the poles of dogmatism and indifference, of enthusiasm and cold-heartedness.

14. The present project comprises the attempt of three friends to verbalize the consensus of their attitudes and ways of thinking about the fundamental truths of ethics. It presents our common convictions historically, the way they really exist in our conscience, and leaves open the scientific question whether and by which other presuppositions these convictions are justified. The project is meant to state those convictions that represent the fundamental truths for us clearly and distinctly, but it does not commit itself to examine how and by which means these convictions originate in our conscience. Therefore, the project has nothing to do with philosophical principles, nor with theological dogmas, but only with facts of our ethical self-consciousness. We have carefully selected the concepts and expressions through which the project represents those facts, and we consider them to be the most suited, until we are set right. We submit them to the scrutiny of conscientious people. Through their help, these concepts will be continually purified from the bias and imperfection of our particular way of thinking and language and thus will approach the universal validity and integrity of sound human understanding.

Part II

Basic concepts of morality and rightfulness in general

15. The following distinctions occur in and by means of that particular self-consciousness which is called conscience. They represent immediately certain facts.

16. We distinguish a mere effect within ourselves—which makes us conscious of ourselves more in a passive than in an active way—from planned action. In performing or refraining from action we are conscious of ourselves as being spontaneously active. The first we call an effect of nature, the other a free act.

17. We distinguish the spontaneous activity of a person, as activity which is characterized by free actions, from the inner activity of animal and organic powers, as well as from the external activity of mechanical powers. We recognize in this spontaneity the distinguishing character of human nature. We call ourselves "persons" because of it and feel uniquely superior to mere things.

18. We distinguish the spontaneity in thinking, under the name of reason, from the spontaneity in willing, under the name of freedom. The spontaneity of reason has a certain and necessary way of acting. The spontaneity of the will, however, determines for itself its way of acting, and it is, therefore, preferably called free. Reason cannot do anything which contradicts itself; it cannot refrain from requiring agreement with itself. This is the law that is the essence of its activity. In thinking, reason complies with it necessarily, and in acting, it necessarily prescribes the acts of the will. Under this law, freedom ought to do what it cannot refrain from doing, and ought to refrain from what it cannot do without contradicting the law.

19. We distinguish the necessary striving in a person (the mere desire) from the self-determination of a person to satisfy or not to

satisfy that desire (decision). The first, necessary striving, is created by pleasure and displeasure and, in its various expressions, it is called appetite, inclination and passion. The second, self-determination, is called proper willing.

20. We distinguish those decisions or actions of the will where the use of freedom conforms to the necessary way of acting or the law of reason, from those where its use contradicts this law. In the first case, we call the actions lawful, in the second, unlawful. The lawfulness of a free action in general is called ethical; the unlawfulness, unethical.

21. Among lawful actions of the will, we distinguish the proper moral ones from the merely rightful ones. Moral actions conform to the law through the inner decision and the intention of a person; rightful actions conform to it through the external appearance of a free deed. Regarding the former, the lawfulness of the action must be the ultimate intended goal of the agent. This ultimate goal does not matter in judging the latter. For example, the payment of debts as an external, free act is a rightful action, even if the debtor internally has no other intention than to escape the punishment of civil law, or the fury of a creditor, or the loss of his credit. The payment of debts only becomes a proper moral action through the intention to freely obey reason. Every moral action is always simultaneously rightful, but not every rightful action is also moral. According to the broad sense in which we are using it, the term ethical shall designate the common character of rightfulness and morality.

In court, this word really means mere rightfulness, or rather the [external]¹ voluntariness of an action.

22. Among unlawful actions, we distinguish immoral and wrongful ones. Immoral actions are those that contradict the law through the inner decision and the intention of the agent, whether they conform to it as an external action or not. Wrongful actions are those that contradict the law as an external, free deed; to that extent, they cannot conform to it as an inner decision. Not paying a debt that one is able to pay is simultaneously immoral and wrongful. The

---

1. What Reinhold seems to have in mind is that the action was not performed under external compulsion.

judicial coercion that a rich creditor exercises over a needy debtor, greatly aggravating his distress, is immoral, but not wrongful.

Every wrongful action is always at the same time immoral—but not every immoral action is also wrongful.

23. The most common precept for morality is the demand that reason imposes on the will, namely, that the will shall adopt conformity to the law of reason as the basis for all free action, and consequently that it will decide for or against the satisfaction of an appetite solely in accordance with its consistency or inconsistency with reason. This most common precept is preferably called the moral law, since all the other prescriptions are subordinate to it.

24. If one calls those determining grounds of actions which are freely assumed maxims of the will, then the content of the moral law runs as follows: Make lawfulness the maxim of all the actions of your will. Or: As a rule, act only according to such maxims as could serve as laws, and which, consequently, cannot contradict themselves, since they are maxims required of all rational beings.

25. The ultimate end that the moral law prescribes to all actions is nothing else but morality, that is, the free rationality of action. Thus, the moral law demands of the will that the latter assert such a free and rational nature through all its actions. In this respect, the law reads as follows: In all your decisions, treat free and rational nature, hence your own personality as well as that of others, as an end in itself, never merely as a means.

26. The most common precept of mere right that reason imposes on the will of a person is the following: A person's external, free action has to be compatible with the external, free action of every other person. Therefore, nobody shall act in a way that contradicts the external freedom of any other person. This most common prescription is called the rightful law, since all other prescriptions are subordinate to it.

27. We distinguish may and must not from mere can and cannot, and ought from mere must. We mean by may and must not that which freedom is allowed or forbidden to do, in order not to contradict the law of reason. By the mere can and cannot, we mean that which freedom is able to achieve regardless of the law.

Ought refers to that which is necessarily prescribed to freedom by the law of reason, but which nevertheless can only happen through freedom. And must means that which cannot occur freely but occurs necessarily according to a mere law of nature.

28. Conscience manifests the freedom of the will particularly through the consciousness of may, must not and ought in contrast to mere can, cannot and must. We can do what we must not do as well as what we may do. Nevertheless, we must not do everything that we can do. We can do what we ought to do without having to do it. Thus, whenever and wherever we must or cannot, ought does not apply. We must breathe and cannot fly—therefore, neither can be thought of as a may, nor as a must not, nor as an ought. We must not slander and ought to pay our debts—both must be seen as acts that we can either perform or not perform.

29. We distinguish right from might, and duty from compulsion. By right, we mean that which freedom may, that is, that which it can achieve rationally. Hence, right is the faculty that the law of reason grants freedom. Might is that which freedom can do, that is, that which it can accomplish with the help of other powers subordinate to it. Nature gives this faculty to freedom, and it is limited by mere laws of nature. Duty refers to that which freedom ought to do, that is, what it rationally cannot fail to do. Thus, duty means the necessity imposed on freedom by the law of reason—a necessity which therefore cannot be a must. By compulsion, we mean that which prevents a free action externally, hence the necessity which counteracts freedom through natural laws and which therefore is a must.

30. We distinguish the internal from the external character of an action. The latter comprises the relationship of an action to its effects which are independent of freedom. By the internal character, we mean the relationship of an action to its ground which lies in freedom and the law of reason. The intrinsic worth of an action consists in its free lawfulness, its intrinsic worthlessness in its free unlawfulness. Its extrinsic worth consists in the usefulness of an action, its extrinsic worthlessness in its uselessness or harm.

The intrinsic worth or worthlessness of an action is judged according to its intention. In regard to it, the action is intrinsically good or evil, decent or indecent. The evaluation of the extrinsic worth occurs according to success, with respect to which an action proves to be successful or unsuccessful, useful or harmful.

31. We distinguish respect and contempt from honor and disgrace, and both from esteem and disdain. Respect and contempt mean the inner recognition of the intrinsic worth or worthlessness of an action. Honor and disgrace are the external recognition of this intrinsic worth or worthlessness. By esteem and disdain, we mean the recognition of the extrinsic worth or worthlessness. The worth of the moral and the worthlessness of the immoral are unlimited; thus, they do not allow for assessment, that is, determining the respective quantity with regard to number, measure and weight. A quantification of effects is only possible in regard to the value of the useful and the valuelessness of the harmful. The intrinsic worth is beyond all assessment—it is invaluable. It alone deserves respect and honor, and the latter should not be confused with mere esteem, for then respect and honor are wasted on extrinsic value, that is, on favors of happiness and nature.

32. We distinguish the capacity for well-being which is achieved through voluntary lawfulness of action, and the incapacity for well-being which is acquired through voluntary unlawfulness, from that capacity and incapacity of well-being which depend on the generosity and parsimony of nature and luck. The self-achieved capacity is called worthiness; the self-acquired incapacity, unworthiness. We think of worthiness as a claim to well-being, inseparable from free lawfulness, and call it merit. Unworthiness we regard as a claim to ill-being, inseparable from free unlawfulness. It is the forfeiture of well-being and is thus called guilt.

Part III

On conscience

33. We differentiate between a conscience which legislates and one which judges. The legislating one is conscious of the law's demands on freedom. By the judging one, we mean consciousness of the fulfillment or transgression of those demands by freedom. One consists in the consciousness of conformity to duty, the legitimacy and illegitimacy of an action that has yet to be performed; the other one consists in the same consciousness with respect to an action that has already been performed. The recognition of the freedom of performed actions is called accountability.

34. We distinguish immediate from mediate conscience. The former we understand to be the consciousness of duty in regard to right and wrong, insofar as this consciousness solely depends on reason and its relation to freedom. By mediate consciousness, we mean the consciousness that goes beyond reason and freedom to depend on external circumstances and knowledge of them.

35. Immediate conscience consists of the immediate consciousness of our freedom and rationality and, thus, of our proper selves as ethical beings. Therefore, it is infallible, as it does not have other subjects besides freedom and rationality. It preferably carries the name conscience, because, as pure self-consciousness, it is infallible and self-evident, hence the most certain among the different kinds of consciousness.[1]

36. We divide mediate conscience into correct and incorrect, and into honest and dishonest conscience. By correct conscience, we mean the correct, by incorrect conscience, the incorrect application

1. This is a play on words in German: *Gewissen* (conscience) and *das Gewisseste* (what is most certain).

177

of the law and of the general decision to observe it. Honest conscience is the sincere attempt to apply the law according to one's best possible conviction—dishonest conscience is the voluntary deception in the employment of the law.

In incorrect conscience, it is neither legislating reason, nor law-embracing freedom that errs, but rather the faculty of judgment, which determines the law's application. Therefore, the claims of incorrect conscience are just as obligatory as those of correct conscience. Thus the will of the conscientious person does not fail as it fulfills these claims. Nor does his reason go wrong, since it requires him to do what he believes to be lawful or to refrain from doing what he believes to be unlawful. Dishonest conscience is a mere mask behind which self-love ordinarily hides from itself. Behind this mask, it artificially adds the illusion of commands of duty to its claims. Under this pretense, amoral actions become moral, and immoral ones are transformed into merely amoral ones. Throughout, dishonest conscience thinks itself virtuous if it encounters good which is generated by nature or luck, or if it does not commit evil merely because it lacked the courage, opportunity or drive to commit that evil.

Part IV

Freedom of the will

37. Of all the things that are certain through conscience, nothing can be more certain than the freedom of the will and the necessity with which reason makes demands on it. This freedom and this necessity, which are certain in themselves, represent the basis and essence of conscience.

Through consciousness of freedom and reason, we become convinced that a human being may not do everything that he can do, but rather that he can do everything that he ought to do. We do not believe that it solely depends on him whether he will be healthy or ill, happy or unhappy, alive or dead. But we are indeed convinced that it does depend upon him whether, in time and eternity, he will be righteous. We are convinced that merit and guilt are the only goods that nature and luck cannot take away from him, that the worth or worthlessness of his person are completely in his own hands, and that, through his freedom, he can not only abide by the moral law—in spite of all the enticements and horrors of sensibility—but also violate it in spite of all its holiness. The consciousness of the correctness and importance of this conviction constitutes our first article of faith. We think of it as the sole saving principle and as the fundamental truth, upon which all the other convictions concerning ethical affairs rest. It must purify all the lesser convictions of those errors that are brought into jurisprudence and moral philosophy by those schools of metaphysics that deny the freedom of the will.

38. Nothing can be as concrete and as evident as the freedom of the will, especially for the conscientious person. His usual state of mind is careful reflection. He tries to sustain this state through his freedom, and knows how to maintain his use of freedom through such reflection. He asks the verdict of conscience concerning every

free action that has to be performed. And, in his own absolute willingness to act according to the decision of that verdict, the reality of his own freedom is evident to him. He finds this freedom also in his feebleness. Far from seeking the cause of this feebleness outside himself, he accuses himself with unwavering strictness before the tribunal of conscience. Every confession of his guilt and each renewed resolution to improve is simultaneously an homage to the moral law and a renewed recognition of his freedom. The conviction of the freedom of the will is as dear to the righteous person as his righteousness itself. Closely related to the firmness and purity of his decision to stick to his duty, it is already contained in this decision, and supports it no less than it is supported by it.

39. The conviction of the freedom of will can be obscured by a manner of thought that is led astray either by the affectation of false knowledge or by an immoral mental attitude, or by both. Thus, it often becomes completely lost and gives way to the opposite conviction.

The vicious person can quickly come to doubt the independence of his ego through the developed and deep-rooted habit to let his actions be determined by mere appetites and a reason that serves them. He feels overwhelmed by the slightest agitation of his ruling passion, considers every difficulty in fulfilling his duty to be an impossibility, can vouch for his promise only as long as it is to his advantage to keep it and, in general, becomes that which the external circumstances under which he lives make him. His consciousness of his freedom decreases proportionately to the increasing difficulty he has with using it. That difficulty is brought about by abuse of freedom. Finally, he confuses the self-inflicted dependence of his volition with the natural dependence of involuntary desire, which he shares with all, even the best, human beings. This dependence becomes overwhelming in him through his indulging in his appetites.

Apart from this natural unscrupulousness, to which vice generally leads, there is also an affected one, to which especially grave and outrageous crimes can lead. The vicious person tries to throw the heavy burden of guilt off himself and to blame nature. The more he wishes his ego to be mere nature, the easier he finds it to persuade himself that it is so. And he continues to tell himself the lie that he does not feel free, until he believes it. The conviction of his freedom, which makes him despise himself, is more than annoying. Thus he attempts to get rid of it and succeeds the faster and the more superficially, the more his talents and culture support him in doing so.

40. Various artificial concepts of freedom are brought about partly through false metaphysical systematic concepts about the essence of the soul and its connection to the body, and partly through an incorrect concept of the will which confuses proper volition with mere desire. According to these artificial concepts, freedom, thought as a natural concept, would indeed be self-contradictory, hence impossible. This is the case, for example, with the systematic concept of materialism, in which the essence of the soul consists of organized matter. The same applies to that concept of volition which explains volition as rationally guided desire (*Appetitus rationalis*). In these representations, freedom is seen as something that cannot be thought. The feeling of freedom, and also accountability, are taken for a natural deception of the uneducated understanding. This deception must be dissolved through philosophical reflection. However, the conscientious person will never be able to appreciate such a conviction, artificially created by speculation. As soon as he acts, he will defeat that conviction with the help of the natural and opposite conviction of his conscience. The more loyal he remains to conscience, the less will he be able to doubt that the contradiction he finds in his scholarly concept of freedom is only apparent and founded on some unknown error in his fundamental scientific concepts.

41. We distinguish original freedom of the will, which belongs to the essence of humankind in general, from the one to be acquired, which belongs to the essence of humanity. The latter presupposes the former. It is present in every human being whose mental powers have been developed so as to enable the use of reason. In contrast, the latter is only expressed in the aspirations of the righteous person. Through his striving it is capable of progressing infinitely in him.

42. Original freedom of the will is effective in every accountable action, hence it is effective in morally good as well as morally evil

acts. Original freedom consists in the faculty to decide. Its activity is essentially different from the effectiveness of reason as well as from the effectiveness of desire, both of which are presuppositions in every decision.

For with the help of self-consciousness, it is possible to distinguish three kinds of activities in every accountable action. Without their difference and interconnectedness, no voluntary action takes place. First, there is the claim of desire (or expression of inclination, excited by pleasure or displeasure); second, the claim of conscience (or the expression of reason, laying down and announcing its law); third, the decision or the activity (function) leading to action that will either satisfy the desire or leave it unfulfilled in accordance with or in contradiction to conscience. Self-consciousness recognizes that the first two expressions are entirely involuntary and necessary, but that on the contrary the last one is voluntary and free.

43. Freedom that has to be acquired is called moral, since it lies in the direction that the moral law prescribes for original freedom. It prefers to manifest itself in:

1) its independence from satisfying desires, inclinations and passions—neither through natural insensibility, nor through artificial indifference toward pleasure and pain, but through careful reflection and conscientiousness;

2) its independence from rightful coercive laws—neither through privileges, nor through cunning or violent frustration of legal coercion—but through voluntarily doing that which otherwise is only done under compulsion. He who offends a rightful coercive law is an evil human being. However, he who needs this law to abstain from evil is not good either;

3) its independence from scientific systems (including its own)—neither through ignorance, nor through indifference to truth, but through the soundness of natural understanding, being guided rather by conscientiousness than by speculation and scholarliness;

4) its independence from habits, tradition, and reputation—neither through passion for innovation, nor through the desire to excel, but through that independence of the spirit from tutelage which consists of the conviction of the end of all ends. This independence is acquired

through autonomous thought, supported by strength of pure will, and is neither obscured nor corrupted by any dominating passion.

44. The end of all ends is preferably called the ultimate end, because no end can be thought to which it could be subordinated by reason, and because no end can be thought that would not have to be subordinated to it by reason. It cannot be anything but morality itself, which in regard to its inner essence is called the good will. As such, it consists neither in a blind drive to so-called kindheartedness nor in wishful thinking, but in a carefully reflected-upon and considered decision and the honest and serious commitment of all powers to fulfill the moral law.

In its freely abstaining from anything unlawful, and its voluntary striving for unlimited lawfulness, the good will is the only thing that—within the world and outside of it, in itself and through itself, under all circumstances and without exception—is good. It gives true worth to all gifts from nature and happiness, and to all acquired skills. It determines the degrees of worthiness of knowing. It partly increases and ennobles, partly substitutes and makes dispensable the joys of life. It partly diminishes life's sufferings, partly rewards them, and is the only one that provides indubitable, not merely imagined, prospects beyond the grave.

Part V

Nature and destiny of man

45. We distinguish in a human being what is given by nature and must be, from what is gained and ought to develop through freedom. Without the help of freedom, mere nature is all that is present and effective in a human being. It is characteristic of human nature not to be mere nature. A human being is not nature, it possesses a nature, and is a free being endowed with natural powers.

46. In regard to this characteristic of human nature, we make a distinction between humanness, humaneness and humanity.

47. Humanness means the essence of human nature, hence it comprises spontaneous activity of reason and freedom of the will that are tied to an animal organism. Self-consciousness distinguishes the animal organism as merely an instrument from the spontaneous activity of reason and the freedom of the will as the proper self.

The self is called soul insofar as one reflects on its relation to the animal organism. If one abstracts from this relation, it is called spirit. The animal organism is called body [*Leib*] in relation to the soul; if it is considered separately, it is called physical form [*Körper*].[1] With respect to the soul, a human being is a person; with respect to the body [*Leib*], the person is human. The body [*Leib*] belongs to the person, while the physical form [*Körper*] is a mere thing.

48. Humaneness is that mere natural disposition which is characteristic for mankind and which distinguishes it from animals. Among the most remarkable peculiarities of this disposition is sympathy (the sympathetic feeling), that is, compassion and shared joy, which accompany mere perception of suffering and joy of other beings. Their disposition is partly grounded in the human organism.

---

1. There is no appropriate equivalent in English for the German distinction between *Leib* and *Körper*.

184

Language use shows that the noun "humaneness" best designates the faculty and expressions of sympathy, while the adjective "human" generally denotes everything that is inseparable from human nature.

49. By humanity we mean that which a human being ought to be and to become through freedom and rationality—hence through the free exercise of his natural talents in conformity with reason.

Humaneness therefore is original and uncorrupted human nature—while humanity is human nature ennobled through freedom and reason. Humaneness is a naturally healthy temperament; humanity is the moral character of humankind.

50. Humanity cannot be conceived without humaneness, but humaneness can be thought without humanity. Somebody who is endowed by nature with an unusual degree of sympathy could fail to raise himself to the level of humanity through the rational use of his freedom. Yet somebody else who is less disposed to sympathy because of his nervous condition[2] can partly improve, partly compensate for this imperfection of his natural disposition through the rational use of his freedom. And, because of this, he will be even more assured of the quality of humanity.

51. The original dispositions of humankind, as distinguished from acquired skills, can be divided into those characteristic for humankind and those shared with other beings. They partly consist in the sensible faculty of representation which is tied to the organism (the mere animal disposition), partly in freedom and reason (the mere ethical disposition). Mankind has the former in common with all animals, the latter with all conceivable spirits. On the other hand, the dispositions of humaneness and humanity are characteristic only for humankind. Humaneness consists in those qualities of body [Leib] and soul that already distinguish human beings as mere natural beings from animals. Humanity is freedom and reason in relation to those qualities (the disposition of a uniquely human quality of being ethical) by which the human mind differs from all the other conceivable spirits.

---

2. Not to be understood in the modern pathological sense.

52. The natural dispositions belonging to humaneness can either degenerate in a human being through the abuse of freedom, hence through its own fault, or be impeded in their development through mere external circumstances, hence without its own fault. In the latter case, natural cruelty and lack of humanity will follow. This condition is called savageness in a human being who has been born and raised outside civil society. However, in the crude citizen of an uncivilized state it is called barbarity.

Acquired inhumaneness (the moral as opposed to the mere natural kind) is the real inhumanity. It shows partly in the lack of culture as the vices of brute cruelty, and partly in the abuse of culture as the vices of artificial inhumaneness or affected humaneness.

53. It belongs to the nature of humanness that a person interacts with other things and other persons. What he shall become and bring about through this interaction is his destiny. So far as this occurs independent of freedom and rationality, it is called fate;—where it depends on them, it is called the ultimate end of humankind.

54. If one looks at a human being as a natural being and disregards the freedom of the will, then it is through the incentives of pleasure and displeasure that things and persons put the power of a human being's soul in action. All of the soul's capacities are then developed by those incentives under the influence of external circumstances. The latter include bodily organism, climate, nourishment, civil institutions, even the energy of a human being's reason (which is merely theoretical if it is not related to the freedom of the will). And even the purposely caused development of the soul's capacities can only be understood as the result of the drive for pleasure which thereby finds its reward.

55. If pleasure and displeasure were the sole incentives of human nature, then the striving for well-being would be the sole destiny of humans—the necessary goal not only of all their actions, but of their entire development. Things would provoke this striving in order to satisfy it, and satisfy it in order to provoke it again. The sufficient cause for manipulating objects would be the drive for pleasure which lies in human beings themselves. The entire success of this manipulation would consist in the conservation and expansion of

this drive, assuming that it would not be disturbed or even destroyed by maladroit handling of things or their unfortunate reaction. A human being would only be what it must be, would only do what it could not refrain from doing, and would refrain from doing what it could not do. It would be a mere natural being, and its destiny mere fate.

56. Regarding a human being in respect to its proper self, which consists of freedom and rationality, its destiny is absolutely necessary through and only through reason. Through freedom, its destiny is made possible. Destiny consists in voluntarily acting in conformity to the necessary spontaneous activity of reason. This means to act morally. The destiny of man's proper self, then, cannot be conceived of as fate, but only as an object of free will, as an ultimate end.

57. If one views a human being simultaneously as a free and a natural being, he will be in contradiction to himself. That contradiction can be resolved continually through reason, and ought to be resolved through freedom—reason being related to nature through its necessary way of acting and to freedom through its spontaneous activity. This resolution is brought about by the moral law, which challenges a human being to use its natural powers as a means for exercising its free rationality and rational freedom, hence to transform the obstacle of freedom into an instrument. Whatever reason commands in its relation to a human being's will (as practical reason), it teaches the human being to perform through its relation to the faculty of knowledge (as theoretical reason).

58. Thus, the destiny of humankind is neither the well-being of a mere animal, however amply endowed and well-trained it may be. Nor is it the morality of a mere spirit. But it is the ennoblement of humaneness through freedom and rationality, striving to form everything that is not free and rational in humanness into an instrument of free rationality, and to use it as such. In short, the destiny of humankind is human morality—humanity.

59. Through reason, which is coherent in itself, morality is the only feature that can be and must be thought of as an end of all ends, that is, as the ultimate end. Freedom of persons can coexist with the nature of things only insofar as nature is a mere instrument

of freedom, and as things are mere means to the ultimate end of persons. As far as this holds true, things and persons share one and the same destiny. And the immediate ultimate end of humankind is simultaneously the mediate ultimate end of the whole of nature.

60. If things are to be used by persons as means and instruments of morality, then they have to be useful to this ultimate end both in themselves and in conforming to their nature. That means that, even insofar as they do not depend on human freedom but are presupposed by it, things must be constituted so as not to inhibit the ethical, but to promote it. In addition, this constitution must be theirs in general and by necessity, not only occasionally and by chance. The character of things as a means and as an instrument of morality must be the cause of their existence and of their constitution. They must necessarily be thought of as the work of a holy creator.

61. In recognizing the fulfillment of the moral law as absolutely necessary, conscience is convinced for that reason of the external possibility of such a fulfillment. Through the command of conscience, reason, on the one hand, makes morality the ultimate end of humankind. On the other, it reasons about the feasibility of this ultimate end. However, through its belief in God, it is united with itself and, through religion, completes its conviction concerning humankind's destiny.

62. So far as humankind's destiny through nature depends on God, and so far as God is the holy being who determines the fate of human beings according to the standard of their moral behavior, humankind's destiny depends entirely on its freedom. It is by no means subject to blind fate.

Part VI

Sound natural understanding

63. The terms understanding and reason designate two different faculties of intellectual power. Only the inseparable unity of their different functions in conviction, the chief result of intellectual power, explains why those terms occur so often interchangeably in everyday language.

64. In the state of mind called conviction, which consists in being conscious of the certainty of a judgment, understanding judges by establishing the content of a conviction to be certain. It does that by analyzing the content into its original parts. Reason, on the other hand, draws inferences by establishing the form of a conviction to be certain. This form consists in interconnecting the parts of the content. Through this, a conviction is achieved.

65. The given meanings of the terms understanding and reason are united in the expression "human understanding." The latter commonly is used synonymously with sound, common, natural understanding. It is the faculty that is characteristic of and shared by all human beings, the faculty to judge and to draw inferences.

66. This faculty is called sound[1] understanding insofar as it is in an appropriate state for humankind's original natural dispositions and destiny.

67. This soundness is called internal soundness whenever it is grounded in a human being's proper self and therefore depends on the practice of its freedom. It is called external soundness whenever it depends on the condition of a human being's other faculties. The external side is partly based on the natural powers of the soul. As such, it depends on the respective strengths of the individual

---

1. Literally: "healthy" understanding.

faculties, for instance, of the power of imagination, of memory, of wit, of sagacity, and so forth, as well as on their harmony. External soundness is also partly grounded in the disposition and health of the body. The latter could be called the physical, while the former would be the psychological soundness of understanding.

68. Understanding in itself (as well as reason) is infallible because it is a particular faculty bound to its own specific laws. Therefore, its soundness or unsoundness can only consist in its use, abuse, or nonuse. Its internal unsoundness really comes about only through abuse by the will. And the external unsoundness only consists in its nonuse or the limitation of its use owing to the shortcomings and faults of other human faculties.

69. Insofar as internal soundness of understanding consists in its use by freedom of the will, its very essence as moral soundness is independent of the merely external soundness. To be sure, it can be initiated, facilitated, and complicated by the latter. However, it can be neither generated nor annihilated by it. If self-consciousness and, consequently, the use of freedom of the will are interrupted by external natural occurrences, neither moral unsoundness nor soundness is the result. Both depend on freedom and therefore remain under the command of the will as long as self-consciousness continues to function. The will remains in command even in moments of deepest physical exhaustion or greatest excess.

70. External, merely natural soundness of understanding, on the other hand, depends on internal and moral soundness. This is partly the case because the will is free and therefore can be good or evil. It either strongly promotes the generation, duration and restoration of the harmony of natural powers of the mind, or it can limit and destroy it. Also, the will has a strong influence on conserving and multiplying the merits, and on reducing and erasing the lacks and faults not only of innate mental powers but also of the organization of temperament, education, and so on.

71. Sound understanding is called common (properly speaking, general) insofar as it expresses itself in convictions that follow from those dispositions of the human spirit which are common to all human beings. In respect to convictions that are characteristic of

particular human beings and dependent on certain external circumstances, that understanding is called particular whose judgments can only be true as long as they do not contradict those of common understanding.

72. As a disposition common to all human beings, common understanding has to be distinguished from merely vulgar (trivial, base) understanding (*sensus communis* from *sensus vulgaris*), which is by no means developed to the level of expression that deserves the name common and sound understanding.

73. Common understanding is called purely natural insofar as it has developed through its mere practice, its daily affairs and its relations, and not because of purposeful and artificial education. It is called educated if it has been developed on purpose and artificially.

74. Educated understanding has to be distinguished both from the affected, overrefined one and from the uneducated or crude one. Common and sound understanding is degraded by affected artfulness that contradicts nature, while crude understanding has not yet risen to the rank of sound understanding.

75. In the above, the difference between understanding and reason has been neglected. The expression philosophizing reason reflects this difference. Linguistic custom only knows educated understanding, not the philosophical one.

76. It is indispensable to determine precisely the difference and interconnectedness between philosophizing and natural reason. It is only too common that the latter, under the improper name of common understanding, is mistakenly contrasted with the former—as one does with the common man in contrast to the nobleman. This leads to the error of placing one's own understanding in one or the other category, either looking down upon common understanding with the noble pride of superior reason, or scorning philosophizing reason with the peasant pride of broad and solid "domestic" understanding [*Hausverstand*].

Part VII

Distinctions and relationships between the natural and the philosophical employment of reason

77. The natural employment of reason as such presupposes inner and outer experience without being willing or able to conceive of the possibility of experience. It derives the latter from the actual existence of experience. The philosophical employment of reason as such leaves the reality of experience undecided until it can account for its determinate possibility independent of the actual existence of experience.

78. Mere natural reasoning begins with nothing but facts, analyzes them into the elements already comprised within them, and never goes beyond them. The conceptual basis and matter of merely elaborating activity as well as its conceptual result refer to intuitions, sensations and emotions. Natural reasoning neither can nor needs to account for the latter, since it knows them only through such concepts that presuppose intuitions, sensations and emotions.

79. Philosophical reasoning, on the other hand, must go beyond every fact, since it is required to ascertain the possibility of each fact insofar as this possibility is determined through itself. Those concepts that can only be asserted through philosophizing cannot be given through mere reflection. They must be produced instead through pure autonomous thought. Philosophy can and may consider the intuitions, sensations and emotions valid only insofar as it is able to strictly account for them through mere reason.

80. The convictions of the merely natural employment of reason consist not only in knowledge but also in belief and opinion. The

knowledge of natural reasoning is not pure knowledge, certain in itself. It presupposes and contains emotions and sensations that are not knowledge themselves; nor can they be attributed to knowledge through the natural employment of reason.

81. Philosophical convictions as such can be neither beliefs nor opinions. They can only be knowledge, that is, a form of knowledge which consists in actions of the spirit as opposed to presuppositions that contain emotions and limitations. As pure knowledge, it is certain in itself—certain solely by virtue of its truth and true by virtue of its certainty.

82. The faculties of imagination, emotion, and sensibility as well as the other faculties of the mind, working together with reason, participate in the natural convictions no less than reason does. Reason, under the conditions of these faculties, therefore does not operate solely according to its own laws. In regard to philosophical conviction, reason is required to be active for and by itself. The remaining faculties of the mind are only permitted to be active as instruments of the free employment of reason, for this employment and by means of it.

83. Merely natural convictions are not developed without our conscious contribution, nor solely through ourselves. They are presupposed by free actions, not produced by them. Thus they can only be mere means, not ultimate ends, of free and rational actions. Philosophical convictions, on the other hand, ought to be developed solely through ourselves, not just through some contributing agency of ours. They are not presupposed by freedom, but are produced by it through reason. They are only conceivable as effects of the kind of activity whose ultimate end is truth for the sake of truth.

84. The truth of a merely natural conviction presupposes physical, psychological and ethical soundness of understanding. Since this can only be accomplished to a certain degree in reality, natural conviction can never be thought to be pure truth itself, but solely its mere approximation. The truth of philosophical conviction, on the other hand, presupposes nothing but freedom and mere reason. It occurs whenever freedom succeeds in making conscious the necessary course of rational action. Thus it does not allow for degrees and is only possible as pure truth—mere rationality of thought.

85. Like everything natural, a conviction is only natural insofar as˙ it is lawful and necessary. Being merely natural, it develops without consciousness of the underlying basic laws. A conviction becomes philosophical by being derived from those underlying laws through the free employment of reason. Therefore, philosophizing reason may recognize a given conviction as natural only if it is able to make conscious the general lawfulness of that conviction. However, natural reason can count as valid the convictions of philosophizing reason only insofar as it finds in the results of these convictions its own convictions.

86. The essence of natural convictions consists in mere outer and inner experience insofar as this is rationally analyzed (developed by reflection). Philosophy is constituted by the science of the laws of those convictions, hence by the science of the possibility of experience as determined through itself (the legal necessity). Therefore, the natural and philosophical employments of reason, like the laws of experience and knowledge of these laws, are independent of each other.

87. Philosophizing does not presuppose experience for the scientific convictions that it asserts and derives from mere reason. Its only premises are freedom and reason, and it has no other principle than the free employment of reason. However, past experience and an exceptional degree of sound disposition and natural development of mental powers are indispensable as the external conditions of the possibility of the free employment of reason. As such, philosophizing reason depends on the state of natural reason.

88. In order to be completely natural, that is, thoroughly lawful, nonphilosophical convictions presuppose not only a perfectly sound disposition of the mind, but also an understanding that is fully developed through experience and natural reasoning. Because of this, nonphilosophical convictions are never possible as absolutely pure and complete natural convictions. Solely because philosophizing reason asserts the possibility (the laws) of experience as determined through itself, it elevates those convictions that can be derived from those laws to the level of legality. By doing that, it raises them to the purity and completeness of natural conviction. Thus, philosophical

employment of reason is an artificial remedy for natural reason by purifying and completing its convictions.

89. The natural and philosophical employments are simultaneously, but in different respects, dependent and independent of each other. Philosophizing presupposes a certain degree of natural soundness and development of spiritual powers, and it is itself a precondition of a higher degree of this soundness and development. Therefore, the two mutually promote each other's progress. Experience and philosophy in themselves are mutually independent. With respect to each other, however, they are only true insofar as they are not only not contradictory, but secure each other somewhat through their harmony.

90. Since the results of true philosophy are nothing but purified and completed natural convictions, they must be conceivable by such concepts and expressible by such propositions as can be understood and found to be true through mere natural reasoning. However, they cannot be discovered and asserted solely through natural reasoning. These sentences, therefore, are called propositions of common and sound understanding in contrast to philosophical theses, which means those propositions that can only be understood and found to be true through the philosophical employment of reason. Although philosophizing is indispensable for humankind in general, it is by no means necessary nor even possible that every human being philosophize in order to participate in spiritual culture, which is furthered by philosophy.

91. The results of ethical philosophy especially must be assertable in terms of the manner of thought and language of the natural employment of reason. Since rightful and moral actions are the common calling of all human beings, the origin of these convictions must be accessible to them all. Therefore, this origin must consist in self-consciousness and in experience. In addition, the assertion and proclamation of the moral law by conscience is a (practical) effect of reason, independent of reasoning and thus of philosophizing.

92. Like all natural convictions, those which concern morality never consist in the free employment of reason. However, they are distinct from all the others in having as their object the employment

that freedom (regarding actions of the will) has to make of reason. Morality and philosophy have in common the fact that both are free employments of reason—one in willing, the other in conviction.

93. The convictions of conscience and of ethics share one and the same content. They are only distinct in that moral philosophy consists in the free, artificial and scientific employment of reason, while conscience consists in the necessary, natural and popular one. The convictions of conscience are derived from mere facts of self-consciousness, those of ethical philosophy from the determinate possibility of these facts through thought.

94. The purpose of the present attempt is to assert not philosophical theses, but propositions of common and sound understanding. It ought to be understood and found true by mere natural reasoning of those educated and interested in moral education. It would thereby be subjected to the scrutiny of natural, not of philosophical reason. Therefore, those among the critics of this attempt who are professional philosophers will only understand its purpose if in their judgment they leave their artificial doctrines aside, and if they are willing and able to assume the standpoint of a mere natural employment of reason. The purpose of this attempt can only be realized if several worthy participants, through their morally sound judgment, correct, broaden and improve its content.

95. So far as the natural employment of reason presupposes feelings and concepts, its cultivation can be divided into the development of feelings as education of the heart, and the development of concepts as enlightenment of understanding.

Part VIII

Education of the heart

96. Through the term heart the customary use of language expresses the disposition toward humaneness insofar as this disposition expresses itself through feelings in general. However, what is mainly expressed by this term is sympathy, or the feeling of compassion and shared joy.

97. Sympathy is aroused by the mere perception of the manifest characteristics of ill-being and well-being. It extends to the sufferings and joys of all sensible beings. This disposition is a characteristic of the human organism. It is originally present in all human beings, though to different degrees.

98. Through this disposition, the drive for pleasure takes on two opposed directions, which limit each other in their effects. As such, it is divided into the selfish and the sympathetic drive. The former expresses itself through the drive for self-preservation; the latter through the drive for sociability.

99. Customary language, which calls the natural disposition toward sympathy "the heart," means by the nature of the heart the relation of sympathetic to selfish feelings. The limitation of selfishness through sympathy, which occurs without the contribution of freedom and reason, is called natural kindheartedness. If sympathy overflows, we speak of natural weakheartedness; if selfishness does, of natural hardheartedness.

100. Sympathy in itself is not moral; likewise selfishness in itself is not immoral. By relating to each other, they produce kindheartedness, weakheartedness and hard-heartedness, but both lack the character of morality and immorality. They cannot be raised to moral ennoblement through the (theoretical) employment of reason. Nor can they be protected against the degeneration into immorality.

101. Comparing one's own state to that of others is one of the most important modifications of the involuntary relationship between sympathy and selfishness through (reasoning) reason. By means of this comparison, the partly existent balance between selfish and sympathetic instinct is elevated to the drive for equality of well-being. This manifests itself in the feeling of displeasure at others' situations that are worse in comparison with one's own, and in the same feeling about one's own worse situation in comparison with others. Through this comparison, it is also possible that the partly existent excess of selfishness over sympathy turns into a drive for inequality of well-being. It is apparent in the feeling of displeasure at the equally good or better situation of others and the pleasure in one's own better situation. Both drives become moral or immoral through the participation of the freedom of the will. One could call them reasoned humaneness or inhumaneness.

102. So far as one distinguishes moral kindness of the heart from merely natural as well as from reasoned, involuntary kindheartedness, one introduces moral feeling into the precisely defined meaning of the term heart. Moral feeling adds the receptivity toward pleasure and displeasure, as it is felt about the conformity and the conflict between freedom and the moral law.

103. Pleasure experienced in moral lawfulness and displeasure experienced in immoral unlawfulness are neither the reasons for moral obligation nor the reasons for the moral decision. They are mere consequences of the consciousness of the moral law on the one hand and, on the other, of freedom, which conforms to or contradicts the law. Pleasure or displeasure accompanies the moral decision, helping to enforce it against the resistance of the appetites. However, they also occur without that resistance, depending on whether freedom turns that decision into action.

"No human being exists without any moral feeling. It would be morally dead if it were completely nonreceptive to this feeling. In medical language, if moral vitality were not able to stimulate this feeling, mankind (as if according to chemical laws) would dissolve into mere animality, and irretrievably mingle with the bulk of other natural beings" (Kant, *The Metaphysical Elements of Virtue*).[1]

104. The moral law possesses dignity, that is, sublimity of worth beyond all comparison with other kinds of worth. It possesses original dignity, that is, a dignity that does not presuppose any other and is the basis for all others. The feeling of this dignity is called respect. It consists in the pleasure of unconditional necessity (inviolability— sanctity) of the law. That necessity, however, carries with it an admixture of displeasure insofar as the compulsion is felt which the law imposes on sensibility.

105. Active respect toward the law is connected to distrust. The latter originates from feeling the obstacles to adhering to the law which have to be fought by freedom. This active respect is called reverence toward the law. It is also connected to trust that originates from the feeling of having partly defeated the obstacles and having achieved the means to conform to the law. Then it is called love of the law.

106. Respect toward morality consists in the feeling of dignity to which freedom is raised in conforming to the moral law. Through such dignity, freedom asserts the superiority of persons over things, and the sovereignty of the will over nature. The contempt for immorality consists in the feeling of unworthiness which freedom acquires by transgressing the moral law. By doing so, freedom destroys the personality, it grants the superiority of things over persons, and it degrades the will as the slave of arational nature.

107. That dignity is revealed and assured to humankind by the dignity of the law. Humankind is called to that dignity through the law and is capable of it through freedom. It ought to resist all charms and horrors of the senses, so as to abide by the law. Therefore, it must be able to do so. Mankind is stronger than the whole of nature through the law and through its own free obedience to it. Nature can only destroy the body [*Leib*][2] through its superior

---

1. My translation.
2. It would have been more consistent for Reinhold to have used "physical form" (*Körper*) in this case.

force. But it can by no means overwhelm the dutiful will. The entire dreadfulness of all kinds of suffering and of death itself becomes the sensible measure of the dignity of personality, which is immeasurable in itself. It becomes the measure by demonstrating to the power of imagination the superiority of the ethical faculty over the physical capacities, of spirit over matter, and of freedom over nature.

108. The feeling of the sublime must not be confused with the feeling of respect. The former is related to the latter but is only connected with it when the dignity of the law is represented in a sensible manner. Sensibility has limits, as does imagination, since it is bound to sensibility in its representations. Beyond those limits, the size of a given object cannot be grasped in an image. The size that is called sensibly immeasurable nevertheless can be conceived of by reason, which can think what is absolutely immeasurable. Thus the intuition of a sensibly immeasurable object (whether it belongs to physical or to ethical nature) can arouse the pleasant feeling of the power of rational nature as exceeding all sensible faculties. At the same time it is accompanied by the unpleasant feeling of the impotence of sensible nature. The heartwarming feeling of the sublime is composed of both these feelings, announcing itself in its higher degrees through both terror and delight.

109. The tendency of imagination toward lawlessness, as expressed in the appetites, can be limited by frequently and purposely arousing the feeling of the sublime. Thereby, imagination does not lose its energy, but is ennobled through pleasure. It gets accustomed to work harmoniously with the moral law without compulsion. That is to say, the power of the senses is bent under the authority of free rationality, the will is elevated above all attractions and horrors of the senses, and delight is generated in the elevation of reason through the humiliation of sensibility. In short, the power of imagination is taught, through the feeling of the sublime, to serve reason and to use the will in acting morally.

110. That figure, shape, or form is beautiful which can be intuited by imagination in a fashion harmonious with the independent activity of reason in thought. The feeling of beauty is pleasure that immediately arises from the harmony between imagination and intellectual

power. It consists in the feeling of delight in the mere form of an object, regardless of its usefulness.

111. The feeling of beauty, aroused frequently and purposely, limits the tendency of imagination toward lawlessness in thought. Thereby, imagination does not lose its energy, but is ennobled through pleasure, and is accustomed to working harmoniously with the intellectual power without compulsion. It gives up its crude barbarity and turns into a useful instrument of the intellectual power striving for truth.

112. The feeling of beauty and the sublime is called taste. As a disposition and in regard to its object, it is essentially different from both moral feeling and sympathy. Through the exercise of taste, above all and immediately, the power of imagination is cultivated, not the faculty of desire nor the will. Imagination needs special attention, through which it is kept disciplined and nurtured, and is taught proficiency for the purposes of reason: truth of conviction and morality of volition.

113. The feeling of propriety, or the externally decent, concerns merely the external form of social behavior of human beings. It consists of sympathy, taste and, in its perfection, also the moral feeling. Thus it is the characteristic expression of the beautiful and ennobled drive for sociability.

114. Sympathy, taste and the feeling of the externally decent make up the humanity of the heart when they are united with the moral feeling. Separated from moral feeling, sympathy degenerates into weakness—weakness that commits injustices out of compassion. Or sympathy is pushed aside by selfish feelings from the very beginning. Taste, then, is not seen as a means anymore, but as the ultimate goal of culture. It turns into the attitude of sensibility, refined by luxury, which is content with external form. And it grows indifferent toward truth and justice, as it is interested in mere entertainment. The feeling of external decency is degraded to hypocrisy, or comes forward as manifest infidelity, by confusing the ethical itself with so-called conventiality and decency.

Separated from sympathy, the moral feeling itself cannot protect against natural hard-heartedness and exaggerated strictness against others. Without taste, the moral feeling is more or less limited in its influence on action through the crude barbarity of imagination. Finally, without the feeling of the externally decent, it cannot be completely secured against indecent and uncivilized behavior, despite its honest disposition.

115. The immediate education of the heart consists in the knowledge of the (above-named) feelings, in part to arouse them and in part to prevent their being confused and mixed. Also it consists in the harmonious exercise of these feelings, through which their vitality is assured against enervation and overstraining. The mediate education of the heart includes the development of concepts, or the enlightenment of the understanding.

Part IX

Enlightenment in general

116. Representations through which objects are determined in consciousness are called concepts. Concepts as representations are distinguished from objects as such. The intuitions in consciousness make up the objects themselves and, therefore, cannot be separated from them.

117. A concept is called clear insofar as with its help its object is distinguished from other objects. Clarity increases with the increasing number of particular objects, species and genera that one distinguishes with the help of concepts from a given particular thing and a given species or genus at hand.

118. A concept would be completely opaque whose object would not be distinguishable from any other object and thus would be indeterminate as an object in consciousness (it could not be thought). Such a concept would not be a concept. There cannot be a completely opaque concept. Every concept, therefore, is clear in regard to that which can be differentiated through it. It is opaque in regard to that which cannot be differentiated through it. However, it is only called opaque or clear if its object is confused with or distinguishable from those objects from which it should be distinguished.

119. A concept is called distinct insofar as it is possible to differentiate among the characteristics that make up its content. Hence, distinctness consists in the clarity of the elements of a concept. Distinctness also allows for degrees. The lowest degree is the consciousness of those characteristics that immediately constitute the content of the concept and that are the result of the first analysis. With each new analysis of the characteristics found by the last analysis, a higher degree of distinctness is reached. The highest degree consists of the characteristics obtained by the last possible

analysis. These characteristics are not analyzable any further, and thus are simple.

120. There is a necessary and natural indistinctness, which is owing to the simplicity of the content of the concept (for example, in the concepts of color, sound, and so forth). It has to be distinguished from the contingent and faulty indistinctness, which is a consequence of either the entirely neglected development of a concept or a development that has not been carried far enough. This kind of indistinctness occurs only in complex concepts, and is called confusedness in contrast to the indistinctness of simple concepts.

121. One can call the clarity of a concept as a whole its external clarity. The distinctness, as the clarity of its elements, can be called its internal clarity. External clarity is brought about by beginning with the given concept and comparing its object with other objects. Internal clarity is produced by stopping at the given concept and analyzing its content.

122. Convictions in general are only possible through clear concepts. And convictions which one can account for are only possible through distinct concepts. The truth and certainty of convictions depend on the attempt to elevate the concepts involved to the utmost clarity and distinctness. Hence truth and certainty of conviction depend on enlightenment.

123. Truth, as the agreement of representation and object, partly rests on the condition that nothing is found in the representation that contradicts the object. And partly, it depends on the fact that everything is contained in the representation that belongs to the full consciousness of the object. The concept cannot contain anything superfluous, and cannot lack anything indispensable. On that basis, falsity consists partly in the faultiness, and partly in the deficiencies of the concept.

124. An incorrect concept that is considered and used as correct is called an error. In order to be completely incorrect, the concept would have to contain nothing of that which belongs to its object. Its object would not be determined through it in consciousness; therefore it would not be a concept at all. Hence, in every error, there is something true mixed with more or less untrue elements.

An error can only be refuted by separating the true from the untrue and recognizing it as true.

125. Ignorance is partly a complete lack and partly a deficiency of concepts. A deficient concept becomes faulty and turns into an error if it is used as a complete one. Utter ignorance certainly is free of error. But it is by no means closer to truth than error.

126. Insofar as enlightenment depends on the clarity of concepts—and therefore on the number of different concepts that are compared—it is called extensive. Insofar as it depends on the precision and completeness of analysis of clear concepts, it is called elucidating (intensive) enlightenment.

127. Extensive enlightenment above all counteracts ignorance, while elucidating enlightenment counteracts error. Separated from elucidating enlightenment, extensive enlightenment would multiply errors through clear but confused concepts. Elucidating enlightenment on its own would prompt partial and false knowledge. It endows the errors caused by deficient concepts with the character of verified truths. Therefore true enlightenment as such can be neither solely extensive, nor solely elucidating.

128. Clear concepts, remembered with the help of symbols, amount to knowledge. Distinct concepts amount to insights of a human being. Knowledge without insight is shallower the more widespread it is. On the other hand, insights without sufficient knowledge are emptier the deeper they are. The proportion of insights and knowledge makes up the actual state of enlightenment.

129. The expression "learned," used for knowledge, designates in its original sense all and only that knowledge which can be acquired through learning and communicated through teaching. As such, it is distinguished from that knowledge which is drawn immediately from experience and produced by autonomous thought. In ordinary use of language, learned knowledge, whose essence is scholarliness, is that knowledge which is distinguished from common knowledge. Learned knowledge is distinguished partly by the importance and rareness of its content, and partly by its scholarly form, whose ultimate purpose consists in thoroughness. The content of common knowledge

is shared, and its form popular.[1] Therefore its main concern is comprehensibility.

130. That which for one nation, and for a certain period, counts as learned knowledge can be common knowledge for another nation in another period. The transition of useful knowledge from the sphere of the scholarly to everyday life is a sign of the progressive enlightenment of a people.

131. So far as scholarly knowledge is conceived through imagination and memory, which means is learned, it makes up the mere matter of knowing—dead scholarliness. This can only be vitalized and raised to proper knowing through insight, achieved through autonomous thought about its objects, and through natural knowledge, drawn immediately from experience.

132. Only insofar as learned knowledge represents at the same time insights can it be called scientific knowledge. Learned knowledge belongs, rather, to the proper sciences when it presupposes autonomous thought, and to mere scholarliness when it depends on memory.

133. Philology has its place at the top of scholarly learning. It consists of knowledge of the instruments of learning. As the science of the fundamental concepts and principles of all knowing, philosophy is the leading science.

134. Philology comprises linguistics, bibliography, and the knowledge of the ancients and of classical models of the works of fine art, and rhetoric. Raised to the level of insight and made into an instrument of specific historical and philosophical science, philology becomes an auxiliary science.

135. Philosophy can be itself a part of scholarliness. It presupposes and incorporates, then, the knowledge of the philosophical theses of older and contemporary superior independent thinkers, and hence consists in the (historical) acquaintance with modes of representation different from one's own. It is not part of scholarliness, however,

---

1. The term *popular* (or German *populär*) nowadays designates the quality of being appreciated and approved of by many people. In Reinhold's time, it did not possess that evaluative tinge, but referred to the quality of being comprehensible to most people.

when it consists in one's own conviction, that is, in a conviction that is only possible through autonomous thought. As such, it can be neither taught nor learned. Because of this, philosophy is the science which must determine the ultimate end of all learning, the interconnectedness of the fields of learning. It must determine the limits of learning, and the value of that which is to be known.

136. Scholarliness, even classical scholarliness, in lacking taste is barbaric and in lacking philosophical spirit is barren. Only with a conjunction of both can it represent a higher enlightenment, which is fitting for the true scholar. .

137. Enlightenment is prevented by whatever contradicts genuine scholarliness. There are different kinds of scholars who obscure understanding. Among them are the scholar who expands his shallow knowledge toward indefinite boundaries (the pansophist), the scholar who lacks the necessary knowledge of his major subject (the ignorant), the one who has not gained insight and therefore does not know that which he is acquainted with (the idiot), or the one who spoils scholarliness by treating it as an ultimate end, not as a means (the pedant). Finally, there is the scholar who degrades learning to a corrupt luxury of the mind by treating it as a mere instrument to entertain the idle and consuming class of the public. (One might call him the fashionable scholar.)

138. The pedant not only neglects natural knowledge; he also neglects all learned knowledge that does not immediately belong to his subject. And he uses the scholarly form when it is only the popular one that should be used. The fashionable scholar, on the other hand, neglects all knowledge and insight which is only possible in the scholarly form, but uses the popular one even when only the scholarly should be used.

139. Enlightenment, the purposively effected cultivation of intellectual power, can be divided into the cultivation of skillfulness, that is, the qualification of the condition of intellectual power to suit various purposes (technical cultivation), and the cultivation of morality, that is, the suitability of intellectual power for the ultimate end of humankind (practical cultivation). Both kinds make up one and the same enlightenment only insofar as skillfulness is cultivated

and employed as a means for morality. They contradict each other if skillfulness is cultivated and utilized as a mere instrument of the capacity to enjoy.

140. The enlightenment of a nation to an intellectual power cultivated for skillfulness can be brought about by the interaction of favorable external circumstances such as climate, location, fertility of soil, trade, industry, wealth, power, and so on. In this case, enlightenment can evolve to a high degree of a refined ability to enjoy and be prudent, but without having morality evolve to that degree of integrity and vitality of attitude and of that determinateness and completeness of conviction which can justifiably be called moral culture. Morality need not even evolve in the class that crucially influences the manner of thought of others.

141. This sort of enlightenment possesses and knows no other incentive but pleasure and displeasure. It enlightens the understanding only to serve sensibility. It judges the completeness of its concepts according to their efficiency in multiplying and refining enjoyment, and the correctness and fertility of knowledge in light of its suitability for the needs of living well. Even the striving for truth is judged merely by the smoothness with which the faculty of judgment has learned to adjust the rules of reasoning to the instability of external circumstances.

142. This kind of enlightenment cannot conceive of a value that could not be measured and counterbalanced in money. Through it, art, scholarly learning, and science turn into objects and instruments of mere luxury for the consuming class, and into marketable commodities for the acquiring class. It reads and writes its books usually out of vanity, or boredom, or hunger, or greed. And it judges their importance in terms of their entertaining or profitable content.

143. The skeptical version of the philosophy of this enlightenment starts out from indifference toward pure truth. The dogmatic version is based on the exclusive acknowledgment of evident reality, the eclectic version on some arbitrary standpoint. In any case, it suppresses the striving for pure knowledge by displaying supreme skillfulness in fighting all thought which aims at pure knowledge. And as the appointed teachers, who adhere to this philosophy,

degrade science, they encourage the unreflective crowd in its un-reflectiveness, delivering it from the painstaking task of autonomous thought.

144. The beaux esprits of this kind of philosophy, who philosophize for the so-called elegant world, endow the half-true concepts of their principles with the appearance of infallibility by representing them in a charming way. They maintain and propagate the delusion of the superfluity of scholarly research and the careful formulation of principal concepts. Thereby they contribute to the spread of their superficial culture.

145. Taste is for these bel esprit philosophers not a means, but the ultimate end of culture. Beauty is the criterion of truth, and philosophy is nothing but the subject for a beautiful composition. Oddity, newness, and the boldness of their ideas secure them the name of independent thinkers. Their main supporters are those members of the public who, because of rank and fortune, are able to live purely for enjoyment. The more they rely on the charms of representation for their pastime, the less they care for truth.

146. In this culture, which is based on enjoyment and aims for nothing but enjoyment, it is natural for the ethical to be reduced to a mere theory of well-being under the name of the doctrine of happiness. This ethics increases and expands its efforts for precisely the same refined and multiple enjoyments that it ought to limit and guide. It justifies the tyranny of the drive for pleasure by granting reason power over the will only under the sanction of this drive. By the common good, it means nothing but well-being. It derives from this common good the obligation of the duties of conscience, as well as the validity of external rights. Even religion (if it still accepts religion as valid) it traces back to heightening enjoyment, when good luck prevails, and to comfort, when bad luck prevails. It attributes the hope for immortality to the longing for enjoyment beyond the grave, and grounds faith in God in the presupposition that the world is arranged completely for the sake of the well-being of human beings and therefore must have an intelligent creator.

147. When the striving for enjoyment becomes the primary and exclusive aim, enlightenment assumes the form described above.

This form is entirely coincidental to enlightenment. The essence of enlightenment consists in the intention to develop the faculty of knowledge in general, but this is completely lacking in this form. The incentive and the objects of enlightenment are thus not taken into consideration.

Part X

Being enlightened about
ethical matters

148. The term enlightenment is used in a narrower but no less common sense to designate the development of the faculty of knowledge with respect to certain concepts, and the improvement of the method of thought about certain subjects. The use of language of the common and sound understanding treats these subjects as the most important ones by preferring to call the clarity of their concepts enlightenment.

149. The concepts whose clarity and distinctness are called enlightenment immediately refer to that which is characteristic for mankind and common to all humans: the affairs of human beings as human beings. Those concepts can consist neither of the knowledge of the artisan, nor that of the artist, nor of the scholar, nor in the insights of the philosopher.

150. Ethical, rightful and moral matters immediately concern the proper self, that is, the free and rational nature of human beings. Therefore, they are equally relevant for all humans. They can only be recognized and settled through freedom and reason, hence only through autonomous willing and autonomous thought. Not only distinct but also clear concepts about these matters are only possible through autonomous thought. Any correct judgment on these matters is rendered possible solely through one's own judgment.

151. Physical objects and, alongside them, physical matters force themselves on a human being from outside. Clear concepts about them arise nearly by themselves through mere reflection on that which is sensed and intuited with sufficient vitality. On the other hand, ethical objects exist only for freedom and through reason.

Concepts about them can only develop from feelings and retain their clarity, as concepts, through autonomous thought.

152. Through its free and rational nature, every human being possesses the disposition and the vocation for this autonomous thought. As a member of civil society, he is called upon from outside by the administration of right to exercise autonomous thought. And because in civil life the development of mental powers is inevitable to a certain degree, a human being is also invited by conscience from within to think autonomously.

153. It is characteristic of autonomous thought that it is only possible if one chooses it. On the other hand, one can be carried along to mere reflection without consciously choosing to do so. Because autonomous thought is necessary for knowing and for exercising duties and rights, and is impossible without a free decision, it is itself a duty.

154. Ignorance in ethical matters is the inability to judge one's proper self and to act through it. This is true tutelage. Since such ignorance can and ought to be removed through autonomous thought but is prolonged through voluntary laziness, it is self-incurred tutelage. In this regard, enlightenment can be called man's release from his self-incurred tutelage.

155. Since political matters are and ought to be rightful, and religious ones moral, the clear and distinct concepts of these matters, too, are rendered possible solely through autonomous thought. They essentially belong to the content of enlightenment in the narrowest sense of the word.

156. Insofar as the concepts about political and religious matters are determined not through the principal concepts of rightfulness and morality, but through custom, habit and reputation, they are partly causes and partly effects of prejudices, that is, of judgments that precede autonomous thought. These are called prevailing prejudices, partly because they concern subjects of general interest, and partly because they make up the customary manner of thought of the large crowd of all classes.

157. Therefore, customary language prefers to call that person unenlightened who has not elevated himself above the prevailing

manner of thought of the rabble of all classes in regard to political and religious matters. Such a person resorts to obscure concepts about what is rightful in political matters, and what is moral in religious matters—even if he possesses a quite extensive juridical, statistical, theological, and so forth, scholarly learning. He is called an obscurantist if he contributes to misunderstanding the rightful character of political affairs and the moral character of religious affairs by unreflective adherence to tradition, custom, and reputation.

158. Autonomous thought about the ethical, thus political and religious affairs, is encouraged by public communication of autonomously conceived concepts. Through the spread and propagation of methods of representation which are founded merely on tradition, custom, and reputation, autonomous thought is impeded. Political laws that aim to uphold those methods of representation and that prevent public communication of autonomously conceived concepts thus are both wrongful and immoral.

159. Public enlightenment consists in the unimpeded public communication of independently thought concepts about ethical, political and religious matters. In this regard, only that state can be called enlightened which recognizes and protects by law that communication as the right of everybody. Such communication must not depend upon the arbitrary will of the government.

160. Only that state which is sufficiently strong in the justice and wisdom of its other laws and institutions is able to assert freedom of the press as an unlimited right. Only then will it not be shaken by any exercise of that right. A people whose writers can endanger the inviolability of the supreme authority is in one of two predicaments: Either its civil constitution is so bad that it would lose nothing through abolishing it; or it is too immature for a better constitution, so that it would lose everything by losing its present one.

161. Administrators of supreme authority, if they attempt to make themselves indispensable as guardians by acting to maintain the tutelage of the people, act imprudently against their own interest no less than they act unwisely against the general interest. For wherever this tutelage continues, it affects the guardians as well as the wards. The guardians rely too much upon ignorance if they pretend to owe

power above all, or solely, to it. For power cannot be maintained without the public conviction of its indispensability and legitimacy— even if that power is achieved through intelligence, boldness and luck. Dominance of public opinion is then either not possible at all, or only by the incidental interaction of external circumstances. These can be neither brought about, nor maintained, through violence and cunning.

Part XI

On genuine and spurious enlightenment about ethical matters

162. Not everybody whose thinking about political and religious matters is above prevalent prejudices automatically knows the rightful and moral character of these matters. It is possible to vividly feel the injustice of certain political institutions and laws as well as the preposterousness of certain notions of folk religion, but not to think about the essence of civil society and of religion through definite and correct concepts.

163. Deluding self-love can divert the feeling of wrong from that which is unjust to that which is inconvenient in just institutions. This happens when the feeling is only awakened through the pressure of unjust institutions and not accompanied by a definite concept of right. Whoever judges folk religion according to the feeling of preposterousness only, and not according to definite concepts of morality (without which no definite concept of religion in general is possible), is bound to think of religion in general as preposterous.

164. When the interest of sensibility becomes the only incentive, enlightenment is directed only by that interest. It becomes inconsistent in itself. Within the same nation, it declares itself to be opposed to the existing state of affairs because this state contradicts part of its interests, but also to be in favor of that same state because it benefits in another part of its interests. This contradiction results in the struggle of new prejudices with old ones for the domination of public opinion.

165. In this struggle, the thinking of those who are favored under the current political state, and who do not want to have anybody

equal to themselves, clashes with the thinking of those who are factually or supposedly oppressed, and who do not want anybody to be superior to them. Superstition, which attempts to be redeemed from natural duties by courting a supernatural being, opposes unbelief, which hopes to gain the same redemption by recognizing natural necessity only.

166. Enlightenment about ethical matters becomes genuine or spurious enlightenment according to the mental attitude and manner of thought with which it starts out.

167. With respect to attitude and manner of thought, genuine enlightenment originates in the ethical. It is the obligatory effort to gain clear and distinct concepts about ethical matters. Therefore, genuine enlightenment is not possible without the serious and honest general decision to fulfill one's duty. This decision makes up the inner essence of a morally good character.

168. Genuine enlightenment presupposes—and by no means produces—morality with respect to this general decision, insofar as this decision depends on the freedom of the will. Immorality, as far as it is not an effect of ignorance and error, cannot be prevented or minimized by enlightenment. On the contrary, it produces spurious enlightenment.

169. However, the decision to fulfill one's duty is serious and honest only if it is accompanied by the attempt to execute it. Execution depends not only on freedom of the will but also on concepts and judgments of the intellect. To that extent, enlightenment is presupposed by morality. The good will alone cannot produce enlightenment, let alone replace it. Enlightenment in this respect is only a particular duty, which cannot be replaced by any other duty, but which is necessary for the fulfillment of other duties.

170. There exists a misunderstanding among certain friends and foes of enlightenment. The former derive the ethical only from enlightenment; the latter think that enlightenment is dispensable or even dangerous for the ethical. This misunderstanding can be partly explained through the fact that the friends of enlightenment fail to see the dependence of the ethical on the freedom of the will and only see that it depends on conviction. And it can also be partly

explained through the reverse phenomenon, namely, that the foes of enlightenment fail to see that the ethical depends on conviction and only see it as dependent on the freedom of the will.

171. The eye of the spirit is clouded without the decision—dependent on the freedom of the will—to fulfill one's duty without exception (that is, without the practical employment of reason). And without illuminating the objects (that is, without the theoretical employment of reason), the spirit is either unable to see anything at all or unable to see it correctly, even with the help of the most healthy vision. The friend who wants to make enlightenment the efficient cause of the ethical wants to see through mere light, disregarding the condition of the eye. However, the foe who views enlightenment as not an essential condition, or even as an obstacle to the ethical, wants to see without light.

172. Those convictions that are grounded in the influence that a morally good attitude has on the manner of thought are called maxims of genuine enlightenment. Such convictions determine the direction of enlightenment.

173. The following conviction is of this kind: that genuine enlightenment consists in a mode of thought that is equally far removed from haughty confidence and cowardly distrust in one's own judgment, from credulity and (pathological) skepticism, from superstition and unbelief, and from the extremes characteristic of political zealousness.

174. The attitude that is at the base of genuine enlightenment is not dogmatic insofar as both imagination and striving to know what cannot be known are absent from it. It is not skeptical insofar as it is not indifferent to problems concerning the ethical. And the attitude is not supernaturalistic insofar as it despises superstition, and not naturalistic insofar as it despises unbelief. Finally, it is not aristocratic insofar as it scorns political oppression, and not democratic, since it disdains political licentiousness.

The theoretical doctrines of the sects known under the names of democratic and so forth are neither completely repudiated through the above-mentioned attitude, nor are they sanctioned through it. These doctrines fall far short of sufficiently distinguishing between what is true and what is false. Furthermore, scientific culture has not yet asserted universally valid, fundamental concepts about them.

175. It is evident for the manner of thought animated through a moral attitude that the true interest of humanity is only known in a one-sided way by each of those sects, and is commonly misunderstood by them. That is a result of their passionate struggle. Therefore, nothing must be feared so much for the interest of humanity than that one party, whichever it may be, gains a decisive victory over the others. It is most desirable that they all limit and neutralize each other.

176. The attitude that is the basis of genuine enlightenment despises the apathy of indifference no less than the fanaticism of partisanship. A definite lack of humanity is presupposed in one who assumes a merely speculative interest and the role of a passive observer in regard to ethical matters.

177. The attitude that is basic to genuine enlightenment enables the unbiased thinker to support justice and truth by discovering and fighting wrong and error on all sides. However, it does not allow him to imitate that arrangement of providence which limits one evil through another, refutes one error through another, and punishes one injustice with another. This terrible undertaking belongs exclusively to the Educator of mankind who is not Himself a human being. Therefore, He Himself is not interested in any evil, cannot err, and cannot commit a wrong act.

178. During a revolution in the mode of thought, even the most unbiased person is, unbeknownst to him and unintentionally, in danger of counteracting his own intention. Such a revolution, occurring within a nation and concerning political and religious matters, inevitably creates conflict between old and new prejudices. The real points at issue are obscured through the passion of the conflicting parties. The unbiased person runs the risk of favoring the error of one party by opposing the error of another party. And if he attempts to protect himself against this danger, he may just totter back and forth between them. It may happen to an emotional heart which is endowed with a lively imagination that it becomes outraged over the horrors that surface from first one, then another party. Hence it

may be pushed sometimes toward one, and sometimes toward the opposite extreme.

179. Genuine enlightenment protects the unbiased thinker against one-sidedness and indecisiveness. It does so by reflectiveness and justice, which are characteristic of its attitude, and through definite concepts, which are characteristic of its manner of thought. Similarly, genuine enlightenment provides such a thinker with the courage to expose himself to being misunderstood by all parties. He will be blamed for being indifferent to truth and right, being cowardly for trying not to alienate any party, or secretly planning to dominate them all.

180. The common characteristic of the attitude of spurious enlightenment consists in having—part voluntarily, part involuntarily—no other internal incentive than pleasure and displeasure. The employment of intellectual power by spurious enlightenment serves solely the drive for pleasure. The common characteristic in the manner of thought of spurious enlightenment consists in knowing no other internal incentive than pleasure and displeasure. It begins with the conviction that in willing, intellectual power is activated only by the drive for pleasure, and that it can only act to serve this drive

181. According to the manner of thought of spurious enlightenment, the ethical or unethical character of a voluntary action depends solely on the correct or incorrect judgment of pleasure or displeasure by the understanding. Pleasure or displeasure is the efficient cause of the decision. The correctness of the judgment depends on the influence of the organism, its temperament, dispositions and capacities, education, habits, the civil constitution, and so on, upon the faculty of desire and, indirectly, on the intellectual power.

182. According to this manner of thought, therefore, there is neither autonomy of reason nor freedom of the will. Reason can do nothing but represent, which means make conscious for a human being the interconnectedness of things (the way they are and have to be). And the will cannot help performing as pleasure or displeasure dictates. The will can be prevented externally only by compulsion from complying with the dictate of pleasure or displeasure, and internally only by ignorance or error. The only freedom of the will

consists in the absence of compulsion or error. Through it, the will only does what it can do, and refrains from doing what it cannot do.

183. This manner of thought declares the will to be internally free insofar as understanding judges correctly. Since the unethical is attributed to incorrect judgments, freedom and accountability are denied relevance. This manner of thought thus negates the difference between immoral actions and merely amoral ones. It finds sufficient reason for moral actions in the externally uninhibited effectiveness of rational desire. For other—immoral or amoral—actions, it seeks this reason in the effectiveness of rational desire that is externally inhibited. In so doing, this manner of thought absolves the will of any guilt, and credits it with necessarily acting well as soon as it is not externally prevented from doing so. Therefore, this manner of thought argues, the will is good by nature.

184. Although the advocates and spokesmen for this enlightenment may differ very much in their theories (as, for example, Helvetius and Rousseau), they still agree on the following: that every human being would and would of necessity act in the same way under the same external circumstances of organism, climate, education, situation, and so forth. In their opinion, wrong in fact is mere misfortune; being guilty of something wrongful rests internally on ignorance and error and externally only upon any coercion that thwarts the development of the natural powers of human beings. According to this manner of thought, the dignity of human nature consists in this inalienable innocence and in this (under the condition of external uninhibitedness) inevitable morality.

185. The kind of enlightenment which consists in the development of intellectual power through the drive for pleasure occurs necessarily and inevitably as soon as its development is not impeded from outside. The manner of thought of this enlightenment expects— not without justification—enlightenment, the ethical and happiness from nonrestrictive external conditions. Freedom is understood and praised as mere freedom from external restraints. The value and significance of a civil constitution in general, as well as the condition of particular constitutions, are judged in terms of this freedom alone.

186. The striving for clear concepts, provoked merely by sensible interest, is more vividly exercised and more easily satisfied by objects of external experience than by objects of inner experience and self-consciousness. Therefore, enlightenment concerning any objects of inner experience—apart from a few exceptions—is largely neglected. The manner of thought of spurious enlightenment believes that it derives the unknown from the known by presupposing that inner experience resides in the objects of external experience, self-consciousness in the sensible world, and thought and volition in mere (physical) makeup.

187. A spirit that finds enjoyment and entertainment exclusively in matter is easily convinced that existence also belongs solely to matter. Progress in the natural sciences promotes this viewpoint. And progress in the cognitive sciences supports it, too. The more the technician, chemist, and philologist investigate and come to know the forces of matter and the less they study the forces of the spirit, the more they will attribute to matter and the less will they doubt that the effects of the soul—which are not well enough investigated—originate from properties of matter to be discovered in the future. They think that ideas about immateriality only occur in the common way of representation and can be ascribed to ignorance of the essence of matter.

188. Historical research, working in accordance with the described manner of thought, is used to seek and find everything that human beings have become in organisms, climates, food, civil constitutions, and revolutions—in short, merely in facts of external experience. This implicitly justifies or confirms the conviction that the entire essence of human beings is based on the composition of certain elements, and that characteristic human behavior depends on the coincidence of external circumstances.

189. Finally, that attitude which does not rise above the sensibly perceptible continually implies the judgment that nothing is real besides the perceptible. This judgment is confirmed by the rich and distinguished rabble through the refinement of its external way of life and even of its manner of thought. The more such people learn to multiply and heighten physical pleasures, the more important

physical nature becomes to them, and the more uninspiring, toil-some, and obscure becomes the idea of another nature.

190. The belief that there is nothing else but matter increases with the interest in this belief. This interest grows with the corruption of morals. One who is a slave of vice likes to give away the internal freedom of doing what he ought to do for the external freedom of doing everything he can do. Internal freedom makes itself known through his conscience, while external freedom is assured to him by unbelief.[1] A slave of vice gladly ascribes merit, which he does not have, to good luck, so that he can ascribe the wrong he has committed to bad luck. He willingly thinks of himself as a mere animal in order to be able to believe that he has never done anything that he could have refrained from doing, and never failed to do anything he could have done.

191. The character of spurious enlightenment is based upon the drive for pleasure and that reasoning[2] which depends on this drive. This is true in regard to its attitude or its manner of thought, or both. Spurious enlightenment takes as its principle the mutual influence that the drive for pleasure and reason have on each other, together with the exclusion of freedom of the will. The character of genuine enlightenment consists in the fact that it presupposes freedom of the will and spontaneity of reason with regard to its manner of thought as well as its attitude. Genuine enlightenment assumes as its principle the harmony between the freedom of the will and the spontaneous activity of reason, for which the drive for pleasure serves as a mere means.

192. Nothing is more evident and certain in itself for the manner of thought of genuine enlightenment than the freedom of the will. It takes this conviction as a basis for all others. To spurious en-lightenment, the opposite of freedom is perfectly clear. Therefore it must assume and circulate incorrect concepts of the ethical, rightful,

---

1. It is unclear which unbelief is referred to. Reinhold probably means unbelief in the free, rational self.
2. Theoretical reason.

and moral. Genuine enlightenment takes freedom of the will as the chief characteristic and thus ends up with correct concepts. It views such freedom as the fundamental truth in the development of the concepts that concern political and religious matters.

Part XII

Some principles and maxims of political enlightenment

193. When the direction of the freedom of the will conforms to the law of reason, it is called right [*Recht*] in a broad sense.[1]

194. The law that does not negate freedom, but presupposes and secures it, can only be derived from reason and can only consist in the necessary course of action of reason. Right can depend on this law only if it simultaneously is to incorporate freedom and legal direction.

195. When the term "right" is used as opposed to the term "a right," it signifies law itself insofar as this determines the direction of the will. As a law that commands, it sanctions only one course of action for the will. As a law that prohibits, it makes possible only the omission of an action. In both of these cases, the law prescribes a decision as necessary. On the other hand, the law may sanction both an action and its omission, leaving the decision to mere choice (the permissive law).

196. The given meaning of the term "right" encompasses both the internal or so-called right of conscience, as well as the external or so-called mere right. The latter is also called "right" without qualification.

197. Since all right is freedom of the will, external right must be different from internal right, just as the external freedom of the will must be different from the internal one. The latter is the faculty

---

1. Alluding to the wider use of *Recht*, Reinhold adds: "In an even broader sense, which is irrelevant here, this term designates everything reasonable, and thus right, occurring through or without freedom. Examples of this are the expressions: to make things right for somebody [*rechtmachen*], self-righteousness [*Rechthaberey*], and right spelling [*Rechtschreibung*]."

of a person to decide; the former is the faculty of a person to act externally on the basis of the internal faculty of freedom.

198. External freedom in itself is inseparable from internal freedom. No external free action is possible without a decision. The decision for an external act is only possible insofar as freedom provides the inner capacity to effect actions externally. However, one and the same external free act can be the result of entirely opposite internal directions of freedom. One and the same external act of the will may have either a moral or an immoral intention. Therefore, freedom as merely internal freedom, which is the basis of the intention, must be accurately distinguished from merely external freedom, which is the basis of an external deed.

199. External freedom, as freedom of the will, should not be confused, as it usually is, with a lack of external constraint, or the external freedom of the external human being. The latter consists in mere unconstraining external conditions. This freedom means the absence of external obstacles for the will, and is denied to it in the presence of obstacles. Freedom of the will, on the other hand, is a quality of the will. It is presupposed by the freedom from external constraint and cannot be annihilated by an external obstacle. Freedom of the will is a faculty of the will which is necessarily included in the concept of external right. It continues to be included in it, even if its exercise is inhibited by illegitimate coercion. Of course, freedom of the will is essentially different from the spontaneity of reason. To act rightfully is to act according to reason; to act wrongfully is to act in contradiction to it.

200. Since the will cannot effect an external act without a decision, its external action is subordinated to the moral law, which is the law of inner freedom. Insofar as external right and wrong consist of actions that conform to or contradict the moral law, they also represent internal right and wrong.

201. However, external right as such is essentially different from internal right. An action that one has an external right to perform may be prohibited by the moral law. Because of that, this action is not transformed into an external wrong. Under different circumstances, an action may be ordered by the moral law and still remain merely

an external right, left open to the exercise of choice. External right must be completely independent of the moral law. The law that is its basis, the juridical law,[2] must be essentially different from the moral law.

202. The essence of external right as such consists only in the external free action of a person who has the right to perform that action. For this person, external right can only be conceived of relative to the external freedom of other persons. The person's action can be legitimate only if it is compatible with the external freedom of any other person. External right leaves it up to the person's choice whether an action is performed. The right to perform makes the action merely permissible. The law that is the basis for external right consists of the following claim of reason: that every person restrict his external free action in such a way that it is compatible with the external action of any other person.

203. Therefore, the juridical law by no means concerns all actions of the will as the moral law does. It concerns only external action, so far as the latter is related to the external actions of others. Juridical law does not prescribe the intention of an act of volition, only its external direction. It does not demand, as the moral law does, the performance or omission of an act. It only requires that the act possess the form of compatibility of one's freedom with everybody else's freedom. It leaves to the discretion of the will whether to perform or not to perform what is compatible with everybody's freedom. Finally, the juridical law requires that the will conform to that external form of compatibility under a specific condition. This condition consists of the fact that a person lives together with other persons and wants to be treated by them as a person, that is, as a free being. The moral law, on the other hand, commands such compatibility unconditionally.

204. The force that one person uses is called aggressive when it is directed against another person's action that is compatible with the

---

2. Kant calls those laws that concern legality (*Legalität*) *juridisch*. I translated Reinhold's term *Rechtsgesetz* as 'juridical law,' thereby staying close to Kantian terminology.

external freedom of all other persons. This force is wrong without exception. The force that counteracts an aggressive force is called defensive. It does not negate the compatibility of the external freedom of persons, but protects it. This form of coercion is permitted by juridical law. As a particular right, called the right of coercion, it is inseparably connected to every right in general, that is, to every action of a person which is not wrong.

205. Personality in its characteristic external faculty, that is, the external freedom of the will of a rational individual, is the original source of all rights. The essence of the conditions on which the exercise of external freedom depends makes up original right. These conditions follow immediately from the character of personality. A person cannot be denied their employment without turning him into a mere thing.

206. Insofar as original right is external right, it accrues to a person on the grounds that, and only insofar as, the person exists in the world through his living body. Original right consists in the right of the person to act through his body on other things and have these other things act on him by way of his body. The elements of original right are inseparable and, therefore, taken together, make up only one single original right. They are: the right to be left alone by other persons, and the right to use things as means.

207. Original right is grounded in the personality and must be granted to every person by every other person. It is unconditional, inalienable, and incapable of being lost. Since it belongs to every person, it is due every individual only insofar as this individual grants it to every other person. The original right of every person is necessarily limited by that of every other person. It is limited in the individual by his behavior toward others. Through the mere social life of several persons, original right is in many ways restricted in its execution. Hence it is, as mere original right, impossible in reality.

208. The free external effectiveness of a person is a right only insofar as the person limits himself to that which is compatible with the free effectiveness of all other persons. Juridical law makes such self-restraint binding for everybody under the condition that everybody else subjects himself to the same self-restraint. External

right remains uncertain and undecided in its existence, as long as persons do not realize that they mutually impose this self-restraint on each other. The reality of right thus depends on its being mutually recognized, through a recognition that is clearly and distinctly stipulated (declared). This mutually stipulated recognition of right is called the original contract. It represents the essential condition of the reality of external right. Through original right, every person is entitled to force all other persons who enter its physical sphere of action and wish to stay there to recognize this contract.

209. The will of a person to exclude others from the use of a thing is called possession. It must be connected to the external capability to enforce this will. If a person has the right to possess a thing, this thing is owned. According to (only theoretically) unlimited original right, all and only that which I possess is mine.[3] According to original right, which is necessarily limited by the social life of persons, only and all of that which I have the right to possess is mine, regardless of whether I possess it or not.

210. Like right in general, the right of ownership can only become real through its explicit, mutually declared recognition. This is called the contract of ownership. As soon as ownership is publicly acknowledged, original right is recognized in its mutually inseparable elements, and the entire original contract is enacted.

211. The original contract can realize right only insofar as it is fulfilled. If it did not have a guarantee of its fulfillment which is independent of mere right and good faith, it would presuppose the reality of right which should be its result. Such a guarantee can only be conceived in an external institution. The latter should be arranged in such a way that the same self-love that entices the will to break the contract deters it from doing so. In such an arrangement, every person who hurts another person would hurt himself at the same time. So far as this institution evenly and always imposes a legitimate compulsion against every action that is illegitimate, it is called coercive law. As such, it belongs to the necessary conditions of the reality of right.

3. That is, is owned.

212. Coercive law can secure the fulfillment of the original contract only if the contract is actually and rightfully applied. If this application were left to the parties themselves—to those who have been violated and in whose favor the coercive law is enacted, or to the violators against whom it has been enacted—then its reality and rightfulness would be equally uncertain. The guarantee presupposed in the application of coercive law can only consist in the affected parties' renunciation of applying it. A strict standard must be laid down, by which the actual and rightful application of the coercive law is determined uniformly for everybody at all times. This is called positive law, and belongs to the necessary conditions of the reality of right.

213. There is no natural law[4] that is independent of the condition of positive law and at the same time substantially different from the right of conscience. Positive law, which is one of the necessary conditions of the sole form of natural law that is possible, can only be conceived of as a well-established rule for judging rightful conduct. It can only be the application of juridical law to certain objects, hence the rightful will of anyone who lives among others.

214. Positive law can secure rightful coercion, and through that right in general, only insofar as subjection to it and its enactment are guaranteed. Therefore, there has to be a guarantee for this subjection and enactment which is different from positive law, but inseparable from it. On the one hand, this guarantee must be in accordance with the rightful will of everybody; on the other, it has to be superior to the wrongful will of everybody. It can only consist in a combination of the physical force of all individuals into a superior power that is rightfully compulsory and linked to positive laws. This union is called the rightful commonwealth. It belongs to the necessary conditions for the reality of right.

215. That condition is called the rightful condition which externally enables every person to exercise his rights and makes it externally impossible for any person to commit wrong. In this state,

---

4. 'Natural law' is the customary translation of *Naturrecht*. Otherwise, I translate *Recht* as 'right.'

external right as such takes place in reality. It is only possible in and through the commonwealth. Thus, the so-called state of nature, the state outside the commonwealth, is only conceivable as being without rights and wrongful.

216. The rightful will of everybody dictates that everybody be treated rightfully, hence that an institution exist through which right can act powerfully and power is exercised rightfully. This will is actualized in reality as the general will by persons who live in society and externally recognize the right to ownership. Whoever joins these persons thereby assents to the general will.

Nevertheless, the will of anybody who decides to live with others may be merely selfish (one cannot presume otherwise with regard to an institution that is supposed to assert right through compulsion). Even then, the selfish will has external rights only insofar as it acknowledges them for others, too. It can only assert its own rights, as it recognizes those of others, if it simultaneously aspires to live in a society as a free being together with other free beings. If the will declares its willingness for such coexistence, it thereby declares its willingness to recognize the rights of others. The rightful general will is not a mere idea, but takes place in reality. Everybody who lives in a commonwealth thereby sufficiently demonstrates this will. The rightful general will is the real foundation of any rightful commonwealth.

217. In regard to this rightful general will, one can disregard the intentions of someone who wants to or is supposed to live with others socially. One can also disregard the intention to uphold right because it is right, as it is prescribed by the moral law. The latter intention would make up a moral general will, if it were presupposed as present in everyone. This will cannot be the basis of a commonwealth maintaining right through compulsion. On the contrary, it would render such a commonwealth superfluous.

218. For the decision to found and maintain a commonwealth, the rightful general will receives 1) everybody's promise to everybody else to contribute to the existence of the rightfully coercive superior power; 2) everybody's promise to everybody else to exercise this superior power rightfully. These mutual promises constitute the civil contract.

219. The general will that makes this contract contains the following three conclusions. They are the essential conditions for the civil contract and as such make up the fundamental laws.

The general will concludes first that everyone's freedom be protected by the power of all in regard to everything that is compatible with the freedom of everybody in the commonwealth. This is the fundamental law of civil freedom, which is distinguished from so-called natural freedom, since the latter, under certain circumstances, can act wrongfully. Under different circumstances, it may not even be able to act rightfully. Civil freedom under any circumstances can only act rightfully.

The general will concludes second that everyone's freedom be limited by the power of all to that which is compatible with everyone's freedom in the commonwealth. This is the fundamental law of civil subjection. Subjection concerns not just the limitation of everybody's freedom through that of everybody else (with the help of civil laws). It also means that subjection is required as a contribution to the application of the laws.

The general will concludes third that the freedom of each individual, as a member of the commonwealth, be simultaneously protected and limited by the power of all. This is the fundamental law of civil equality. By virtue of this equality, there cannot be persons who are suppressed by the law, or persons who are favored (privileged) by it in a rightful state.

220. The wrongful private will attempts to enforce its own freedom against the freedom of others. It therefore lays down the following maxims, which are contradictory to the principles of the commonwealth. According to certain external circumstances, it wishes:

1) that everybody's freedom be limited by the superior power of a single or a few persons (principle of political oppression).

2) that everybody's freedom be limited by everybody's superior power (principle of political anarchy).

3) that the freedom of many people be limited by the superior power of a few, or the freedom of a few by the superior power of many (principle of political inequality, which manifests itself either in privileged classes or in the rule of the mob [sansculotism]).

221. The means for securing the ultimate end of the commonwealth, that is, for securing right, make use of irresistible power. They consist in the positive laws, the physical forces of the individuals united in a single power, and the connection of this power to the positive laws. Only through this connection does the rightful general will, manifested in the positive laws, become power, and the united power of all secure right. This rightful power, conceived as an effective capacity, is called the supreme authority. It can only be thought of as belonging to[5] the commonwealth.

222. This supreme authority cannot be exercised by all, irrespective of how small the commonwealth may be. This is evident because, if it were otherwise, it would have to be in the hands of those for whom as well as those against whom it ought to be enacted. Unanimity of thought and harmony in attitudes are necessary for determining the method of exercising authority. Without these, this authority would never be effective. The more people are in the commonwealth, however, the less likely will unanimity and harmony be achieved. A supreme authority, therefore, is only conceivable for the general will if the will chooses to have it administered through representation.

223. For its rightful reality, representation presupposes the promise of those to whom it has been entrusted to accept it and to exercise it for the ultimate end of the commonwealth. The others have to promise to subject themselves to the representatives. This mutual promise is called the contract of subjection. It is part of the necessary conditions for the reality of right. Only through this contract can the commonwealth be conceived as a state, as a society that is autonomous through power and right.

224. Because there is no authority that is superior to the supreme authority, either within the state or outside of it, the predicate of sovereignty accrues to the supreme authority. So far as it has the right to enact and reject laws, to compel and not to be compelled, it possesses the predicate of majesty. The rightful general will can exercise the supreme authority only through representation. Therefore,

5. Literally: "being owned" (*Eigentum*).

the above-mentioned predicates belong solely to such representation. Individual administrators possess them according to their position. However, all other members of the commonwealth, taken together, do not participate in those predicates. Since they do not possess a general will for the exercise of the supreme authority, they subject themselves to the representatives.

225. With regard to the civil original contract, which is the basis of the state as the commonwealth, each individual participates in the rightful general will, is a member of the commonwealth—a citizen—and in this capacity equal to everybody else in the state. However, with regard to the contract of subjection, which underlies the commonwealth as state, the citizens are essentially unequal as commanding and obeying ones. The ones who administer the supreme authority are authorities and magistrates; the others who are subjected to the supreme authority are subjects and private persons. All members of the commonwealth, including authorities and magistrates, make up the nation. By excluding authorities and magistrates, they make up the people.

226. The particular manner in which the power of the commonwealth is bound to positive laws is called a civil constitution. A civil constitution that is determined through rightful laws is called the Constitution.[6]

227. If right, with the help of power, is to be realized in a commonwealth, then the supreme authority in its entirety must be transferred to the representatives of the general will. Without that, no unity of the power of all, no irresistible power, could exist. But the exercise of this authority should be split up, so that the individual administrator would exercise it only in parts. This would prevent the authority from falling prey to its administrators' arbitrariness and from being abused. Superior power is only conceivable as external right if it guarantees everybody's rights. It forfeits this character when it endangers

6. In German, there exist two different terms for "constitution," *Verfassung* and *Constitution.* In order to render Reinhold's distinction between *Staatsverfassung* and *Constitution,* I translate the former as 'civil constitution' and the latter as 'Constitution.'

everybody's rights. Rightful superior power must be organized to secure everybody's right against any despotic exercise of the power of all people, as well as against the violence of any single individual.

228. The supreme authority is only conceivable as an autonomous union of power and right, insofar as it exercises this power without limitation from outside. Therefore, the representatives of the supreme authority must distribute its administration among themselves, so that only in their union can they employ the irresistible power of the rightful general will. In isolation, however, they should be incapable of applying the power of all to oppress anyone.

229. Without the distribution just described, supreme authority becomes merely the private will of its administrator—whether it rests undivided in the hands of several administrators, or just one. Such an administrator is not subject to the juridical laws, which would limit him externally. He is bound to the ultimate end of the state by nothing but his conscience. The state then ceases to be a commonwealth (*Respublica*) and becomes a possession (*Res privata*) of the despot, who is not the head of state, but becomes its master. Everything he orders to its disadvantage is his right, and anything beneficial he orders is a sign of his mercy. The commonwealth ceases to be a state by becoming a patchwork held together by a changeable despotic will and by chance and not a thoroughly lawful whole existing through itself. This civil constitution is called despotic.

230. A supreme authority that limits itself is divided into the right to determine the civil constitution of the commonwealth through laws—the constitutive supreme authority—and into the right to administer the commonwealth according to its legal constitution—the constituted supreme authority. Both authorities make up a rightful whole on the condition that they exclude each other. The constituted supreme authority has no right to change the Constitution. And the constitutive authority ceases to exist when the Constitution is completed; it only assumes its rights when something in the Constitution must be changed.

231. The right to administer the state according to its legal civil constitution—the constituted supreme authority—is divided into the following parts:

the right to determine the application of the Constitution through general precepts that are eternally valid—the constituted legislative authority;

the right to apply the physical power of the state according to the laws by issuing commands (precepts for particular cases)—the executive authority;

and the right to apply legal punishments, intended for the transgression of laws, to particular cases through judgments—the judicial authority.

232. The way in which the constituted supreme authority is administered in accordance with the civil constitution is called the form of government. It is either monarchical, if it is headed by a single individual, inherited or elected. Or it is aristocratic, if it is administered by several persons from certain estates. Or it is democratic, if it is administrated by several persons who have been elected by the citizens for a certain period of time. The form of government is republican if the legislative and executive authorities are constituted independently of each other. It is mixed if the laws proposed by the legislative body need the sanction of the executive authority. It is a monarchical republic if the administrator of the executive authority who also sanctions the laws is a single individual. Which of these forms of government is legitimate depends on its suitableness under given circumstances. It cannot be determined through the mere concept of right.

233. The science that determines the legitimacy of the institution of a commonwealth, constitutional law, must be distinguished from statesmanship (politics), the science of the suitableness of this institution. Since the ultimate end of the state lies in nothing but external right, statesmanship can only consist of knowledge about the general and particular external conditions that are required for instituting a commonwealth. It also consists in applying the principles of constitutional law to those conditions. Otherwise, it becomes the destructive as well as despicable art of justifying and maintaining despotism.

234. The most general external condition for building a commonwealth consists in relating selfishness to the rightful institution. If the commonwealth is to exercise right through power, it

must bind the individual to the rightful institution through that individual's personal advantage. Because of this, selfishness is the most general political incentive. It must be used effectively for the advantage of right by the prudence and power of the administrators of the state.

235. The rightful foundation of the state has to be distinguished from the political foundation, and both have to be distinguished from the historical one. The rightful foundation is the civil contract produced by the general will. The political foundation consists of selfishness, prudence, and power. The historical foundation rests partly with the public conviction that a rightfully coercive superior power is indispensable. It is constituted in part by the inability of the weak and the thirst for power of the strong, and in part by accidental events, wars, peace treaties, revolutions, and so forth.

236. A civil constitution can neither evolve rightfully nor last politically if it guarantees the right of the individual only through the arbitrary employment that can be made of the united power of all. The despotism of such a civil constitution, be it monarchical, aristocratic, or democratic, is sanctioned by the rightful general will only if it fulfills the following conditions:—It must be limited by the same external circumstances, habits, and customs through which it evolved at least to the extent that it protects the lives of the greater part of a people and what they own;—it must offer the external condition for the gradual transition from the state of savageness through barbarity to political and moral culture;—and through the destruction of such a despotic constitution, all the security of right would have to be negated which had prevailed through it at least to a certain degree. The rightful general will can want only rightful reformation, not violent revolution.

237. A civil constitution is only perfect, that is, generally purposeful and legitimate, insofar as it enables the private will of the administrators of the supreme authority to do all, and only that, which can be the object of the rightful general will. Nothing but the law should be superior to the magisterial power, and it should only be capable of acting legally. The attempt to continuously bring actually existing civil constitutions closer to this perfection is a duty

of conscience, but it is also, of necessity, brought about and initiated by mere natural disposition.

238. The self-love of the subjects continuously counteracts the external limitations imposed upon it by the magisterial authority. And the self-love of the rulers counteracts the external limitations that the interest of their subjects inflicts on the rulers' power. Both represent in every real civil constitution ineradicable seeds—one of anarchy, the other of despotism. Only insofar as each limits the other in their opposing expressions, they make up a politically necessary condition for the civil constitution and administration to be equally far removed from anarchy and despotism. They help in founding the continuing development toward a completely rightful form of commonwealth.

239. By confusing the merely rightful foundation with the political one and vice versa, the contradiction in the principles of constitutional law is initiated and sustained. Thus, the tendencies of despotism and anarchy are favored even by well-meaning leaders of public conviction (unbeknownst to them and involuntarily). By favoring despotism and anarchy, they sanction the manners of thought which in modern times conflict with each other under the titles of aristocratic and democratic parties.

240. The so-called democrats lose sight of all the civil conditions that cannot be derived from the abstract concept of humanness. Their concept of humanness is indeterminate and incorrect. The aristocrats, on the other hand, neglect specific essential characteristics of human nature in favor of political modifications of the three estates. The democrats do not wish to recognize the citizen in terms of anything else but what he brings with him into this world, that is, independent of the external circumstances under which he is born. The aristocrats by no means want to acknowledge anything but what a human being has actually become through external circumstances, education, descent, custom, and the existing civil constitution. The democrats restrict the rank of humankind to the people. The aristocrats place the noble estate above the rank of humankind, and degrade the common person by placing him below that rank.

241. Well-meaning politicians and leaders of public opinion pro-mote many destructive measures in the mistaken belief that the well-being of all—general happiness—or morally good conduct, or both at the same time, are the ultimate end of the state. However, the state is and can only be the realization of mere external right. The development of external wealth as well as morality itself must be subordinated as means by the administrators of the state. Morality and happiness can be promoted by legislators and rulers only insofar as they support external right.

242. External right, and therefore the external freedom of all, is the ultimate end of the state and of the politically legitimate activity of its leaders. However, for the teaching profession, and for the ethically legitimate activity of scholars and writers, external freedom is not an ultimate end for moral cultivation, but only a means for the ultimate end of morality. That kind of enlightenment which knows, praises, and intends nothing but external freedom, is as contrary to reason and as ruinous as that kind of politics which attempts to foster internal freedom through wrongful restrictions on external freedom.

Part XIII

Some principles and maxims of religious enlightenment

243. Through internal freedom of the will, a human being is conscious of his superiority over mere nature, and thus also of the independence of his fate from nature. He acknowledges as unconditional and irresistible only those limitations on his will and that direction of his fate which are imposed on him by a being that possesses more power than himself over nature. To acknowledge the legislation and guidance of a (higher, supernatural) being distinct from nature has always been called religion.

244. Acknowledgment of the limitations on the will and of the direction of fate by an irresistible natural necessity, which governs absolutely, contradicts all freedom of the will in general. It is called irreligion.

245. To recognize the limitations on the will and of the direction of fate by the mere (arational) choice of a being distinct from nature is called false religion. It contradicts the freedom of the will in its obligation to act according to its own convictions—an obligation imposed on it by reason. Hence, such a view contradicts it in the exercise of its moral faculty.

246. Recognition of the limitations on the will and of the guidance of fate by the will of a being distinct from nature which creates and rules nature according to the law of rational freedom is called true, genuine religion. It only contradicts the decision of a human being to act contrary to its own convictions; hence, it contradicts the exercise of his immoral faculty.

247. We call a natural effect that which happens owing to a necessity that is conditional, lawful,[1] and identifiable. The sum of things

---

1. A consistent translation would have 'legal', since Reinhold uses *gesetzlich*. But 'lawful' makes more sense in the context of natural necessity.

that are natural effects by virtue of their qualities and occurrences is called the physical world. Every final cause of a natural occurrence and quality can be discovered by natural research. Since every cause must itself be the natural effect of another natural cause, nature is infinitely comprehensible. Only as a whole is it incomprehensible.

248. Unconditional necessity, since it contradicts all freedom, would be blind fate (*Fatum*), regardless of whether it is conceived as a cause or as the inner essence of nature. Therefore, it is incomprehensible, since it consists of something self-contradictory, which cannot be thought.

249. As the final cause of all conditional necessity, unconditional freedom is incomprehensible only because it is absolutely presupposed by everything comprehensible. It is called God insofar as it is deemed to be the cause of nature, from which it is different. In this respect, it acts necessarily in conformity with reason. Its action is considered to be the activity of a will.

250. To find such a cause of the world to be necessary, that is, to be convinced of the existence of God, is called the fundamental truth of religion. Among those convictions that directly belong to religion, it does not presuppose any other conviction but is presupposed by all others.

251. This fundamental truth has never been doubted by common, sound understanding. However, philosophizing reason has contradicted itself in disputes among its past advocates. The disagreement of the disputing parties is represented in the following assumptions:

1) The existence of God can be known through rational insight. (Chief proposition of naturalistic theists.)

2) The existence of God can only be believed through supernatural revelation. (Chief proposition of supernaturalistic theists.)

3) The nonexistence of God can be known through rational insight. (Chief proposition of dogmatic atheists.)

4) No verifiable conviction, either of the existence or the nonexistence of God, is possible. (Chief proposition of skeptical atheists.)

252. It cannot escape the attention of merely natural reason, which belongs to none of the parties, that each of these chief propositions is accepted by only one of the four parties. The other three reject it. On

the other hand, the contrary assumptions to those four propositions are held to be true by each of the three parties against the one holding it. The contrary assumptions are:

1) No conviction of the existence of God is possible through knowledge.

2) Neither is such a conviction possible through revelation.

3) Neither philosophical knowledge nor historical belief concerning the nonexistence of God is possible.

4) Nevertheless, an answer concerning the question of God's existence which satisfies reason is possible.

253. The claims contained in the above contrary propositions must pertain to any conviction of natural reason regarding the existence of God. Its content has to be verified by philosophizing reason, which is internally coherent. However, such a natural conviction must not presuppose philosophy or scholarliness, nor revelation.

254. The only employment of reason in which this conviction can be grounded must be transcendent, because it has a supernatural subject. At the same time, it must not be artificial (philosophical, metaphysical), but has to be based on the nature of reason itself. It should be no less accessible to the nonphilosopher than to the philosopher.

255. This transcendent employment of reason, which is natural for human beings, is that which mere reason imposes upon the freedom of the will in prescribing the moral law to it. Freedom ought to use reason transcendently by complying with the law. This transcendent employment of reason immediately makes itself known to self-consciousness in and through conscience.

256. This employment of reason is self-evident for conscience insofar as its conviction is not obscured by affected manners of thought or impure attitudes. It is called practical in the terminology of the newest philosophical school.[2] This school claims that the practical employment of reason is misunderstood in the systematic concepts of the four above-mentioned parties. Such misunderstanding is pre-

---

2. Kant's critical philosophy.

sumed to be the reason for the past discord of philosophizing reason with itself, as well as with natural reason, about the fundamental truth of religion.

257. The way conscience establishes that fundamental truth seems to be comprehensible for natural reason in the following manner.

258. Conscience requires us absolutely to assert that the moral law is the sole and universal incentive and rule of all free actions. The essence of the moral law consists in the unconditional necessity of fulfilling this requirement. The fulfillment of the moral law consists in the decision that all free actions shall be performed in conformity with the moral law, in the serious resolution to solely let the law rule over us, and in the honest attempt to carry out this intention. That resolution, combined with the attempt to carry it out, is called holiness in attitude. Without it, no inner righteousness of the deed is conceivable. Whoever does not accept the moral law as his sole guiding principle for all free actions, whoever excludes even one action from his moral decision, has not accepted the moral law at all as a guiding principle. He uses it only as a mask for the satisfaction of his appetites, which then conform to the law only externally and by accident.

259. Resolution and aspiration are absolutely necessary through reason, and possible through the inner freedom of the will. This is as certain as the moral law itself, because that law consists in that absolute necessity; without it such freedom is inconceivable. Conscience itself is nothing but the immediate certainty of this necessity and this freedom. Only through that inner freedom—which belongs to us and is therefore a faculty of finite beings—can we begin to understand the decision to act morally. And only through that inner freedom is the attempt to carry out the moral decision comprehensible—insofar as it depends on that decision. The decision and the attempt to carry it out thus make up the inner possibility of fulfilling the law. The external possibility of that aspiration depends not only on our freedom but, since it is external, also on the nature of things. Therefore it relies upon all of physical nature and the character of its objects to help external freedom of the will attain its aspiration by providing it with the required resources.

260. Fulfilling the moral law through a conviction based on the cognition[3] of nature, that is, through knowledge, presupposes cognition of the whole of physical nature and of the inner essence of its parts. Neither philosophizing, nor natural reason, has ever doubted that this cognition is impossible through the merely natural employment of reason. The conviction by natural reason that it is externally possible to fulfill the law is possible not by cognition but only as mere faith.

261. It has been demonstrated by the above-mentioned new school that such cognition is precluded for philosophizing reason, too. This school has discovered the misunderstanding that has caused lengthy quarrels to take place, partly between the sects of dogmatic philosophy about the alleged reality of such a cognition, and partly between dogmatists and skeptics about the verifiability of all cognition in general.

262. The external possibility of fulfilling the moral law, just like the internal possibility, cannot be the subject of natural or philosophical knowledge. Conscience takes it to be true only because, and as far as, it is presupposed by the inner necessity of the moral law. The external possibility is neither comprehended nor comprehensible; it is taken to be certain merely through the infallible guarantee of the moral law. That means that conscience believes in it.

263. The external possibility of fulfilling the moral law, which conscience takes to be certain, can only be conceived as certain and as well established in itself under certain conditions, since it is merely external to and independent of the will of persons. It must be assumed to be a necessary consequence of the organization and constitution of nature. This nature is, on the one hand, independent of that will; on the other hand, it necessarily conforms to the

---

3. Throughout this work, I translate the terms *Erkenntnis* and *Wissen* both as 'knowledge'. However, in this and the next article, Reinhold distinguishes between *Erkenntnis* as the process of knowing and *Wissen* as the result of this process. Thus, I translate *Wissen* as 'knowledge' and *Erkenntnis* as 'cognition'. I do not translate *Erkenntnis* as 'cognition' elsewhere because the customary rendering is 'knowledge' as in 'faculty of knowledge' (*Erkenntnisvermögen*).

moral law. It is conceivable only as possessing the character of an instrument of morality.

264. This character necessarily accrues to nature only insofar as it is conceived to be the effect of a cause that is infinite and free, and one that intends the fulfillment of the moral law as an ultimate end through nature. This cause is called omnipotent, since all of nature depends on its effects, and holy, since it acts according to the moral law (which is its form). Conscience believes nature to be the work of God.

265. This belief, laid down in the inner sanctuary of conscience, is aroused, enlivened, and affirmed from outside through the perception of the purposiveness of physical nature in its large and small appearances. This purposiveness, which is perceived externally, only suggests an ultimate end in general without being able to identify it. It is related to the ultimate end announced through conscience. And together, they make up the complete argument establishing the existence of God.

266. The complete and, as such, absolutely necessary fulfillment of the moral law presupposes the perfect development of the faculties of knowledge and desire in order to guarantee the complete execution of the moral decision. Thus, it presupposes a degree of enlightenment of the understanding and of discipline of the appetites which in a free finite being can only be conceived in terms of an infinite progress. Hence, this is only comprehensible in the infinite continuity of the personality of this free being.

267. To be convinced through knowledge of this continuity, the cognition of the difference and interconnectedness of the inner essences of soul and body would be necessary. This cognition is impossible for natural reason—in its own judgment as well as in the judgment of philosophizing reason, which is coherent in claiming this inability of natural reason.

268. The above-mentioned school has acknowledged that this cognition is impossible for philosophizing reason as well. After the lengthy, futile efforts of philosophizing reason to achieve this cognition, the school has discovered the misunderstanding that lies at the bottom of such efforts.

269. The immortality of the soul, as well as its mortality, is not the subject of possible knowledge, be it natural or artificial. Conscience takes it to be true because, and insofar as, it is presupposed by the inner necessity of the complete fulfillment of the moral law. The immortality of the soul is assumed, that is, believed without being comprehended and comprehensible in itself because of the mere but infallible guarantee of the moral law.

270. The belief in immortality is supported by belief in God. For God is thought of as the being that has brought into existence the persons and things necessary for the fulfillment of the moral law. Through His omnipotence He has the faculty, and through His holiness the will, to grant to finite free beings the infinite continuity that is needed to fulfill this ultimate end.

271. This conviction, founded in the inner sanctuary of conscience, is awakened, enlivened, and confirmed externally through the appearances of the unethical, especially in the imperfect state of public (civil and religious) institutions, which have been set up by human beings for the sake of rightfulness and morality. For that state shows to conscience, which is convinced of the inner necessity of the moral law, that the destiny of humankind is not completely realized on this side of the grave.

272. Therefore, the conviction of the existence of God and of immortality does not constitute knowledge, since it is grounded neither in historical nor in reasoned cognition of its objects. However, it is not mere opinion either, which means it does not take something to be true for reasons that are preponderant but not complete. Sufficient reason for the conviction is given completely in and through conscience. It provides a basis not for cognition, but for belief. That means that it is a conviction that assumes that the reality of its object is absolutely certain without knowing it through insight.

273. Owing to its inner essence, the degree of this conviction can only conform to the determinate precision and correctness of the ethical concepts, and to the purity and vitality of the ethical feelings.

274. The acknowledgment of the moral, therefore supernatural, creator of the world consists partly in conviction (theoretical religion), and partly in attitude (practical religion). Attitude by all

means presupposes conviction. As religiosity, attitude can be distinguished from conviction or religion, insofar as the will is capable of acting contrary to its own conviction. Religion, on the other hand, turns into false religion or irreligion, if it is not supported by true religiosity.

275. The essence of religion as a conviction consists in the belief that the moral law is the ultimate end of the universe, expressing the will of the creator of the world. On the other hand, the essence of religiosity, or of the attitude suitable for religion, rests in the decision and the attempt through our actions to assert as universally valid the moral law as God's will. In and through our free actions such an attitude expresses enduring respect for God.

276. The essence of religiosity is concerned partly with God's holiness and partly His omnipotence. The former attitude rests in freely respecting the will of the Almighty, which consists in the moral law and therefore is holy. The latter is based upon the fear and hope in regard to the will of the Holy, which decides our well-being in light of our good conduct, and our fate according to our worthiness.

277. Respect for God is only conceivable through respect for the moral law. The moral law is by no means respected because it is the will of the Almighty. On the contrary, the Almighty is respected only because He Himself is the moral law, and thus holy. Therefore, reverence and love of God are only possible as the reverence and love of the law as His will. Whoever observes the law loves God.

278. Fear and hope regarding the Almighty represent religiosity only insofar as they are necessary consequences of the respect for the law, and not arbitrary effects of self-love. They necessarily follow from that respect as far as it requires and expects from the omnipotence of the Holy that the fate of a finite free being will be determined by the moral employment of its freedom.

279. Moral (naive) fear and hope, which follow from this conviction and attitude, have to be distinguished from amoral (slavish) fear and hope, which are unconnected to that conviction and attitude. Moral fear and hope by no means limit the moral employment of freedom of the will. On the contrary, they secure it along with careful reflection, which is indispensable for freedom. Moral fear and hope

suppress the excess of involuntary appetites and mitigate the fear and hope of finiteness through the fear and hope of the eternal.

280. The consciousness of the moral law and the moral decision are vitalized through respect for the Holy, that is, by representing the moral law as realized in God's will. And in cases when the conviction of the possibility of fulfilling one's duty is obscured by particular difficulties, then the respect for the Holy will elucidate that conviction.

281. Since the conviction characteristic of religion is best called faith, the lack of such conviction is called unbelief, and its faultiness, superstition.

282. Complete lack of religious conviction is either positive unbelief or negative unbelief. Positive unbelief is related to being persuaded of the nonexistence of God and of the mortality of the soul. Negative unbelief occurs without being thus persuaded.

One is in a state of negative unbelief either because one cannot come to a conclusion by oneself about the grounds of religious conviction (skeptical unbelief), or because one does not know those grounds at all. The latter is the case either of ignorance owing to a state of crude savageness for which one is not guilty, or of ignorance owing to a state of an immoral life of pleasure for which one is guilty.

283. The attitude of unbelief—irreligiosity—is positive insofar as it explicitly excludes consideration of God from moral decision-making. It does so either from immorality, if it does not acknowledge any incentive of the will apart from reasoned self-love. Or it does so out of morality, incorrectly assuming that the consideration of God is not compatible with the purity of the moral decision. The attitude of unbelief is negative insofar as it simply does not consider God in its moral decision-making, but it does not explicitly and voluntarily exclude this consideration.

284. The delusion of superstition, which contradicts the truth of religious conviction, is positive if it more or less explicitly denies the holiness of God as the proper object of religion. It is negative if it loses sight of it without explicitly denying it.

285. The attitude of superstition is positive insofar as it attempts to please God through actions that contradict the moral law. It does so

out of mere fear and hope, and by excluding respect for holiness. It is negative insofar as its respect for holiness is involuntarily obscured and outweighed by fear and hope regarding God's omnipotence.

286. Religious conviction, as well as superstition and unbelief, is theoretical if it is grounded in a manner of thought. It is practical if it is initiated and supported by attitude. The theoretical principle of religion is conscience produced by the right concept of the moral law. The practical principle is conscientiousness produced by the moral decision. Similarly, the theoretical principle common to unbelief and superstition consists in an incorrect concept of the moral law; the practical principle consists in immorality.

287. In true religious conviction, God is distinguished from nature, just as freedom and the moral law are distinguished from natural necessity and mere natural laws. In the manner of thought of superstition and of unbelief, God is not distinguished from nature in this way. On the contrary, unbelief confuses Him with nature, and superstition sets Him in conflict with it.

288. The manners of thought of superstition and of unbelief both begin with equally wrong, yet mutually opposed concepts of freedom. Therefore, they are both prevented from arriving at the correct concept of the moral law. Evaluated in its most extreme consequence, superstition becomes supernaturalism when it is established in the form of a doctrine. Unbelief, in its most extreme consequence, becomes naturalism when thus developed. Supernaturalism views freedom of the human will as mere licentiousness and as merely the faculty to act immorally. Naturalism, on the other hand, looks at freedom as mere rationality and merely as the faculty to act morally. Each party grants the will only one half of that faculty that constitutes its real freedom according to the testimony of conscience.

289. Supernaturalists understand the freedom of our will as nothing but the capacity and inclination to act immorally. They usually think of it as an inherited propensity toward evil, which cannot be given up in a natural way. This makes it necessary for them to regard moral evil (sin) as the only capacity of the will acting on its own. In addition, they must look upon ignorance and error about everything that belongs to religion as the only capacities of human reason when

reason acts on its own. Therefore, they believe that a human being can only become capable of religious conviction and actions agreeable to God, if his freedom is transformed supernaturally. Likewise, religion can only be conceived of as a gift of revelation, and true morality as an effect of grace.

290. For the supernaturalists, the will of God is by no means a demand of mere reason which announces itself immediately through conscience and which reason imposes upon freedom. It is, on the contrary, a completely incomprehensible choice that is substantially different from that demand of reason. The demands of this arbitrary will imposed upon human beings are only recognizable through supernatural disclosures, only credible through miracles, and refer to many mysteries. Above all, they require blind faith and blind obedience. And as exercises of religion, they require that actions have no utility for the world in order to be worthy of God. Therefore, these actions must be performed out of supernatural inspirations and impulses. While those actions that occur out of respect for reason—the so-called virtues of the heathens—must be, if not vicious, then at least of no interest in the eyes of God.[4]

291. The naturalists mean by the freedom of our will nothing but the rationality of desire. Thus freedom is for them the mere absence of such obstacles that would render impossible the harmonious development of the faculty of desire and of intellectual power. Hence, the naturalists are forced to explicitly deny all freedom to immoral actions. They concede no other actions to freedom (what they call freedom) than those which they call moral, but which in their conception consist in mere expressions of reasoned desire. Natural necessity for them contains the final cause of everything that exists and occurs. Therefore, they regard as externally different effects of one and the same natural necessity both the involuntary balance of thoughts and appetites, which is for them morality, as well as the involuntary preponderance of the appetites over the thoughts, which is for them immorality.

---

4. Reinhold refers here to Wolff and others who had pointed to the virtuousness of the Chinese in order to present evidence for the possibility of morality without a revealed religion.

292. For the naturalists, the moral law is a manifestation of desire (a natural law), necessary under certain circumstances, and only valid for certain phenomena (the moral ones). It is not the demand of reason imposed upon freedom of the will that is different from the effectiveness of desire and of reason. The immoral phenomena are ruled by a different natural law, which, like the other law, is obeyed only when, and insofar as, it cannot be contravened.

293. Naturalists at most accept a deity that is a primordial being without inner freedom, one that does not act but only has some effects. This being only does that which it cannot refrain from doing, and does not do what it is incapable of doing. It is only active from and through mere natural necessity. The naturalists either attribute to this primordial being (theoretical) reason, which, as they know it, is the activity of mere representing. Or they deny reason to it, holding reason to be an exclusive property of human nature. In the former case they call that being God; in the latter case, infinite nature.

294. Naturalism confuses the deity with nature because it denies freedom of the will to the deity. Supernaturalism sets the deity in contradiction to nature because it denies rational activity to it. Both misjudge the deity because, and insofar as, they seek the idea and the convincing argument for God apart from the consciousness of freedom and of the law of the will, that is, apart from conscience.

295. Conscience consists in the immediate consciousness of this law and this freedom. This consciousness is independent of all philosophizing about freedom and the law of the will. For that reason, it can act effectively and independently when philosophizing reason errs or makes guiltless artificial errors. Conscientious naturalists and supernaturalists therefore, compelled by their moral feeling, attribute the characteristic of complete free rationality, that is, holiness, to the deity, which they theoretically misjudge. They borrow this characteristic from conscience, but their thinking about it is indistinct.

296. For that reason, the religion of conscientious naturalists and supernaturalists obtains that degree of subjective truth which is proportionate to the conscientiousness, vitality, and purity of their moral feeling. The objective falsity of their artificial systematic concepts is partly corrected, and partly made less harmful, through this subjec-

tive truth. If the subjectively true and objectively false religion of the supernaturalists is called supernatural religion, and that of the naturalists is called natural religion then, in contrast to them, the religion that is subjectively and objectively true must be called moral religion. Its feeling and concept are drawn from conscience.

297. This religion is in its essence a mere matter of conscience. As such, it is a conviction of mere natural reason, and is the exclusive possession of common sound understanding. Because of that, it is neither an artificial effect of philosophy, nor a supernatural effect of revelation. It is not a metaphysical doctrine, nor a political device. Nor is it a manner of thought which exclusively belongs either to any naturally privileged classes, or chosen ones of grace, or the rabble of all classes. This religion does not by any means establish morality; rather, it is established through the disposition to morality. Therefore, this religion can neither produce nor substitute for moral conviction, since it partly presupposes that conviction and partly completes it. It is nothing but the complete, consistent, moral conviction itself—the harmony of reason commanding absolutely through conscience, and deliberating within itself aided by the faculty of knowledge about the ultimate end of nature. It is the harmony of mind and heart founded through morality. And it is the mode of thought of humanity knowing itself, hence it is the mode of thought of the unanimous striving for moral enlightenment and discipline. Blessed are those whose hearts are pure, for they shall see God. (Matt. 5, 8.)

German-English Terms

allgemeingeltend	universally accepted as valid
allgemeingültig	universally valid
Anlage	disposition, capacity
Aufklärung	enlightenment
wahre	true
falsche	false
echte	genuine
unechte	spurious
äussere,-r	outer, external
äusserlich	outer, external
Begehren	desire
Begierde	appetite
bestimmt	determinate, definite
Bestimmung	destiny
Bewusstsein	consciousness
Bildung	education, self-cultivation
bürgerlich	civic
Constitution	constitution
Denkart	manner of thought
Eigentum	what is owned
Eigentumsrecht	right of ownership
Einsicht	insight
Endzweck	ultimate end
sich entschliessen	to decide
Erkenntnis	knowledge, cognition
Form	form, structure
Geist	spirit
gelehrt	learned, scholarly
Gelehrsamkeit	learning, scholarliness

Gemüt	mind
Gerechtigkeit	justice
Gesetz	law
Gesetz, moralisches	moral law
gesetzlich	legal
Gesetzlichkeit	legality
Gesetzlosigkeit	lawlessness
gesetzmässig	lawful
Gesetzmässigkeit	lawfulness
gesetzwidrig	unlawful
Gesinnung	attitude
Gesundheit (des Verstandes)	soundness
Gewissen	conscience
Gewissensrecht	right of conscience
Grundsatz	principle
Handlung	action, act
Humanität	humanity
Immoralität	the unethical
Inhalt	content
innere,-r	inner, internal
innerlich	inner, internal
Innerlichkeit	inwardness
Kenntnis	knowledge
Körper	physical form
künstlich	artificial
Lehrbegriff	systematic concept
Lehre	doctrine
Lehrgebäude	doctrinal edifice, doctrine
Lehrsatz	doctrinal claim
Lehrstück	doctrinal claim
Leib	body
Menschenverstand, gemeiner, gesunder, natürlicher	common sense

Menschheit	humankind, humanness
Menschlichkeit	humaneness
Moral	ethics
moralisch	ethical
Moralität	the ethical
Philosophem	philosophical thesis, claim
philosophieren	to philosophize
raisonnieren	to reason
Recht	right
natürliches Recht	natural law
Recht(e)	right(s)
rechtlich	rightful, juridical
rechtlicher Zustand	rightful state
Rechtlichkeit	rightfulness
rechtlos	lawless
rechtmässig	legitimate
Rechtmässigkeit	legitimacy
rechtschaffen	righteous
Rechtschaffenheit	righteousness
Rechtsgesetz	juridical law
Rechtslehre	jurisprudence
Reinheit	purity
Religiosität	religiosity
Richtigkeit	rightness, correctness
Schulbegriff	scholarly concept
schulgerecht	having a scholarly form
Selbstdenken	autonomous thought, independent thought
selbstisch	selfish
Selbsttätigkeit	spontaneous activity, spontaneity
Sitten	morals
Sittenlehre	moral philosophy

sittlich	moral
Sittlichkeit	morality
Staatsrecht	constitutional law
Staatsverfassung	civil constitution
System	system
Überzeugung	conviction
ungesetzlich	illegal
unmoralisch	unethical
Unmündigkeit	tutelage
Unrecht	wrong
unrechtmässig	illegitimate
unsittlich	immoral
Unwert	worthlessness, valuelessness
Urrecht	original right
Verfassung	(civil) constitution
verkünstelt	affected
Vermögen	faculty, power
Vernunftmässigkeit	reasonableness
Vernunftwidrigkeit	unreasonableness
Vormund	guardian
Wert	worth, value
widerrechtlich	wrongful
Willen	will
Willkür	choice
Wissen	knowledge
Zurechnung	accountability
Zwang	coercion, compulsion
Zwangsgesetz	coercive law
Zwangsrecht	right of coercion

English-German Terms

accountability	Zurechnung
action, act	Handlung
affected	verkünstelt
appetite	Begierde
attitude	Gesinnung
autonomous thought, independent thought	Selbstdenken
body	Leib
capacity	Anlage
choice	Willkür
civic	bürgerlich
civil constitution	Staatsverfassung
coercion, compulsion	Zwang
coercive law	Zwangsgesetz
cognition	Erkenntnis
common sense	gemeiner, gesunder, natürlicher, Menschenverstand
conscience	Gewissen
consciousness	Bewusstsein
constitution	Constitution
constitutional law	Staatsrecht
content	Inhalt
conviction	Überzeugung
correctness	Richtigkeit
cultivation	Kultur
to decide	sich entschliessen
definite	bestimmt
desire	Begehren

destiny	Bestimmung
determinate	bestimmt
disposition	Anlage
doctrinal claim	Lehrsatz, -stück
doctrinal edifice	Lehrgebäude
doctrine	Lehre
education	Bildung
enlightenment	Aufklarüng
true	wahre
false	falsche
genuine	echte
spurious	unechte
ethical	moralisch
the ethical	Moralität
ethics	Moral, Moralphilosophie
external	äussere,-r; äusserlich
faculty	Vermögen
form	Form
guardian	Vormund
humaneness	Menschlichkeit
humanity	Humanität
humankind	Menschheit
humanness	Menschheit
illegal	ungesetzlich
illegitimate	unrechtmässig
immoral	unsittlich
inner	innere,-r; innerlich
insight	Einsicht
internal	innere,-r; innerlich
inwardness	Innerlichkeit
juridical	rechtlich
jurisprudence	Rechtslehre
just	gerecht

justice	Gerechtigkeit
knowledge	Erkenntnis, Kenntnis, Wissen
law	Gesetz
lawful	gesetzmässig
lawfulness	Gesetzmässigkeit
lawless	gesetzlos
learned	gelehrt
learning	Gelehrsamkeit
legal	gesetzlich
legality	Gesetzlichkeit
legitimacy	Rechtmässigkeit
legitimate	rechtmässig
manner of thought	Denkart
mind	Gemüt
moral	sittlich
moral philosophy	Sittenlehre
morality	Sittlichkeit
morals	Sitten
natural law	natürliches Recht
original right	Urrecht
outer	äussere,-r; äusserlich
what is owned	Eigentum
philosophical thesis, claim	Philosophem
physical form	Körper
to philosophize	philosophieren
power	Gewalt, Vermögen
principle	Grundsatz
purity	Reinheit
to reason	raisonnieren
reasonable	vernunftmässig
religiosity	Religiosität
right	Recht
right(s)	Recht(e)

right of coercion	Zwangsrecht
right of conscience	Gewissensrecht
right of ownership	Eigentumsrecht
righteousness	Rechtschaffenheit
rightful	rechtlich
rightful state	rechtlicher Zustand
rightfulness	Rechtlichkeit
rightness	Richtigkeit
scholarliness	Gelehrsamkeit
scholarly	gelehrt
scholarly concept	Schulbegriff
having a scholarly form	schulgerecht
selfish	selbstisch
soundness	Gesundheit (des Verstandes)
spontaneity	Selbsttätigkeit
spontaneous activity	Selbsttätigkeit
structure	Form
system	System
systematic concept	Lehrbegriff
tutelage	Unmündigkeit
ultimate end	Endzweck
universally accepted as valid	allgemeingeltend
universally valid	allgemeingültig
unlawful	gesetzwidrig
unreasonable	vernunftwidrig
value	Wert
valuelessness	Unwert
will	Willen
worth	Wert
worthlessness	Unwert
wrong	Unrecht
wrongful	widerrechtlich

Bibliography

Works by Karl Leonhard Reinhold

Auswahl vermischter Schriften. 2 vols. Jena: Mauke, 1796, 1797.

Beyträge zur Berichtigung bisheriger Missverständnisse der Philosophen. 2 vols. Jena: Mauke, 1790, 1794.

Beyträge zur leichtern Uebersicht des Zustandes der Philosophie beym Anfange des 19. Jahrhunderts. Hamburg: Perthes, 1801–3.

Briefe über die Kantische Philosophie. 2 vols. Leipzig: Göschen, 1790, 1792. New edition by Raymund Schmidt, Leipzig: Reclam, 1923.

Ehrenrettung der Lutherischen Reformation gegen zwey Kapitel in des K. K. Hofraths Herrn J. M. Schmids Geschichte der Teutschen nebst einigen Bemerkungen über die gegenwärtige katholische Reformation im Oesterreichischen. Jena: Cuno's Erben, 1789 [1788, according to von Schönborn].

"Einige Bemerkungen über die in der Einleitung zu den metaphysischen Anfangsgründen der Rechtslehre von I. Kant aufgestellten Begriffe von der Freiheit des Willens." In his *Auswahl vermischter Schriften,* 2:364–400.

"Gedanken über Aufklärung." *Der Teutsche Merkur* 3 (July, August, and September 1784). Reprinted in K. L. Reinhold, *Schriften zur Religionskritik und Aufklärung 1782–1784,* 352–96.

Herzenserleichterung zweyer Menschenfreunde, in vertraulichen Briefen über Johann Casper Lavaters Glaubensbekentnis. Frankfurt and Leipzig: Weidmann, 1785.

Korrespondenz 1773–1788. Edited by Reinhard Lauth, Eberhard Heller, and Kurt Hiller. Stuttgart: Frommann-Holzboog, 1983.

"Revision des Buches: Enthüllung des Systemes der Weltbürger-Republik." *Der Teutsche Merkur* 2 (May 1786): 176–90.

Schriften zur Religionskritik und Aufklärung 1782–1784. Edited by Zwi Batscha. Bibliothek der Aufklärung 1. Bremen and Wolfenbüttel: Jacobi, 1977.

"Ueber das Fundament der moralischen Religion." In his *Beyträge zur Berichtigung bisheriger Missverständnisse der Philosophen,* 1:295–368.

Über das Fundament des philosophischen Wissens: Über die Möglichkeit der Philosophie als strenge Wissenschaft. Edited, with an introduction, by Wolfgang Schrader. Hamburg: Meiner, 1978.

"Ueber das Verhältniss der Theorie des Vorstellungsvermögens, zur Kritik der reinen Vernunft." In his *Beyträge zur Berichtigung bisheriger Missverständnisse der Philosophen*, 1:255–338.

"Ueber den philosophischen Skepticismus." Preface to *Untersuchungen über den menschlichen Verstand*, by David Hume. Translated by M. W. G. Tennemann. Jena: Verlag der akademischen Buchhandlung, 1793.

"Ueber die neuesten patriotischen Lieblingsträume in Teutschland: Aus Veranlassung des 3. und 4ten Bandes von Hrn. Nicolai's Reisebeschreibung." *Der Teutsche Merkur* 3 (August 1784). Reprinted in K. L. Reinhold, *Schriften zur Religionskritik und Aufklärung 1782–1784*, 406–40.

Ueber die Paradoxien der neuesten Philosophie. Hamburg: Perthes, 1799.

"Ueber die teutschen Beurtheilungen der französischen Revolution. Ein Sendschreiben an den Herrn Hofrath Wieland. Im Februar, 1793." In his *Auswahl vermischter Schriften*, 1:66–121.

Verhandlungen über die Grundbegriffe und Grundsätze der Moralität aus dem Gesichtspunkte des gemeinen und gesunden Verstandes, zum Behuf der Beurtheilung der sittlichen, rechtlichen, politischen und religiösen Angelegenheiten. Lübeck and Leipzig: Friedrich Bohn, 1798.

Versuch einer neuen Theorie des menschlichen Vorstellungsvermögens. Prague and Jena: Wiedtmann und Mauke, 1789. Photomechanical reproduction, Darmstadt: Wissenschaftliche Buchgesellschaft, 1963.

Works by Other Authors

Albrecht, Michael. "Thomasius—kein Eklektiker?" In *Christian Thomasius 1655–1728.* Edited by Werner Schneiders. Hamburg: Meiner, 1989.

Allison, Henry E. *The Kant-Eberhard Controversy: An English translation together with supplementary materials and a historical-analytic introduction of Immanuel Kant's "On a Discovery According to which Any New Critique of Pure Reason Has Been Made Superfluous by an Earlier One".* Baltimore: Johns Hopkins University Press, 1973.

———. *Kant's Theory of Freedom.* Cambridge: Cambridge University Press, 1990.

———. *Lessing and the Enlightenment: His Philosophy of Religion and Its Relation to Eighteenth-Century Thought.* Ann Arbor: University of Michigan Press, 1966.

Altmann, Alexander. "Aufklärung und Kultur: Zur geistigen Gestalt Moses Mendelssohns." In his *Die trostvolle Aufklärung. Studien zur Metaphysik und politischen Theorie Moses Mendelssohns*, 276–85. Stuttgart: Frommann-Holzboog, 1982.

Ameriks, Karl. "Kant's Deduction of Freedom and Morality." *Journal of the History of Philosophy* 19 (1981): 53–79.

Baggesen, A. H. "Reinholds Todtenfeier, den 5. August 1823: Ein maurerisches Denkmal." *Zeitschrift für Freimaurerei*, 1:95–112. Altenburg: Literatur-Comptoir, 1824, printed as a manuscript for brothers.

Barnard, Frederick M. "Rightful Decorum and Rational Accountability: A Forgotten Theory of Civil Life." In *Christian Thomasius 1655–1728*, edited by Werner Schneiders, 187–98. Hamburg: Meiner, 1989.

Batscha, Zwi. "Reinhold und die französische Revolution." *Jahrbuch des Instituts für Deutsche Geschichte* 2 (1973): 67–100. Edited, with an introduction, by Walter Grab. Forschungszentrum für Geschichte, University of Tel Aviv.

Beck, L. W. *A Commentary on Kant's Critique of Practical Reason.* Chicago: University of Chicago Press, 1960.

———. *Early German Philosophy: Kant and His Predecessors.* Cambridge: Belknap Press of Harvard University Press, 1969.

———. "The Fact of Reason: An Essay on Justification in Ethics." In his *Studies in the Philosophy of Kant*, 200–14. Indianapolis: Bobbs-Merrill, 1965.

————. "Kant's Strategy." In his *Essays on Kant and Hume*, 3–19. New Haven: Yale University Press, 1978.

————. "Toward a Meta-Critique of Pure Reason." In his *Essays on Kant and Hume*, 20–37. New Haven: Yale University Press, 1978.

Becker, Carl L. *The Heavenly City of the Eighteenth-Century Philosophers*. New Haven: Yale University Press, 1932.

Behrens, C. B. A. *Society, Government and the Enlightenment: The Experiences of Eighteenth Century France and Prussia*. New York: Harper and Row, 1985.

Beiser, Frederick C. *The Fate of Reason: German Philosophy from Kant to Fichte*. Cambridge: Harvard University Press, 1987.

Beyer-Fröhlich, Marianne. Introduction to *Pietismus und Rationalismus*. Deutsche Literatur. Sammlung literarischer Kunst- und Kulturdenkmäler in Entwicklungsreihen. Edited by Heinz Kindermann. Series [25]: Deutsche Selbstzeugnisse. 10 vols. Edited by M. Beyer-Fröhlich. Vol. 7. Leipzig: Reclam, 1933.

Birtsch, Günter. "Freiheit und Eigentum: Zur Erörterung von Verfassungsfragen in der deutschen Publizistik im Zeichen der Französischen Revolution." In *Eigentum und Verfassung: Zur Eigentumsdiskussion im ausgehenden 18. Jahrhundert*, edited by Rudolf Vierhaus, 179–92. Göttingen: Vandenhoeck und Ruprecht, 1972.

Blanning, T. C. W. "The Enlightenment in Catholic Germany." In *The Enlightenment in National Context*, edited by Roy Porter and Mikuláš Teich, 118–26. Cambridge: Cambridge University Press, 1981.

Bloch, Ernst. "Christian Thomasius, a German Scholar without Misery." In his *Natural Law and Human Dignity*, translated by Dennis J. Schmidt. Cambridge: M.I.T. Press, 1986.

————. *Thomas Münzer als Theologe der Revolution*. Gesamtausgabe, vol. 2. Frankfurt am Main: Suhrkamp 1969.

Bödeker, Hans E. "Menschheit, Humanität, Humanismus." In *Geschichtliche Grundbegriffe: Historisches Lexikon zur politisch-sozialen Sprache in Deutschland*, edited by O. Brunner, W. Conze, and R. Koselleck, 3:1063–1128. Stuttgart: Klett-Cotta, 1972ff.

————. "Zur Rezeption der französischen Menschen- und Bürgerrechtserklärung von 1789/1791 in der deutschen Aufklärungsgesellschaft." In *Grund- und Freiheitsrechte im Wandel von Gesell-*

schaft und Geschichte: Beiträge zur Geschichte der Grund- und Frei-heitsrechte vom Ausgang des Mittelalters bis zur Revolution von 1848, edited by Günter Birtsch, 258–86. Göttingen: Vandenhoeck und Ruprecht, 1981.

Bodi, Leslie. *Tauwetter in Wien: Zur Prosa der österreichischen Auf-klärung 1781–1795.* Frankfurt am Main: Fischer, 1977.

Borchmeyer, Dieter. *Höfische Gesellschaft und französische Revolu-tion bei Goethe: Adliges und bürgerliches Wertsystem im Urteil der Weimarer Klassik.* Kronberg: Athenäum, 1977.

Brandt, Reinhard. "Revolution und Fortschritt im Spätwerk Kants." In *Aufklärung als Politisierung—Politisierung der Aufklärung,* edited by Hans E. Bödeker and Ulrich Herrmann, 211–21. Hamburg: Meiner, 1987.

Braubach, Max. *Von der Französischen Revolution bis zum Wiener Kongress.* Gebhardt Handbuch der Geschichte, vol. 14. Munich: dtv, 1974.

Breazeale, Daniel. "Between Kant and Fichte: Karl Leonhard Rein-hold's 'Elementary Philosophy'." *Review of Metaphysics* 35 (June 1982): 785–821.

Burkhardt, Frederick H. Introduction to *God. Some Conversations,* by Johann Gottfried Herder, 1–64. Translated by F. H. Burkhardt. New York: Hafner, 1949.

Cassirer, Ernst. *The Philosophy of the Enlightenment.* Translated by Fritz C. A. Koelln and James P. Pettegrove. Princeton: Princeton University Press, 1951.

———. *Rousseau, Kant, Goethe. Two Essays.* Translated by J. Gut-mann, P. O. Kristeller, and J. H. Randall. Princeton: Princeton University Press, 1947.

Cloeren, Hermann-Josef. "Philosophie als Sprachkritik bei K. L. Reinhold: Interpretative Bemerkungen zu seiner Spätphilosophie." *Kant-Studien* 63:2 (1972): 225–36.

de Levie, Dagobert. *Die Menschenliebe im Zeitalter der Aufklä-rung: Säkularisierung und Moral im 18. Jahrhundert.* Berne: Lang, 1975.

Eckermann, J. P. *Conversations with Goethe.* Translated by Gisela C. O'Brien, selected, with an introduction and annotated index, by Hans Kohn. New York: Ungar, 1964.

Epstein, Klaus. *The Genesis of German Conservatism*. Princeton: Princeton University Press, 1966.

Erhard, Johann Benjamin. *Über das Recht des Volks zu einer Revolution und andere Schriften*. Edited, and with an epilogue, by Hellmut G. Haasis. Frankfurt am Main: Syndikat, 1976.

Erhardt-Lucht, Renate. *Die Ideen der Französischen Revolution in Schleswig-Holstein*. Neumünster: Wachholtz, 1969.

Feiereis, Konrad. *Die Umprägung der natürlichen Theologie in Religionsphilosophie: Ein Beitrag zur deutschen Geistesgeschichte des 18. Jahrhunderts*. Leipzig: St. Benno, 1965.

Fichte, Johann Gottlieb. "Beitrag zur Berichtigung der Urteile des Publikums über die französische Revolution." In his *Schriften zur Revolution*, edited by B. Wilms, 81–289. Frankfurt am Main: Ullstein, 1973.

Fink, Gonthier-Louis. "Wieland und die Französische Revolution." In *Christoph Martin Wieland*, edited by Hansjörg Schelle, 407–44. Darmstadt: Wissenschaftliche Buchgesellschaft, 1981.

Friedenthal, Richard. *Goethe: Sein Leben und seine Zeit*. Munich: Piper, 1963.

Gay, Peter. Introduction to *Deism: An Anthology*, edited by P. Gay, 9–26. Princeton: Van Nostrand, 1968.

Gliwitzky, Hans. "Carl Leonhard Reinholds erster Standpunktwechsel." In *Philosophie aus einem Prinzip: Karl Leonhard Reinhold*, edited by Reinhard Lauth, 10–85. Bonn: Bouvier Verlag Herbert Grundmann, 1974.

Göpfert, Herbert G. "Lesegesellschaften im 18. Jahrhundert." In *Aufklärung, Absolutismus und Bürgertum in Deutschland*, edited by Franklin Kopitzsch, 403–11. Munich: Nymphenburger Verlagshandlung, 1976.

Grab, Walter. *Norddeutsche Jakobiner: Demokratische Bestrebungen zur Zeit der Französischen Revolution*. Frankfurt am Main: Europäische Verlagsanstalt, 1967.

Grave, S. A. *The Scottish Philosophy of Common Sense*. Oxford: Clarendon Press, 1960.

Habermas, Jürgen. *The Structural Transformation of the Public Sphere. An Inquiry into a Category of Bourgeois Society*. Translated by

Thomas Burger with the assistance of Frederick Lawrence. N.p.: Polity Press (with M.I.T.), 1989.

Hampson, Norman. "The Enlightenment in France." In *The Enlightenment in National Context*, edited by Roy Porter and Mikuláš Teich, 41–53. Cambridge: Cambridge University Press, 1981.

Hamann, Johann Georg. "Brief an Christian Jacob Kraus vom 18. Dezember 1784." In *Was ist Aufklärung?* edited by Ehrhard Bahr, 17–22. Stuttgart: Reclam, 1974.

Henrich, Dieter. *Konstellationen: Probleme und Debatten am Ursprung der idealistischen Philosophie (1789–1795)*. Stuttgart: Klett-Cotta, 1991.

Herder, Johann Gottfried. *God. Some Conversations*. Translated by Frederick H. Burkhardt. New York: Hafner, 1949.

———. "Wort und Begriff der Humanität." (Excerpts from his *Briefe zur Beförderung der Humanität*.) In *Was ist Aufklärung?* edited by Ehrhard Bahr, 36–42. Stuttgart: Reclam, 1974.

Hersche, Peter. *Der Spätjansenismus in Österreich*. Vienna: Verlag der österreichischen Akademie der Wissenschaften, 1977.

Hertz, Frederick. *The Development of the German Public Mind: A Social History of German Political Sentiment, Aspirations and Ideas*. Vol. 2, *The Age of Enlightenment*. London: Allen and Unwin, 1962.

Hinske, Norbert. "Wolffs Stellung in der deutschen Aufklärung." In *Christian Wolff 1679–1754*, edited by Werner Schneiders, 306–19. Hamburg: Meiner, 1983.

———, ed. *Was ist Aufklärung? Beiträge aus der Berlinischen Monatsschrift*. 4th rev. ed. Darmstadt: Wissenschaftliche Buchgesellschaft, 1990.

Hobbes, Thomas. *Leviathan*. Edited and abridged, with an introduction, by John Plamenatz. London: Collins, The Fontana Library, 1962.

Holzhey, Helmut. "Philosophie als Eklektik." *studia leibnitiana* 15 (1983): 19–29.

Hume, David. *An Enquiry concerning Human Understanding*. Edited by Antony Flew. La Salle: Open Court, 1988.

———. *A Treatise of Human Nature*. Edited by L. A. Selby-Bigge. N.p., 1888. Reprint, Oxford, 1973.

Kant, Immanuel. *Critique of Judgment*. Translated, with an introduction, by J. H. Bernard. New York: Hafner, 1951.

———. *Critique of Practical Reason*. Translated, with an introduction, by L. W. Beck. Indianapolis: Bobbs-Merrill, 1959.

———. *Critique of Pure Reason*. Translated by Norman Kemp Smith. London: Macmillan, 1953.

———. *Foundations of the Metaphysics of Morals and What Is Enlightenment?* Translated, with an introduction, by L. W. Beck. New York: Macmillan, 1959.

———. "Idea for a Universal History from a Cosmopolitan Point of View." In his *Kant on History*, edited and translated by L. W. Beck, 11–26. Indianapolis: Bobbs-Merrill, 1963.

———. *The Metaphysical Elements of Justice*, pt. 1 of *The Metaphysics of Morals*. Translated, with an introduction, by John Ladd. New York: Macmillan, 1965.

———. *Philosophical Correspondence 1759–1799*. Edited and translated by Arnulf Zweig. Chicago: University of Chicago Press, 1967.

———. *Prolegomena to Any Future Metaphysics*. The Mahaffy-Carns translation extensively revised, with an introduction, by L. W. Beck. Indianapolis: Bobbs-Merrill, 1950.

———. *Religion Within the Limits of Reason Alone*. Translated, with an introduction, by Theodore M. Greene and Hoyt H. Hudson, with a new essay "The Ethical Significance of Kant's *Religion*" by John Silber. New York: Harper Torchbook, 1960.

———. "Über den Gemeinspruch: Das mag in der Theorie richtig sein, taugt aber nicht für die Praxis." In his *Schriften zur Geschichtsphilosophie*, edited, with an introduction, by Manfred Riedel, 118–65. Stuttgart: Reclam, 1974.

———. "Was heisst: Sich im Denken orientieren?" In his *Schriften zur Metaphysik und Logik 1*, edited by Wilhelm Weischedel. Werkausgabe, vol. 5. Frankfurt am Main: Suhrkamp, 1978.

———. "What Is Enlightenment?" In his *Foundations of the Metaphysics of Morals and What Is Enlightenment?* translated, with an introduction, by L. W. Beck, 85–92. New York: Macmillan, 1959.

Keil, Robert. *Wiener Freunde 1784–1808: Beitraege zur Jugendgeschichte der deutsch-oesterreichischen Literatur*. Beitraege zur Geschichte der deutschen Literatur und des geistigen Lebens in Oesterreich. Edited by Jakob Minor, August Sauer, and Richard M. Werner, vol. 2. Vienna: Carl Konegen, 1883.

Klemmt, Alfred. "Die philosophische Entwicklung Karl Leonhard Reinholds nach 1800." *Zeitschrift für philosophische Forschung* 15 (1961): 79–101, 250–77.

———. *Karl Leonhard Reinholds Elementarphilosophie: Eine Studie über den Ursprung des spekulativen deutschen Idealismus.* Hamburg: Meiner, 1958.

Klippel, Diethelm. "Naturrecht als politische Theorie: Zur politischen Bedeutung des deutschen Naturrechts im 18. und 19. Jahrhundert." In *Aufklärung als Politisierung—Politisierung der Aufklärung,* edited by Hans E. Bödeker and Ulrich Herrmann, 267–94. Hamburg: Meiner, 1987.

Knigge, Adolf Freiherr. "Philo's endliche Erklärung und Antwort." In his *Freimaurer- und Illuminatenschriften* 1, *Sämtliche Werke,* vol. 12. Nendeln, Liechtenstein: KTO Press, 1978.

König, Alfred P. *Denkformen in der Erkenntnis: Die Urteilstafel Immanuel Kants in der Kritik der reinen Vernunft und in Karl Leonhard Reinholds "Versuch einer neuen Theorie des menschlichen Vorstellungsvermögens".* Bonn: Bouvier Verlag Herbert Grundmann, 1980.

Koselleck, Reinhart. *Kritik und Krise: Eine Studie zur Pathogenese der bürgerlichen Welt.* Frankfurt am Main: Suhrkamp, 1973.

Kuehn, Manfred. "The Early Reception of Reid, Oswald, and Beattie in Germany: 1768–1800." *Journal of the History of Philosophy* 21:4 (Oct. 1983): 479–96.

———. "Kant and the Refutations of Idealism in the Eighteenth Century." In *Man, God, and Nature in the Enlightenment,* edited by D. Mell, Th. Braun, and L. Palmer, 25–35. East Lansing: Colleagues Press, 1988.

———. *Scottish Common Sense in Germany, 1768–1800. A Contribution to the History of Critical Philosophy.* Foreword by L. W. Beck. Kingston and Montreal: McGill-Queen's University Press, 1987.

Laemmle, Peter. "Unterhaltungen über Politik und Revolution." In *J. W. v. Goethe,* edited by Heinz L. Arnold. Munich: text und kritik, 1982.

Lange, Victor. *The Classical Age of German Literature 1740–1815*. New York: Holmes and Meier, 1982.

Lauth, Reinhard. "Fichtes und Reinholds Verhältnis vom Anfange ihrer Bekanntschaft bis zu Reinholds Beitritt zum Standpunkt der Wissenschaftslehre Anfang 1797." In *Philosophie aus einem Prinzip: Karl Leonhard Reinhold*, edited by R. Lauth, 129–59. Bonn: Bouvier Verlag Herbert Grundmann, 1974.

———. "Nouvelles recherches sur Reinhold et l'Aufklaerung." *Archives de Philosophie* 42 (1979): 593–629.

———. "Reinholds Vorwurf des Subjektivismus gegen die Wissenschaftslehre." In *Philosophie aus einem Prinzip: Karl Leonhard Reinhold*, edited by R. Lauth, 225–76. Bonn: Bouvier Verlag Herbert Grundmann, 1974.

Leibniz, Gottfried Wilhelm. *Philosophical Papers and Letters*. A selection translated and edited by Leroy E. Loemker. Chicago: University of Chicago Press, 1956.

Lessing, Gotthold Ephraim. "Anti-Goeze." In his *Werke*, vol. 8. Munich: Hanser, 1979.

———. "Ernst und Falk: Gespräche für Freimäurer." In his *Werke*, vol. 8. Munich: Hanser, 1979.

———. *Laocoön, Nathan the Wise, Minna von Barnhelm*. Edited by William A. Steel. "Nathan the Wise" translated by Steel. London: Dent; New York: Dutton, 1970.

Locke, John. *An Essay Concerning Human Understanding*. Edited, with an introduction, by John W. Yolton. London: Dent, 1961.

Martens, Wolfgang. "Bürgerlichkeit in der frühen Aufklärung." *Jahrbuch für Geschichte der oberdeutschen Reichsstädte* 16 (1970): 106–20.

———. *Die Botschaft der Tugend: Die Aufklärung im Spiegel der Deutschen Moralischen Wochenschriften*. Stuttgart: Metzler, 1968.

Mendelssohn, Moses. *Gesammelte Schriften. Jubiläumsausgabe*. Stuttgart: Frommann-Holzboog, 1981.

———. "Orakel, die Bestimmung des Menschen betreffend." In his *Gesammelte Schriften*, 1st vol. of vol. 6, *Kleinere Schriften*, 19–25.

———. "Über die Frage: Was heisst aufklären?" In *Was ist Aufklärung?* edited by Ehrhard Bahr, 3–8. Stuttgart: Reclam, 1974.

Möller, Horst. "Die Bruderschaft der Gold- und Rosenkreuzer: Struktur, Zielsetzung und Wirkung einer anti-aufklärerischen Geheimgesellschaft." In *Freimaurer und Geheimbünde im 18. Jahrhundert in Mitteleuropa*, edited by Helmut Reinalter, 199–239. Frankfurt am Main: Suhrkamp, 1983.

"Der 'moralische Bund' Reinhold's und der 'Einverstandenen': Beiträge zur Geschichte der maurerischen Reformbestrebungen in Deutschland, 1." In *Latomia* (Freimaurerische Vierteljahrs-Schrift), edited by Th. Schletter and Th. Merzdorf, 1–16, 132–45. Leipzig: Weber, 1861.

Nisbet, H. B. " 'Was ist Aufklärung?' The Concept of Enlightenment in Eighteenth-Century Germany." *Journal of European Studies* 12 (1982): 77–95.

Oelmüller, Willi. *Die unbefriedigte Aufklärung: Beiträge zu einer Theorie der Moderne von Lessing, Kant und Hegel.* Frankfurt am Main: Suhrkamp, 1979.

Palmer, Robert R. *The Age of Democratic Revolution: A Political History of Europe and America, 1760–1800.* Vol. 1, *The Challenge*, vol. 2, *The Struggle*. Princeton: Princeton University Press, 1959.

Philosophie aus einem Prinzip: Karl Leonhard Reinhold. Edited by Reinhard Lauth. Bonn: Bouvier Verlag Herbert Grundmann, 1974.

Porter, Roy. "The Enlightenment in England." In *The Enlightenment in National Context*, edited by Roy Porter and Mikuláš Teich, 1–18. Cambridge: Cambridge University Press, 1981.

Prauss, Gerold. *Kant über Freiheit als Autonomie.* Philosophische Abhandlungen, vol. 51. Frankfurt am Main: Klostermann, 1983.

Ratz, Alfred E. "Ausgangspunkte und Dialektik von C. M. Wielands gesellschaftlichen Ansichten." In *Christoph Martin Wieland*, edited by Hansjörg Schelle, 379–98. Darmstadt: Wissenschaftliche Buchgesellschaft.

Reid, Thomas. *Essays on the Intellectual Powers of Man.* Cambridge: M.I.T. Press, 1969.

Reimarus, Hermann Samuel. *Apologie oder Schutzschrift für die vernünftigen Verehrer Gottes.* Edited by Gerhard Alexander, 2 vols. Frankfurt am Main: Insel, 1972.

Reinhold, Ernst. *Karl Leonhard Reinhold's Leben und litterarisches Wirken.* Jena: Frommann, 1825.

Röttgers, Kurt. "Die Kritik der reinen Vernunft und K. L. Reinhold: Fallstudie zur Theoriepragmatik in Schulbildungsprozessen." In *Akten des 4. Internationalen Kant-Kongresses Mainz. 6.–10. April 1974, Teil II. 2: Sektionen,* edited by Gerhard Funke, 788–804. Berlin: de Gruyter, 1974.

Sauer, Werner. *Österreichische Philosophie zwischen Aufklärung und Restauration: Beiträge zur Geschichte des Frühkantianismus in der Donaumonarchie.* Studien zur österreichischen Philosophie, vol. 2. Würzburg: Königshausen und Neumann; Amsterdam: Rodopi, 1982.

Schiller, Friedrich. *On the Aesthetic Education of Man.* Translated, with an introduction, by Reginald Snell. London: Routledge and Kegan Paul, 1954.

Schindler, Norbert. "Der Geheimbund der Illuminaten—Aufklärung, Geheimnis und Politik." In *Freimaurer und Geheimbünde im 18. Jahrhundert in Mitteleuropa,* edited by Helmut Reinalter, 284–318. Frankfurt am Main: Suhrkamp, 1983.

Schmidt-Biggemann, Wilhelm. "Emancipation by Infiltration: Institutions and Personalities of the German 'Early Enlightenment'." In *Enlightenment in Germany,* edited by Paul Raabe and W. Schmidt-Biggemann, translated by Patricia Crampton, 45–58. Bonn: Hohwacht Verlag, 1979.

———. *Theodizee und Tatsachen: Das philosophische Profil der deutschen Aufklärung.* Frankfurt am Main: Suhrkamp, 1988.

Schneiders, Werner. *Die wahre Aufklärung: Zum Selbstverständnis der deutschen Aufklärung.* Freiburg and Munich: Alber, 1974.

———. Preface to *Einleitung zur Sittenlehre,* by Christian Thomasius. Hildesheim: Olms, 1968.

Schrader, Wolfgang. "Systemphilosophie als Aufklärung: Zum Philosophiebegriff K. L. Reinholds." *studia leibnitiana* 15 (1983): 72–81.

Silber, John R. "The Ethical Significance of Kant's *Religion.*" Introductory essay in Kant, *Religion Within the Limits of Reason Alone,* translated, with an introduction, by Theodore M. Greene and Hoyt H. Hudson. New York: Harper Torchbook, 1960.

Smith, Ronald Gregor. *J. G. Hamann, 1730–1788: A Study in Christian Existence.* With selections from his writing, translated by R. G. Smith. New York: Harper and Brothers, 1960.

Stolzenberg, Jürgen. *Fichtes Begriff der intellektuellen Anschauung: Die Entwicklung in den Wissenschaftslehren von 1793/94 bis 1801/02.* Deutscher Idealismus. Philosophie und Wirkungsgeschichte in Quellen und Studien, vol. 10. Stuttgart: Klett-Cotta, 1986.

Stuke, Horst. "Aufklärung." In *Geschichtliche Grundbegriffe: Historisches Lexikon zur politisch-sozialen Sprache in Deutschland,* edited by O. Brunner, W. Conze, and R. Koselleck, 1:243–342. Stuttgart: Klett-Cotta, 1972.

Thomasius, Christian. *Einleitung zur Sittenlehre.* Edited by Werner Schneiders. Hildesheim: Olms, 1968.

Timm, Hermann. *Gott und die Freiheit: Studien zur Religionsphilosophie der Goethezeit.* Vol. 1, *Die Spinozarenaissance.* Frankfurt am Main: Klostermann, 1974.

van Dülmen, Richard. *Der Geheimbund der Illuminaten: Darstellung, Analyse, Dokumentation.* Stuttgart: Frommann-Holzboog, 1975.

———. *Die Gesellschaft der Aufklärer: Zur bürgerlichen Emanzipation und aufklärerischen Kultur in Deutschland.* Frankfurt am Main: Fischer, 1986.

Vaughan, Larry. *The Historical Constellation of the Sturm und Drang.* New York: Lang, 1985.

Vierhaus, Rudolf. "Absolutismus." In his *Deutschland im 18. Jahrhundert: Politische Verfassung, soziales Gefüge, geistige Beziehungen,* 63–83. Göttingen: Vandenhoeck und Ruprecht, 1987.

———. "Aufklärung und Freimaurerei in Deutschland." In *Freimaurer und Geheimbünde im 18. Jahrhundert in Mitteleuropa,* edited by Helmut Reinalter, 115–39. Frankfurt am Main: Suhrkamp, 1983. (Identical reprint from *Das Vergangene und die Geschichte: Festschrift für Reinhard Wittram zum 70. Geburtstag.* Göttingen, 1973.)

———. "Deutschland im 18. Jahrhundert: Soziales Gefüge, politische Verfassung, geistige Bewegung." In *Aufklärung, Absolutismus und*

Bürgertum in Deutschland, edited by Franklin Kopitzsch, 173–91. Munich: Nymphenburger Verlagshandlung, 1976.

———. "The Historical Interpretation of the Enlightenment: Problems and Viewpoints." In *Enlightenment in Germany*, edited by Paul Raabe and Wilhelm Schmidt-Biggemann, translated by Patricia Crampton, 23–36. Bonn: Hohwacht Verlag, 1979.

———. "Patriotismus." In his *Deutschland im 18. Jahrhundert: Politische Verfassung, soziales Gefüge, geistige Beziehungen*, 96–109. Göttingen: Vandenhoeck und Ruprecht, 1987.

———. "Politisches Bewusstsein in Deutschland vor 1789." *Der Staat* 6 (1967): 175–96.

———. " 'Sie und nicht wir': Deutsche Urteile über den Ausbruch der Französischen Revolution." In his *Deutschland im 18. Jahrhundert: Politische Verfassung, soziales Gefüge, geistige Beziehungen*, 202–15. Göttingen: Vandenhoeck und Ruprecht, 1987.

von Schönborn, Alexander. *Karl Leonhard Reinhold: Eine annotierte Bibliographie*. Stuttgart: Frommann-Holzboog, 1991.

Was ist Aufklärung? Edited by Ehrhard Bahr. Stuttgart: Reclam, 1974.

Weyergraf, Bernd. *Der skeptische Bürger: Wielands Schriften zur Französischen Revolution*. Stuttgart: Metzler, 1972.

Whaley, Joachim. "The Protestant Enlightenment in Germany." In *The Enlightenment in National Context*, edited by Roy Porter and Mikuláš Teich, 106–17. Cambridge: Cambridge University Press, 1981.

Wieland, Christoph Martin. "Das Geheimniss des Kosmopoliten-Ordens." In his *Werke*, edited by Fritz Martini and H. W. Seiffert, 3:550–75. Munich: Hanser, 1967.

Wolff, Christian. "Rede von der Sittenlehre der Sineser." In *Das Weltbild der deutschen Aufklärung: Philosophische Grundlagen und literarische Auswirkung: Leibniz—Wolff—Gottsched—Brockes—Haller*, edited by F. Brüggemann. Deutsche Literatur: Sammlung literarischer Kunst- und Kulturdenkmäler in Entwicklungsreihen. Edited by Heinz Kindermann, series [15] "Aufklärung," vol. 2. Leipzig: Reclam, 1930.

Zahn, Manfred. "Fichtes, Schellings und Hegels Auseinandersetzung mit dem 'logischen Realismus' Christoph Gottfried Bardilis."

Zeitschrift für philosophische Forschung 29:2 (1965): 201–23, 453–79.

Zimmerli, Walther Ch. " 'Schwere Rüstung' des Dogmatismus und 'anwendbare Eklektik': J. G. H. Feder und die Göttinger Philosophie im ausgehenden 18. Jahrhundert." *studia leibnitiana* 15 (1983): 58–71.

Index

Freemasonry: and German enlightenment, 7, 111–18; in Germany,
109–11; morality and politics, 112–15;
religion, 115–18; Reinhold, 118–23,
150; reforming, 121–23
Freemasons, 18, 95
French Revolution, x, 5, 19, 21, 72, 92,
110, 120, 151; German reaction, 92–96;
conspiracy theory, 95; Reinhold, 102–8
Friedrich II, 5, 13, 37, 79, 92, 94, 111,
112
Fundamental Concepts, The, 121–23
Fundamental philosophy, 104–5, 107,
140, 142–44; Reinhold and Kant, 134,
136–39

Garve, Christian, 13, 128, 143
Göchhausen, Ernst A. A. von, 116–17
God, 11, 17, 27, 35, 45, 47, 67, 69, 73,
77, 78, 81, 160, 250; existence, 8–9, 67,
70, 79, 81–86, 131, 151, 240–41, 245;
belief and faith, 80, 140, 151, 188, 245;
will, 88, 246–47, 249; as Educator, 218;
omnipotence, 245, 248; respect, 246;
revelation, 249
Goethe, 15, 16, 17, 75, 81, 106, 112, 121,
152
Good, supreme, 82–83
Guilt, 176, 179, 180, 220

Hamann, J. G., 15, 16, 18, 20, 75, 126
Happiness, 4, 10, 18, 19, 41, 42, 44–45,
47, 48, 51–52, 63, 69, 79, 85, 86, 96,
97, 100, 151, 176, 183, 209, 220, 238;
as part of supreme good, 82
Heart, 31, 80, 84, 107–8, 197, 251;
humanity, 35, 201; evil, 55; religion,
87; education, 143, 148, 196, 202;
enlightenment, 152
Hegel, 81, 108
Herder, J. G., 15, 16, 17, 18, 21, 27, 28,
75, 81, 93, 95, 106, 112, 126, 152
Heteronomy, 48, 50, 52, 54, 55, 57, 59,
83; self-determination, 52; actions, 53;
morality, 63
History: Reinhold, 106–8; Illuminati, 114
Hobbes, Thomas, 92, 97, 113
Holiness, 82, 242, 248, 250
Holy, 244, 246, 247; human will, 86

Human nature, 15, 39, 44–45, 47, 56, 63,
65, 73, 127, 172, 184, 185, 186, 211,
212, 220, 237, 250; viciousness, 55;
autonomy, 65; negative view, 65
Humaneness, 148, 184–85, 186, 197, 198,
254, 257
Humanism (Renaissance), 65
Humanity, 39, 46, 47, 63, 109, 121, 148,
152, 153, 185, 186, 187, 251, 253,
257; essence of, 181; of the heart, 201;
interest of, 218
Humankind, 107, 147, 161, 169; essence
of, 181
Humanness, 91, 97, 184, 186, 237, 257
Hume, David, 5, 15, 16, 70, 76n25, 81,
124, 126, 131–32, 135

Idealism, German, 17, 153
Illuminati, 18, 26, 84, 95, 96, 110–11,
113–19
Immoral: actions, 52, 53, 54, 57, 63, 178,
220, 248, 249; wrongful, 173, 174
Immortality, 36, 82–86, 77, 80, 150, 151,
245
Imperative, 53–54; categorical, 49, 58,
130
Inclinations, 40, 52, 53, 55, 56, 146, 173,
182; motives, 50
Independent thinkers, 102, 105, 168, 169
Inner experience, 145–46
Intellectual intuition, 61, 145
Intelligible and phenomenal worlds, 133

Jacobi, Friedrich Heinrich, 16, 76, 77, 78,
79, 141
Jacobins, 110; German, 94, 95, 120;
French, 101, 105
Jansenism, 22, 65, 66, 72–74
Jensen, 121
Joseph II, 5, 22, 28, 73, 99, 118; Austria,
25–26
Josephinism, 24, 28–30; enlightenment,
72
Justice, 63, 213, 218, 219, 253, 257; virtue
of, 44; theory, 98

Kant, 19, 28, 33, 34, 48–64, 75, 93,
103, 107, 108, 142, 144, 145, 150,
151, 153, 160n2; on Reinhold, ix;
concept of enlightenment, x; human